JOHN HILLABY'S
WALKING IN BRITAIN

David Bellamy

JOHN HILLABY'S
WALKING IN BRITAIN

EDITED BY JOHN HILLABY

COLLINS
8 GRAFTON STREET, LONDON W1X 3LA

DEDICATED TO WALKERS EVERYWHERE,
ESPECIALLY THOSE CONCERNED ABOUT WHAT THEY SEE

Great care has been taken to ensure that all factual
information contained in this book is accurate. Any
errors which appear are the responsibility of the
Publisher and not that of the Tourist Boards for
England and Scotland. Any opinions or subjective
views are those of the Authors and do not necessarily
reflect the opinion or policy of the Publisher or the
national Tourist Boards.

All photographs courtesy of Britain on View
(BTA/ETB), except those on pp. 179–81 and 191
(top) which are courtesy of John and Katie Hillaby.

Paintings courtesy of David Bellamy.

Published in association with the National Tourist
Boards of England and Scotland.

First published 1988 by
William Collins Sons & Co Ltd
London · Glasgow · Sydney
Auckland · Toronto · Johannesburg

British Library Cataloguing in Publication Data
John Hillaby's walking in Britain.
1. Walking—Great Britain
I. Hillaby, John
796.5'1'0941   GV199.44.G7
ISBN 0 00 412272 0

Filmset in Goudy Old Style by Ace Filmsetting Ltd,
Frome, Somerset

Printed and bound by Cronion S.A., Barcelona, Spain

CONTENTS

Preface 6

Prologue · *The Ways of Walkers* · John Hillaby 7

CHALK · Adam Nicolson 10

The River that Loops through London 18
THE THAMES PATH · Miles Jebb 19

Greatest among the Green Roads 24
THE RIDGEWAY PATH · Hugh Westacott 25

Dreamers and Distance Slayers 32
A WALK AROUND THE BLOCK
Richard Mabey 33

Facing up to Realities 40
WILD WEATHER SKETCHING
David Bellamy 41

The Threatened Wilderness 52
WALKING ON DARTMOOR
Brian le Messurier 53

The Great Roller-Coaster 60
THE SOUTH-WEST PENINSULA PATH
Hugh Westacott 62

Some Aspects of the Principality 74
WALKING IN SOUTH WALES
Brian J. Ford 75

Spirit of Dyfed 84
THE PEMBROKESHIRE COAST PATH
David Bellamy 86

Master of Unorthodoxy 94
OFFA'S DYKE PATH · Stephen Pern 96

Some Thoughts on Snowdonia 104
WALKING IN NORTH WALES
Showell Styles 106

Away from it All 112
AROUND THE HEARTLAND · Geoff Allen 113

Character of the Cotswolds 119
COTSWOLD EDGE · Mark Richards 120

Some Notes About Loners 128
WITHIN WALKING DISTANCE
Ronald Blythe 130

The Way Things Go Wrong 136
LINCOLNSHIRE · Brett Collier 138

The Peak District 146
BOG-TROTTING AND OTHER
DELIGHTS · Roland Smith 147

Footprints in the Peat 156
THE PENNINE WAY · Hugh Westacott 158

In Turner's Footsteps 168
THE STRIDING DALES · Roland Smith 170

Some Youthful Ideas 177
WALKING IN THE FAMILY WAY
Kathleen Burton 178

Spiritual Trails 184
THE ATHLETES OF GOD · John Hillaby 185

Poetry and Places 192
AUDEN'S LANDSCAPE · Adam Nicolson 194

Food for Foot-men 202
EATING HIGH · Christopher Driver 204

Crowds and Cloudy Loneliness 208
LAKELAND WALKING · Hunter Davies 210

The Ins and Outs of Gaeldom 218
WEST HIGHLAND WAY · Stephen Pern 219

The View From the Top 228
CAPE WRATH TO FORT WILLIAM
Ivan Rowan 231

By Courtesy of Butlin's 238
THE BIG WALK · Anon 239

Eagles, Wildcats and Walkers 244
HIGHLANDS OF THE EAST
Cameron McNeish 246

Epilogue · John Hillaby 252

Index 254

Acknowledgements 256

PREFACE

Britain, the most famous of the world's off-shore islands, is unique in many respects. In south-east Kent it lies within sight of its parent, the continent of Europe. Geologists tell us that the great breakthrough, the flooding of our protective Straits, occurred late in their concept of time, a mere twelve thousand years ago. This means that our circulatory seas are a temperate barrier against climatic extremes and for some freakish reason which nobody can explain we are endowed with almost every geological system known, from examples of the oldest to the most recent.

For what has now become Britain's most popular, most progressive recreation, that of getting the feel of the land on foot, this is a fact of tremendous importance. Where better can we walk than somewhere usually not too far from where most of us live? Mountains, moorlands, rolling downs, forests and estuaries, the ins and outs of the tops of 6,000 miles of majestic sea cliffs, all are there, ready for exploration and enjoyment.

Books about individual walks are common-place but no other one, we believe, has brought together such a variety of articles by Britain's fore-most authors and journalists including Ronald Blythe, Adam Nicolson, Richard Mabey, Hunter Davies and Showell Styles.

John Hillaby is pre-eminently qualified to introduce each one of them and to write about walking in Britain himself since in 1968 his deservedly famous *Journey Through Britain*, a walk from Land's End to John o' Groats, was described by David Holloway of *The Daily Telegraph* as 'surely the best travel book written since the war.' A feature of this authoritative and lavishly illustrated work – some water colours for which have been specially commissioned – is that it depicts our countryside as it appears today and not in some real or imaginary past.

THE WAYS OF WALKERS

PROLOGUE

Walking along a well-found track on the North Yorkshire Moors one night I recall a steady wind that blew as if engaged on the full-time job of keeping the sky polished and bright. Ventures in the dark, as Stephen Graham once put it, are not unlike a visit to the opera: if you want to see all the stars it's best to have a good stall. When the wind lessened a little towards dawn, a solitary golden plover piped a plaintive *too-lee*, a distant call, at first almost inaudible to human ears but not to fellow plovers who, recognizing rivalry, answered boldly from their own tracts of barren sandstone and ling until the whole moor rang with that fine equipoise of syllables. Not to be outdone in the real-estate business, the curlew took wing and poured liquid complaints into the choral contest. They were joined by larks rising to the apex of cones of sound and pipits too, falling spirals of birds unable to perch in the sky for so long as their more tuneful cousins. I would have held back the rising sun. But life is not composed of mere lengths of time so much as breadth of experience, sometimes more pleasureable in retrospect than in the labour involved.

Many years ago an arduous traverse of the Ben Assynt ridge in the Western Highlands kept me in a state of mental and physical suspense for several hours when that most nebulous of opponents, a blanket of cloud, dropped like a theatre curtain during an incautious venture on to an incoherent scree. As on Dartmoor, near the start of that long walk, an all-enveloping mist reduced visibility to a few yards. I did all that could be done. I stayed put until it drifted away, knowing that at worst I carried the best of insurance, a small tent to crawl into. Unpredictable setbacks and frustrations are hugely offset by a sense of invincibility, a condition of vital importance to a walker on his own.

As a light foot-man, heavy perhaps in years but whimful still, I have no stomach for communal tramps conditioned by the pace of the slowest who, disregarding contours, crash through wet peat, mud and streamlets as if they didn't exist. The well-conditioned walker puts to good account some of the dramatic arrogance of the trained actor who, though tired out after a long performance, is ever mindful of his craft and sweeps forward to the final curtain for his last bow as if treading on air.

Yet after walking alone for over half a century, I married an athletic and uncommonly sympathetic woman and a courageous one too since, for our honeymoon, she readily agreed to follow a succession of tracks from the shores of the Lake District back to our apartment in Hampstead by way of the northern moors, Lincolnshire and Norfolk. How well we matched each other in our different ways may be judged when, a year or two later under conditions mostly difficult and, now and again, perilous, we struck due north over the central Pindos mountains on a zigzag route from Athens to the ancestral home of the old gods on Mt Olympus in southern Macedonia.

My job in this book's great variety show of Britain, scripted by authorities in their particular fields, is simply to lift the curtain and say a few words about the performers. Among much you will discover is that walking with children is an affectionate art, a powerful bonding mechanism unrecognized, I suspect, by far the majority of child therapists more concerned about eliminating town-bred quirks than about encouraging youngsters who scramble so delightedly up and down paths, roll on the grass and seem so thoroughly involved in the adventure of it all.

Before meeting the cast we might take a look at the whole stage, noting the build and shape of Britain as you may see it transmitted from a low-flying satellite. If one draws a line from the mouth of the Tees to the mouth of the Exe it's apparent that most of the masses of hills and mountains lie to the Celtic north and west – for some of us the best of walking country – whilst the major stretches of plain and lowland lie to the southern and eastern regions, once the domain of the Saxons. Yet in nature there is rarely a sharp line between geographic zones but rather does the one fade gradually into the other.

To give some variety the contributions that follow have been arranged so that they swing from one side of the country to the other, but in a northerly direction just as one would embark on a well-planned walk to ensure that you are not looking into the sun. Knowing that there are many with a passionate regard for the Downs, the Wolds and the Fens where the tent-pole of the sky is almost always higher than on Helvellyn or in the ever-gloomy trough of Glen Coe, I have tried to remain impartial in my role of compère but it goes hard to suppress the predilections of a Northerner.

Almost everywhere today we see the qualitative shrinking before the quantitative. We are in danger of developing the surface habits of the hurried as against the earned experience and destinations of those of us who delight in travelling under our own power. Walking is a way of reviving a very old way of life once shared by mendicant friars, beggars, bards, wandering artisans and pilgrims. As Henry James remarked somewhere, landscape is character and walking – which is a form of touching – is like making love to the landscape and letting it return that love throughout our whole being.

It is a privilege to introduce our distinguished contributors, the light foot-men, the marathoneers, the meditative strollers, professional guides, the peat-plodders, countryside wardens, travel writers, a food taster, a mountaineer and an old friend of mine who can't be persuaded that he's

marvellously mad. If to all these you add a scientist, a mystic and a weather-defying water colourist, all are as much pilgrims at heart as ever Chaucer wrote about in those famous *Tales*.

It is fitting, therefore, that Adam Nicolson, a

man of many parts, should open our accounts with some thoughts about the stuff over which those early pilgrims both walked and rode on their way to Canterbury – chalk, found beneath the undulating downs of much of England's grasslands.

The Stiperstones in Shropshire.

CHALK

ADAM NICOLSON

It comes as a shock to learn that there is far more chalk in France than in England; that there are chalk downs in Alabama and Western Australia; that Danes, Poles, Germans, Russians and Arabs can all think of chalk as one of their rocks. Chalk is *not* English. This brutal geological betrayal denies everything we know most deeply about the rock. It is – isn't it? – the most English of all substances, shaping that inherited picture of our country as the deep, solid, reliable thing we all want it to be. Chalk, in this received version, is England made visible. Downs and wolds, combes and clunch – those are some of the root words of England. And it is unfair that we cannot in all conscience make the claim that chalk is really ours.

But you must forget all that. Forget that it was French botanists in the late nineteenth century who first properly investigated and understood the wonderful complexities of the chalk sward and remember instead that it was Daniel Defoe who called the chalklands the 'fine carpet-ground of England, soft as velvet and the herbage sweet as garden herbs underfoot', where the mutton of the sheep which grazed there was already flavoured with thyme before they walked into the butcher's yard. And you must forget, too, for the moment, that only 2.7 per cent of English chalk is now coated in that wonderful grass, which is more than grass. And forget, above all, that well over half of that small proportion has been preserved only because the soldiers and tanks who play war games on top of it are by nature indifferent to botany and the productivity of the soil.

Chalk is the zone for forgetting. Go for a chalk walk and abandon all the boring strictures of realism. Forget the news. Put on that comforting mind-filter that sees only the large, expected shapes, that collects and stores only those details which confirm the prejudice. Abandon scepticism, return to ignorance, to that country where expectation meets experience face to face and greets it warmly. There are no agonies there, only the 'kicked clover and buttercups hissing with the edges of our shoes', the 'broadcast shadows of clouds and limes', the 'outward and visible signs of a great thought'. It is the country where quotation is king, where millions have walked before you and seen what they wanted to see. There's no Wordsworthian emergence here, none of that cloak-wrapped Yeatsian heroism of the single figure on the rock-girt ridge. Chalk is the rock where you *join in*, where even if you are alone – and it is always best to be alone – you are accompanied by armies of ghosts, living and dead, who are all doing and thinking the same thing: that chalk is wonderful and chalk is English.

It is a landscape folded into the creases of the mind. 'That long straight line of the Downs in which a curve is latent,' Edward Thomas wrote. That is the essence of chalk. It is the realm of latency, where everything is promised, part-buried and unexpressed, and where the essence is hidden but hinted at, in the way that sometimes heavier, looser clothes can reveal the form beneath them without revealing it, displaying, without display, the essential substance.

It begins a hundred million years ago, half a revolution of the galaxy, when all the constellations were different and the night sky was unrecognizable. We were at sea, and, with the drifting of the continents, about ten degrees further south. You must imagine the Aegean washing over the older beds, the warm, easy currents flowing gently over the sands and clays, the gault and the greenstone of the Weald. It was a dry time. The land bordering the sea was low, flat and lifeless, a pale desert. No rivers flowed but in the clear tranquillity of the chalk sea life flourished. Some tiny shells, 1/125th of an inch across, have been recovered from the chalk and, seen through an electron microscope, their intricate forms are revealed. Some, which were free-floating, consist of scoops stacked upward and outward in baroque sundaes; others, living on the bottom, spiral outwards like the infinitely larger ammonites. But even these microscopic creatures can be thought of as the giants of the chalk sea. The great mass of life there was the plankton. Most of them have rotted away, leaving nothing, but one family of vegetable plankton, the *Haptophyceae*, were different. At the almost inconceivable scale of about 1/5000th of an inch, their cell walls were hedged around with coccoliths – little flowers, like the heads of scabious, made of calcium carbonate. When the individual

plankton died and the soft parts of its body rotted away, a tiny cluster of these exquisite rosettes floated down through the clear sea to settle on the bottom. And it was those flowers, broken and whole, which made the chalk.

You can think of it, as Jacquetta Hawkes did, as an infinitely slow snowstorm, a gradual drifting and gathering of tiny white skeletons over 35 million years. The chalk is a graveyard, as white as death. For those millions of years, as the dinosaurs enjoyed their last period of dominance and the tiny mammals crept about unseen at night, the seafloor itself was sinking and the gathering of the coccoliths kept pace, piling up above their predecessors layer on layer, so that in some parts the depth of chalk may have reached 3,000 feet or more. You must imagine the slowness of it, the white ooze thickening at about 1/12th of an inch a century. If I stand on the beach at the bottom of a

The gently curving chalk hills of the South Downs near Edburton, West Sussex.

LEFT: *The cliffs and lighthouse at Beachy Head.*

RIGHT: *Goodwood House in West Sussex, coated in discreet grey tweed.*

chalk cliff, the time elapsed between my feet and the top of my head represents nearly 90,000 years of the life and death of the chalk sea.

This is chalk – landscape made by the dazzling persistence of DNA, a plankton cemetery, a transmutation of those clouds of floating life into this present mass of rock, each down a communal fossil.

Within its matrix, chalk holds its darker twin: flint. In every way they sit either side of a balance. Chalk is soft, rounded, white, animal. Flint is hard, strange in shape, black and mineral. Chalk crumbles and is porous, flint is brittle and chips. The silica of which flint is made almost certainly came at one time from the bodies of animals which lived in the same chalk sea. They may have been like certain sorts of modern sponge which build intricate siliceous skeletons. But where the chalk bodies came to rest one on top of the other, these skeletons were somehow dissolved by the water that percolated through the chalk and reconstituted in hard, black, crystalline nodules. They rest on harder chalk bands which regularly interrupt the body of the rock and which probably represent those moments when the chalk sea became shallower and the skeleton ooze dried

and stiffened. You see them now in the cliffs at Beachy Head or in a chalk pit, seaming the whiteness as pinstripes in reverse.

So while chalk retains almost intact the memory of its animal origins, flint has been abstracted, returned to the mineral. A tiny proportion of a flint stone is water and it is the water that keeps it black. When that water is drawn out of the skin of each nodule by the chalk that surrounds it, the black is rimmed there with a coarse white desiccated rind.

Flint has a quality which most chalk lacks: you can build with it. Any walk in chalk country will be a walk *on* chalk but *through* flint. Crude flint walls, the individual stones broken to fit, line a path like banks of rotten teeth. The squared black faces of knapped flints gloss the front of many chalkland churches, sometimes chequerboarded with freestone, sometimes, miraculously, squeezed into the spaces of some flushwork tracery. Where the chalk meets the sea, flint cobbles, like hazelnuts on a fruit-cake, are pushed into the faces of houses. It is not really a material for the nobility. Only at Goodwood in West Sussex does flint dress a palace, coating the house in discreet grey tweed. And even there it looks

slightly strange, because flint is not an aristocratic thing, but intractable and obstinate, the black subconscious of the chalk, unsuited to the ease of a great house.

Most chalk is too soft to build with, but there are some compacted layers in the country where it is hard enough – if well roofed and set on solid foundations – to be used as a building stone. You will find a barn here and there with this hard chalk called clunch built into the walls, often mixed with brick and flint and greenstone rag to patch or strengthen it. The chalk is sometimes a little green if it is a damp north-facing wall. Otherwise it will be scuffed and dusty, where the passing cows have rubbed at it.

If used inside, of course, there are no problems. There are chalk vaults in Westminster Abbey. The Lady Chapel at Ely Cathedral is filled with tiny parsley-like carvings cut all too easily into the willing chalk. Such softness invites all the excesses of over-elaboration, but to match the austerity and simplicity of the material itself, it must be used plainly. No chalk building is as beautiful as the white, doll-like Ashdown House on the Berkshire Downs just south of the Ridgeway. It is there, in its seventeenth-century straight-forwardness, that chalk reaches its cleanest perfection, feminine and delicate, with the idea of the softness of chalk built into the look and feel of the house, so that, like the Downs themselves, it bridges the genders, somehow positive and negative, recessive and assertive at the same time.

I think of Ashdown as the culmination of everything in the chalk, the point where its contradictory and paradoxical qualities are for once made explicit. But to bring it out into the open like that is, in a way, to remove yourself from the real meaning of this magical rock. Granite and basalt push themselves at you, uncompromised and definite; the slates have a darkness and meanness in them; the oolitic limestone is a friendly, amenable thing, offering itself for use; the clays clog you at every step; the sands disintegrate underfoot; the mountain limestone is brittle and elevated, making dramatic gorges and brain-like pavements; the sandstones, perhaps unfairly, I think of as somehow meaningless – not imposing themselves, but shaped by other forces. But what all those rocks share is a *singular* nature, an obviousness and directness which, to my mind, chalk can never have, because chalk can be everything and anything.

At the heart of this ambiguity of chalk is its relation to water. The two are married. The coccoliths are not packed solidly together. They are relatively rigid, they jam up against each other and up to half the volume of a block of chalk is made up of the spaces between them. A down is a sponge and after heavy rain every cubic yard of the chalk beneath your feet will be filled with as many as 80 gallons of water. (And this water, incidentally, when sunk deep in the chalk, will be thick with dissolved silica – flints that have yet to come into being.)

Chalk is only half chalk. Water runs through it, sinking as far as it can until it reaches a harder layer, the floor, in fact, of the sea on which those first coccoliths settled. And there the water runs out to emerge as springs at the foot of the Downs, where villages gather, and where streams begin to eat away at the impermeable clays of the valley.

That is the great water paradox of chalkland: by offering no resistance to water, by allowing water to run through it like a stream through the fingers of your hand, chalk can survive the passage of water far better than a harder, more obstinate rock. Resistance by not resisting, survival by indifference to attack, by absorbing into its body the very forces which are the downfall of other rocks! Above all others, it is this quality of chalk that has given us the downland.

Of course, that is not entirely true. Even the most mildly acidic of rainwater, with tiny amounts of carbon dioxide dissolved in it, will eat away at the chalk. The colder the water, the more carbon dioxide it can contain and the more acid it will become. If in experiment a block of chalk is first saturated, frozen solid and then thawed, it will disintegrate into a shapeless heap of white dust. Exactly this process has been crucial in the shaping of downland. When you see those rounded in-and-outs of the downs, the half-sudden combes and the blunt-nosed headlands, the dry valleys furzed over in part with juniper on one side, what you are looking at – faintly clothed by the passage of time – are the margins of the last Ice Age. Here in this inexplicable landscape is the work of acid cold. It is not – at least in southern England – the coarse abrasion of the glaciers, but the work of massive, penetrative frosts and their consequent destructive thaws. Just as the block lost all form in the experiment, you must imagine in those brutal springtimes as the Ice Age waned the almost literal disintegration of the chalk ridge at these places, a massive and sudden slumping of the chalk into the valley. Watch the edge of a trifle at the moment after the spoon has taken its scoop, as the soft cliff slumps down leaving a combe behind it. That was the shaping moment in the history of our chalk. It only happens after a frost which has penetrated very deep, and we have not had one for about 8,000 years.

All this is latent, hidden, forgotten in the presence of the chalk. But you will find on a chalk walk that a strange reversal takes place and what is present becomes somehow buried under what is past. It is easy to ignore the present here because it is a country, in Richard Jefferies' words, that is 'alive with the dead', where the square miles of modern wheat are in some strange way coated with the long-gone and irrecoverable turf, where those prehistoric bumps and hollows which the receptive chalk retains (I treasure one in particular on Walker's Hill above the Vale of Pewsey: it is called Adam's Grave) assume an importance and significance far beyond the few square yards that

The rounded in-and-outs of the South Downs near Glyndebourne in East Sussex.

they occupy. Our vision of chalk pre-selects for its own pleasure. It identifies the hidden as the obvious and the pleasing as the important.

Don't poo-poo this wonderful faculty of mind. Remember Samuel Palmer inflating the roundness of the downs above the Darent Valley in Kent so that their figure and outline in his pictures matched the moon's. Forget the idiocy of archaeologists tunnelling into Silbury Hill to discover what was buried in this greatest of chalk monuments (nothing). And remember instead the ancient practice of spring-time dancing on top of the same artificial hill, when according to William Stukeley, the eighteenth-century antiquarian, 'the country people . . . make merry with cakes, figs, sugar and water fetched from the swallow-head or spring of the Kennet.'

Indulge the romance of geology. Allow the chalk to loiter in the recesses of the mind as a nebulous half-presence, as rounded as the downs, a source of comfort. Spend a whole day reading Sir Thomas Browne on top of a remote and unvisited barrow. Don't look for one which modern scientists have picked over and analysed for evidence of the economy of Bronze Age Britain. Think instead of the Dr Toope of Marlborough who found some workmen one day in 1685 digging bones out of barrow. 'I quickly perceived they were humane,' he wrote to John Aubrey, 'and came next day and dugg for them, and stored myself with many bushells, of which I made a noble medicine that relieved many of my distressed neighbours.' That's the right approach.

Smell the turf, if you can find it. Think of those

The greatest of chalk monuments,
Silbury Hill in Wiltshire.

botanists who have identified individual red fescue plants on the Downs that may be 1,000 years old. And others, appreciating the sheep as the maker and keeper of turf, who have meticulously worked out that the pressure of a typical downland ewe's foot on the sward is 0.94 kilograms per square centimetre (a cow's is 1.56). This is exactly right, apparently, to keep the turf consolidated without either crushing it or damaging the soil underneath. And celebrate the devotion to science of yet other botanists who have faithfully trotted after downland sheep all day to record the production of 1.8 kilograms of what they call 'fresh faeces . . . typically produced in numerous small pellets of about 2 grams each' – far nicer and better for grass than a cow's 34 kilograms 'produced in twelve or more pats.' It

takes a moment or two to realize that those dedicated men weighed the things. It is then that you appreciate the real meaning of the word 'fresh'.

So have a wonderful time. Think of those migrating birds who identify the chalk ridges from the air and use them to mark their flyways south. It will undoubtedly be better for you to avoid the famous paths. The Ridgeway, for example, is now practically unusable for long stretches, especially in the winter. But all you need do is get the map out and find a path for yourself. Or better, get a few sheets of the Geological Survey as well, where the chalk is shown in various shades of green, and simply follow those careful, inviting strips – the angelica on the great cake of England – as far as the horizon will lead you.

THE RIVER THAT LOOPS THROUGH LONDON

Seen from the air on an indifferent day, London is a smudgy sprawl given coherence only by a tortuous river which, in its lower reaches, seems determined on tying itself up in loops that much resemble the Greek letter Omega. Years ago I recall flying upstream in one of those small adventurous things with two wings and fans at the front. We came in low over Greenwich, seeing on either side the twin ridges of Blackheath and Hampstead as if on shelves of smoke. With its mock-turtle Gothic fabric, Tower Bridge appeared until the pilot, mindful perhaps of his obligations in terms of altitude, throttled up to the regulation height and, as we headed for Reading and Oxford, the Thames below broke up into feeder streams that I couldn't put a name to.

Royal river? Liquid history? Treacherous river, said James Bone in *The London Perambulator*, since it has twice signalled London to the enemy by day and by night. But these are mere epithets. David Piper put the matter plainly when he wrote that 'the Thames was there before London was, and the Thames is why London is where it is.' In 51 BC, Caesar called it *Tamesis* which, as I understand it, is cognate both with a Celtic river name and a tributary of the Ganges. It means dark. I don't know why unless it was that a prehistoric Thames which flowed north of Hampstead Heath carried much mud and clay.

The clouds browse on the hills above the metropolitan river, a fact which, coupled with a ceiling of hot air and pollution, may account for recent successions of almost tropical downpours. A friend who lives near Reading assures me you don't often meet with this new kind of London Peculiar much upstream. In what's fashionable to call ecological terms, aren't we dealing, essentially, with two distinct profiles of the same confluent waterway? One deep, burdensome and fettered and the other fishful and relatively free. Miles Jebb, very wisely I think, has chosen to follow the upper Thames above Kew where, refreshed by the Beverley Brook, the Brent and tributaries lower down, it ambles round west and north to its traditional source beyond Cricklade.

Though more than once I have walked from the Tower to Hampton Court in a vigorous day's going, I have yet to explore 'the stripling Thames' beyond Oxford. Come this spring and I'll be hanged if I don't do it in the warm and informative company of this distinguished pedestrian.

J.H.

THE THAMES PATH

MILES JEBB

A statue of Old Father Thames surveys the operation of his highest lock, St John's Lechlade. As is normal for river gods, he is in a recumbent position, looking like some ancient Roman just after a heavy feast. All his life, one supposes, he has been lounging around in the muddy river bed among the rushes or floating about in the mainstream with only the occasional swim for exercise. But I have some bad news for Father Thames. Despite his age and dignity he will shortly be obliged to be less lazy. He will have to get up on his hind legs and start walking, for the Thames Path is about to be created.

It is true that there has for long been a path along the bank of the Thames for much of its length. This path came into existence for towing barges: gangs of men known as 'halers', or teams of horses, pulled at ropes secured to the barges' masts. The towpath was much improved nearly two hundred years ago when barge traffic was at its peak, and it was extended as far upstream as Lechlade, where a canal linked the Thames to the Severn. But the commercial use of the Thames rapidly declined with the building of the railways and the towpath fell into disuse, especially on the upper reaches of the river, where what had once been a firm gravel path became in some sections an impenetrable mass of thistles and nettles. Worse, it became unwalkable because of the closure of the ferries, for the towpath frequently changed banks, sometimes at bridges but as often connected by special towpath ferries. Bank erosion and private encroachment caused further punctures. As a result, by the middle of this century one could only walk along the Thames in a non-continuous way, or by deviating from it by unsatisfactory sections of paths or roads.

But thanks to a recent (and, some would say, belated) decision by the Countryside Commission, a continuous path from the source will soon be established, with all the awkward spots ironed out, with new bridges and with clearances, keeping beside the river virtually all the way. What is more, such is the enthusiasm for a Thames Path that it is planned to extend it right through London and the tidal reaches as far as the Thames Barrier, with routes on both banks from below Kingston Bridge.

This immediately raises the question of the quality of the Thames Path as a walk, and it must be frankly recognized that the tidal (or London) part of it is, to put it mildly, urban. To be sure, there are some fine old town centres, especially upstream of Putney Bridge. There are also buildings and monuments of national importance, especially in Westminster and the City of London. But there are an awful lot of industrial plants, tower blocks, concrete tunnels and walkways, road crossings and disproportionate developments. At many places the route deviates from the river embankment. So most of this part of the Thames Path is inherently for those kinds of walkers who do not demand a natural scene and are not too bothered by noise and traffic. For students of architecture, yes; for fitness walkers, yes; but for most readers of this book, no. In my view, the Thames Path only qualifies as a great long-distance trail upstream of Kew.

Compared to most of the rest of the world, the whole of rural southern England is a sort of garden: a place where certainly not everything is perfect, where needless destruction sometimes occurs; but still, from its manicured appearance, its intricacy, its delicate patterns of hedges and trees, far more like a garden or a park than what goes by the name of countryside in most of the world. When we walk, for instance, the South Downs Way or the Cornish Coastal Path, we are in part attempting to escape from an enclosed and cultivated environment, and we relish particularly those rare places on the trail where nothing can be seen except what is entirely natural and untamed. But the Thames Path provides no such illusions, for it runs right through the most luscious and leafy part of the country without any really wide views. Just as the best gardens comprise distinctive parts with different characteristics and themes, often with carefully contrived surprises, the visual prospect along the Thames Path is constantly changing, our eyes guided step by step and not by any distant scene. Gardens also should be relevant to architecture; mullion windows glimpsed through the magnolia, rusty-red walls behind the roses. And so it is on the Thames Path, where we come upon so many old church towers and amazingly varied houses and a sequence of bridges which serve to punctuate the course of the path. And then, of course, gardens must have water: small ones have ponds, large ones have lakes, streams or cascades. The Thames Path is a water-path, and the patterns and reflections on the flowing river beside us are as lively and ephemeral as the cloud formations above us.

In effect, the whole scene is artificial, as is our path itself. For prehistoric man never walked for long distances up the Thames: he rowed or punted up it. So in contrast to the great ridgeways which from time immemorial were essentially walking routes, the Thames is really a boat route where walkers are merely the subsequent, not the original, users.

However, walkers have no reason to be ashamed of this apparently junior status. On the contrary, it is they rather than those afloat who are nowadays more in touch with the spirit of ancient times. For, excepting the competitive rowers, the simple exertion of physical energy has largely ceased upon the waters of the Thames. It is a fine sight to see a racing eight go by, striking the water in clean, crisp, confident harmony; but all too often, as we walk beside the river, we only see scenes of complete lethargy among our fellow humans. At regular intervals, each with expensive gear and tackle, the motionless fishermen are seated comfortably. Passing along the river is a procession of cabin cruisers with what seem to be incredibly fat people lounging on deck or fingering the wheel. And on summer weekends a general mass of humanity sunbathing, picnicking or kissing.

All these types gaze upon the lithe figure of the long-distance walker with what seems to be a certain degree of contempt that anyone should be so foolish as to use his legs when he could so easily sit or ride. What is distressing about the cabin cruisers is that despite the strict speed limits they still damage the river banks with their wash, and of course they break the spell of the river by the hum of their engines and the often unsightly flashiness of their superstructures. By their wash and bulk they have served to drive away the punts and small skiffs that were once so popular on the Thames. Frankly, I just wish there were fewer of them.

Fortunately, the cruisers and the loungers tend to peak on summer weekends and from November till April they disappear. All the better, then, to walk in the dark half of the year. One of the great advantages of our mild climate is that long-distance walking can be enjoyed throughout all twelve months, but nowhere are the relative advantages of winter greater than on the Thames Path. Flooding, that chronic hazard of the winter – which used to obliterate whole sections of the towpath up-river – is now very rare thanks to rigorous water control. And mud, which can be so bothersome at any time, is nowhere to be found on a really frosty day, quite apart from the gravelled mileages along the lower stretches.

Thus, firmly footed, we set out in bracing winter along the silent and fast-flowing river, so much more exciting than the placid stream of summer: a purposeful mass of gunmetal grey, with swirling eddies and flotsam of twigs. The spindly forms of bushes and trees, black at a distance, change to subtle colours when close – trunks piebald,

The Thames at Lechlade in Gloucestershire.

stained, furrowed, lichened, and branches yellow, purple or brown, the oaks still with leaves, the hazels already with catkins, the alders guarding their buds. In hoar frost under a bright blue sky crystalline patterns sparkle on the grass and white ice shines on the water-meadows. Or else, whenever visibility is poor due to fog or mist or drizzle or failing light, the path is never dull, for strange shapes and forms are always looming, revealing themselves as walls or plants or bridges.

The phrase 'the stripling Thames' has become something of a cliché in describing the river above Oxford. It comes from a poem by Matthew Arnold and reminds us that in walking the Thames Path we walk all the way with history and literature as ghostly companions, both trying to whisper stories of every reach, every village, if only we would listen to them. Far more than on any of

The Thames at Kelmscott, above Oxford.

Does this mean that the Thames Path is only for literary folk in search of William Morris or Alexander Pope? Not at all; for ignorance can still be bliss in a physical sensation so basic as walking, and the path along the non-tidal Thames can be used simply as the best long-distance trail for walkers or runners in the London area, where 'centurions' can conveniently do their hundred miles in twenty-four hours at any time, and traffic-free; or where lovers of the hills of the north can go for energetic training walks on winter weekends. At the other extreme, it is there also for families out for short strolls, for pub-crawlers or naturalists, in fact for everyone, thanks to its extreme accessibility.

Conforming to its reputation as a peaceful and undramatic river, rockless and gorgeless and with hardly a hill in sight, the source of the Thames is almost laughably obscure. Any imaginative thoughts of the mighty Nile flowing from Lake Victoria or the Sorge gushing out of the limestone at Fontaine de Vaucluse, or even of the rival Severn springing from high on Plynlimmon, must be banished from our minds. Rejecting the claims of the seven-springed Churn to be the true Thames fount, we pursue our path through fields, often having to take on trust that the sluggish ditch of water beside us is truly the Thames. We find ourselves walking beside Father Thames's made-up bed which he has for the moment vacated; he rises sometimes near Kemble, sometimes nearer to Ewen; between Ashton Keynes and Waterhay Bridge he plays a trick and avoids his official route; only very seldom does he spring from his official source on Trewsbury Mead.

Long-distance walkers who become infuriated with multiplicity of gates and stiles would better end their walk at Cricklade rather than pursuing the wily old god to his lair. For the head of the Thames Path, like the tidal tail, though full of curiosity, somehow lacks the impelling thrust which the greater part of it provides for walkers, the challenge to get up and go which it shares with our other splendid official walking routes in Britain.

our other national trails, true appreciation can only be obtained by reading as well as walking, for so much is hidden from the outward eye. This is always a problem for long-distance walkers. Many are not prepared to sit down to a study session before their walk, and, once started, are equally reluctant to break pace by pausing to consult a guidebook. But there it is; and it remains a challenge to combine experience with understanding.

GREATEST AMONG THE GREEN ROADS

Britain is criss-crossed with very ancient highways and smaller subsidiary tracks known to villagers and others who respect them as the Green Roads. The discovery of flint tools, jet beads and fragments of ogham lettering on a number of trails such as the Maiden Way that led to The Wall, High Street above Hawes Water and Rumbolds Way that winds around Ilkley Moor, probably from the Irish Channel to the North Sea and thought by some to be a gold route to Gaul, shows clearly that these prehistoric roads were tramped down by the Celts and their predecessors long before the Legions landed behind Caesar and Claudius. For a nucleus, a veritable *omphalos* of Green Roads, there is no finer conjunction of the trails of antiquity than can be viewed with awe in the vicinity of Stonehenge and Avebury. I stress that word awe, meaning reverential wonder, since archaeologists are all too often mealy-mouthed about their pernickety craft. They delve and date but rarely stand and stare.

On that conjunction around Salisbury Plain, the Dorset Downs, the Mendips, the Cotswolds, the Ridgeway and the extensions of the North and South Downs come close to a common centre as does the hub of an outward-whirling Catherine wheel under Newton's superficially simple principle of action and reaction. Paths beget paths and one of the greatest of them in terms of distance – it's a slice out of a much longer track – is the Ridgeway.

Adam Nicolson has convinced us that chalk ridges are by no means confined to England. Early post-glacial invaders must have encountered them, perhaps in Artois and Flanders. On those lightly clad hills of Wessex they were relatively safe from the hostilities of Wild Wood. There those adventurous fellows could slash and burn, hunt and, eventually, graze domesticated beasts. And there they built chambered tombs and stone circles for rituals, the relicts of which are among our national treasure.

Hugh Westacott, a well known author and guide, starts his tour on the north-eastern rim of the Chiltern Hills where from slopes of wild thyme, orchids, dogwood, viburnum, hawkweeds and gentians you may look down on some of the finest beech woods in Britain. He indulges us in a walk through time.

J.H.

THE RIDGEWAY PATH

HUGH WESTACOTT

And see you marks that show and fade,
  Like shadows on the Downs?
O they are the lines the Flint Men made,
  To guard their wondrous towns.

Trackway and Camp and City lost,
  Salt Marsh where now is corn –
Old Wars, old Peace, old Arts that cease,
  And so was England born!

  From *Puck's Song* by Rudyard Kipling.

The dry statistics of the Ridgeway Path are easily told. The route runs from Ivinghoe Beacon in Buckinghamshire for 89 miles to Overton Hill which lies on the A4 some 12 miles south of Swindon. All other long-distance paths have clearly defined beginnings and endings in towns and villages so why should this particular route start from the top of a hill in the Chilterns and end obscurely at a main road 2 miles from the village of Avebury? The answer is simple, and is what makes the Ridgeway unique. It was created originally to follow part of the prehistoric ridgeway track which once ran from Wells-next-the-Sea in Norfolk to Axmouth in east Devonshire.

It is a pleasant route which passes through few towns and villages and much of it is surprisingly remote from the teeming millions who inhabit southern England. In the 40 miles from Streatley to Overton Hill there is only one small village, Ogbourne St George, and a handful of houses beside the path. When compared with other long-distance routes in southern England it does not rate very high in the scenic stakes; it is finer than the North Downs Way but it cannot, in my opin-

ion, match either the South Downs Way or the Cotswold Way. Yet no Englishman who has wondered idly about the mysterious grass-covered bumps and hollows on the downs and the stark stone circles of Stonehenge and Avebury that the fingers of time have left behind can fail to be moved by its historical associations. In order to get the maximum enjoyment from this easy walk it is essential to have some understanding of the story of the Ridgeway and the role that it has played in our history.

Ten thousand years ago the landscape of southern England looked very different from how it does today. Instead of a smiling, manicured pattern of neat fields, copses and stands of timber, the naked chalk hills were lightly clothed in vegetation. The river Thames had neither locks to control the flow of water nor bridges to provide access from one bank to the other. It was shallow, slow and sluggish, nearly a mile wide in places, and with dangerous marshes along its strand. England was still joined to Europe by a narrow isthmus and would not become an island for another two thousand years. The thick forests provided an ideal habitat for wolves, bears, wild pigs and deer which were hunted by the primitive nomadic tribes who followed the game that, together with fish from the rivers and wild berries, nuts and fruits, formed their staple diet.

These nomads had very little effect on the landscape and it was not until some time between the years 4000–3000 BC that the first farmers arrived in Britain and, in the course of the next few hundred years, firmly imprinted their presence on the countryside. Nobody can be certain why they sailed their frail craft from France to establish a

new life in a strange land but at least two plausible theories have been advanced. It has been suggested that the Neolithic farmers who spread across Europe had no understanding of crop rotation or the nitrogen cycle and would farm a patch of land until it was exhausted and then move on. Eventually they reached the English Channel where they could see the white cliffs of what is now Dover from vantage points near present-day Calais and Boulogne. No doubt with some trepidation they made the crossing. The second theory is that fishermen from northern France were blown out to sea by a storm, made a landfall on our shores, liked what they saw and later brought their families and wordly goods to their new-found land.

Their first task was to clear some of the primeval forest, which was accomplished by slashing, burning and turning domestic animals loose, to make enclosures in the forest that the settlers were then able to cultivate. As the population increased the amount of forest gradually lessened, leaving the chalk hills denuded of trees.

These Neolithic farmers are known to archaeologists as the Windmill Hill people from the causewayed camp excavated on the hill of that name, just north of Avebury, which is typical of many similar structures in southern England. These enormous enterprises are usually sited on hills and comprise a series of concentric earth banks and ditches. Contrary to popular opinion, they were not designed primarily as fortifications

because excavations have revealed that they were used as cattle enclosures with the people living outside in thatched huts. Doubtless they could be defended for a short time during a skirmish but they could not hold out for long as they had neither springs nor wells and every drop of water had to be carried up from the plain.

The increasing population encouraged growth in the trading of the necessities of Stone Age life. After food, flint was their most basic requirement. From this substance, widely found in the chalk of southern England, Neolithic man constructed remarkably efficient axes, hammers, knives, scrapers and arrow heads, making high-quality flint a much prized commodity. Scientists can identify the source of some flint implements and there is evidence that the best flint which came from the prehistoric mines near Brandon in Norfolk was widely traded throughout England.

Four thousand years ago it was natural for trading routes to follow the lines of the chalk hills which dominate the landscape of the southern half of the country. The North and South Downs, the Chilterns, the Berkshire Downs, together with their subsidiary ridges, provided the easiest routes for moving about the country. The forest was far less dense on the hilltops; chalk does not become waterlogged like the heavy wealden clays found in the valleys, and passage for man and beast was relatively easy. This is how the route we know as the Ridgeway Path came into being.

ABOVE: *Ivinghoe Hills, Buckinghamshire. A white lion has been cut into the chalk. One end of the Ridgeway Path is at Ivinghoe Beacon.*

RIGHT: *Avebury Stone Circle, Wiltshire. The other end of the Ridgeway Path is two miles from the village of Avebury.*

Our Neolithic ancestors left several outstanding monuments on or close to the Ridgeway. At Avebury, 2 miles from the western end of the modern long-distance path, they constructed a stone circle so large that a medieval village was subsequently built within the confines of the great ditches. The diarist and antiquarian, John Aubrey, was moved to comment that the monument surpassed Stonehenge 'as a cathedral doth a parish church'. A few hundred yards away, and clearly associated with it, is Silbury Hill, the largest manmade hill in Europe, which so impressed the Romans that they diverted their main road from London to Bath around it. This extraordinary structure is 130 feet high, 126 feet wide, covers 5.5 acres and is surrounded by a ditch 125 feet wide and 30 feet deep. It has been excavated several times, the most recent under the full glare of television, but although we know that it was constructed carefully and ingeniously, we know next to nothing about its function. It does not appear to be a tomb nor was there ever a structure on its summit. One intriguing theory is that it represents the Great Earth Mother in the birth or squatting position, a kind of statue in soil, and it has been suggested that the site was chosen because the spring over which it is built floods at certain times of the year, symbolizing menstruation.

At West Kennett, a mile or so from the end of the Ridgeway Path, is an enormous long barrow or chambered tomb built to house the important dead of the Windmill Hill people and there is another, known as Wayland's Smithy, a stone's throw from the path near Ashbury close to the Uffington hill fort.

In about the year 2400 BC the Beaker people started to arrive in Britain from the Rhine delta. The superior technology of their bronze tools soon supplanted flint implements but it seems that they accepted, or perhaps shared, the religious beliefs of the Windmill Hill people. At any rate they continued to use Avebury and also enlarged Stonehenge. The Beaker people are best known for their ubiquitous pottery which gave their culture its name.

The last wave of prehistoric settlers to enter Britain were the Iron Age Celts who came here about the year 700 BC. They lived in farms and small villages, kept cattle, sheep and pigs and grew corn which was stored for winter use in underground granaries. It is believed that the large flocks of sheep that they kept were responsible for clearing the last of the scrub on the downland hills, leaving them with the appearance that they now have. The famous White Horse near Uffington Castle is their work, too.

The Celts covered southern England with defensive hill forts and there are no less than four – Letcombe Castle, Uffington Castle, Liddington Castle and Barbury Castle – occurring on a 23-mile stretch of the Ridgeway Path. They were definitely built for defence but, as is the case with the Neolithic hill forts, unless the water table was higher then or dew ponds were constructed, they lacked water and could not be held for long against a siege. During the Roman occupation of Britain they fell into disuse but after the Romans withdrew and the Saxons invaded, these forts were re-occupied by Romano-British forces defending the upper Thames valley. Indeed, an important battle took place at Barbury Castle in AD 556 which resulted in a resounding defeat for the Saxons. They were garrisoned again in the ninth century as a defence against the Danes who were attempting to push south from the Thames. King Alfred won a significant battle over the Danes in 878 at Ethandune, the modern Edington, 20 miles from Barbury Castle.

In the medieval period the arts of fortification and siege warfare had advanced so far that the Ridgeway forts were obsolete and even the route itself fell into disuse except for local traffic. It might have been forgotten altogether were it not for the coming of the turnpikes. For centuries cattle, sheep and pigs had been driven on the hoof from as far away as Scotland and Wales to provide fresh meat for the London markets. They travelled slowly along the main roads, churning up the surface and infuriating faster travellers by their leisurely pace. The Turnpike Acts required tolls to be paid and the money raised was used for the repair and upkeep of the roads. Overnight the drovers were looking for alternative routes which they could use without payment and thus the Ridgeway gained a new lease of life. Once the railway network spread droving itself died and the

White Horse Hill at Uffington, Oxfordshire, one of many Celtic hill forts in southern England. The White Horse is thought to be a product of the Iron Age because of its resemblance to designs on coins of that period.

Ridgeway again fell into disuse, until its future was assured by its designation as a long-distance path by the Countryside Commission.

Unless entirely lacking in historical imagination, nobody can fail to be moved by such an extraordinary pageant of history. The scenery is pleasant, if unremarkable, but every step of the way is redolent of history and you will be travelling in the footsteps of our prehistoric forbears. Set off with a spring in your tread, joy in your heart and treat the journey as a pilgrimage through time with your goal the wonderful prehistoric complex of Avebury.

The pilgrimage starts auspiciously from Iving-hoe Beacon, the only really steep hill on the route, which is capped with a 2,500-year old Iron Age fort. From its ramparts where Celtic tribesmen once maintained their lonely vigil we can see a cement factory and a seventeenth-century wind-mill in working order. At Tring we are reminded of our industrial past as we cross the Grand Union Canal and the main London to Edinburgh railway which utilize a gap in the chalk hills. At Georgian Wendover, described by Defoe as 'mean and dirty' but now pullulating with ladies in yuppie tweeds, visit the attractive Red Lion described by Robert Louis Stevenson and enjoy the excellent savoury bar snacks. A few yards away is the public library, an outstanding example of the best in modern architecture, at once contemporary yet wholly in sympathy with its Georgian neighbours.

From Wendover we walk through glorious beechwoods where, within living memory, bodgers worked in huts in the woods making chairs and tables for the Buckinghamshire furni-ture industry, and amble through the grounds of Chequers, the country home of the Prime Minis-ter. If the Queen's chief minister is in residence large men, incongruously dressed in black bowler hats and brown suits, patrol this section of the path, or lurk in the woods staring suspiciously at innocent wayfarers.

At Princes Risborough we join the Icknield Way, yet another ancient trackway which can still be traced, although long stretches now form part of the modern road system, from Wells-next-the Sea in Norfolk to Goring where it meets the Great Ridgeway. The name may be derived from Boudicca's tribe, the Iceni, who gave the Romans so much trouble, or possibly from the old English word for oxen. It passes under the M40 motorway

The Thames from the bridge at Streatley, where the Ridgeway Path descends from the hills to cross the river. This narrow stretch of water where sleek pleasure craft now glide was much wider and a formidable natural barrier in prehistoric times.

where we can smugly remind ourselves how fortunate we are to be experiencing the landscape through the soles of our boots instead of hurtling past isolated in a tin box on wheels. By the time we pass Nuffield churchyard, the last resting place of the motor magnate William Morris, we have turned our backs on the Icknield Way to follow the top of Grim's Ditch, one of the many extraordinary prehistoric boundaries which run for miles through southern England, until we reach the river Thames at Streatley.

This narrow stretch of water where sleek pleasure craft now glide was much wider and a formidable natural barrier in prehistoric times. The lychgate in North Stoke churchyard was a gift from Dame Clara Butt, a statuesque singer who gave recitals of patriotic songs dressed as Britannia, her ample figure swathed in the Union Jack, a helmet on her head and a sceptre in her hand. As we stroll here through pleasant water meadows we shall pass under Brunel's handsome viaduct built to take God's Wonderful Railway to Bristol and see, on the opposite bank, the Beetle and Wedge Hotel which H. G. Wells used as a model for the Potwell Inn in *The History of Mr Polly* and from where George Bernard Shaw went rowing. In South Stoke is a noncomformist chapel built by Selina, Countess of Huntingdon. The slightly eccentric Countess was a missionary for Methodism among the aristocracy and believed that her title gave her the right to appoint chaplains to the army.

From Streatley we climb on to the lonely downs where the Ridgeway proper begins. Cwichelm, a Saxon king, is remembered in the place names of Cuckhamsley Hill and nearby Scutchamer Knob. The latter is probably a Saxon burial mound and may have been used as a moot or meeting place. From here we get distant views of Didcot power station and the Atomic Energy Research Establishment at Harwell.

All about us are traces of prehistoric mound, ditch and barrow as we reach Letcombe Castle, the first of the Ridgeway's prehistoric forts, followed by Uffington Castle, where it is worth descending to the road to look back on the White Horse. Nobody can be certain of its date but modern scholars incline to the belief that it is a product

of the Iron Age because it resembles figures on coins of the period. It measures 365 feet long and is 130 feet high and drawing the outline on the hillside must have posed considerable technical and drafting problems. Close by is the reputed site of the slaying of the dragon by St George.

Wayland's Smithy, which derives its name from the Saxon legend that Wayland, the smith of the gods, would shoe your horse if money were left by the barrow, is a magnificent chambered tomb dating from about 3000 BC and is the next point of interest before descending to cross the M4 motorway. We skirt the summit of Liddington Castle, much loved by the naturalist Richard Jefferies who lived for most of his life hereabouts, and pass close to the site of the deserted village of Snap, abandoned in the nineteenth century in an unsuccessful attempt to turn this section of the Wiltshire Downs into a vast sheep range.

The pleasant village of Ogbourne St George is our next landmark and then we cross Smeathe's Ridge to reach the splendid ramparts of Barbury Castle where once, in the silent watches of the night, the Romano-British defenders prepared themselves for the morrow's battle against the invading Saxons. On Avebury Down, 2 miles from the official end of the long-distance path, we turn south-west to follow the ancient Herepath for a mile and a half into Avebury to avoid the anti-climax of finishing our walk at a featureless junction on the A4 trunk road.

But before descending to the great stone circle, pause for a few minutes and reflect on your journey. Press yourself close to the English earth and, if the Old Gods are kind, you may be rewarded by hearing whispers from the past: the whistling flight of an arrow loosed by a nomadic hunter; the heartfelt prayer uttered to the Great Earth Mother by a Neolithic farmer to ensure that spring will come and his children will not starve; the fluting of a bronze trumpet at ceremonies in the Great Stone Circle; the measured tramp of a Roman cohort marching from Londinium to Aquae Sulis; the despairing sounds of battle on the slopes of Barbury Castle as the Saxon shield ring breaks; the frenzied lowing of cattle as the drovers urge their herds towards London; and rejoice and be glad that these things are part of our heritage.

DREAMERS AND DISTANCE-SLAYERS

'The earth calls aloud for the passionate dreamer.' I can't trace the quotation but the line came back with uncommon force the other morning, early, when walking round Hampstead Heath as I have done for so many years. I went out intent on confirming that a pair of those cheerful little birds, the reed bunting, the male with his black cap, epaulettes and white collar, had returned to nest on the fringe of one of our ponds. I thought I had heard its melodic song that begins slowly and ends in a flourish the previous morning but couldn't be sure. And I had other matters to think about. What could I say about our next contributor, Richard Mabey, that interfered neither with his leisurely style, so deceptively simple, nor his philosophy touched on in *Second Nature*, the anthology he edited which had to do with forging practical and philosophical links between the arts and the conservation of nature and landscapes?

In between wondering whether the words about the dreamer had been written by Walt Whitman or John Cowper Powys and their relevance to *Second Nature*, I walked straight past the pond and didn't think about buntings again until I was all but home. So there is clearly philosophy in what you'll be reading in a few moments. As for myself I am rarely a stroller and may well seek to justify the urge to brisk along after you've enjoyed, as I hope you will, the courses of our other fellow-travellers on foot. But be sure that I'm conscious of that for which I've been nicely reproved by repeating what happened to me once in the great cathedral city of Metz.

I had walked there and with a pressing need to pick up some transferred money in Strasbourg was anxious to be off, but not before trying to find the last known home of Rabelais. After getting lost, twice, an elderly and very dignified street cleaner volunteered to guide me there with his brush over his shoulder, like a rifle. But in a leisurely roundabout way. Sensing my impatience, he stopped. He turned to me and said, 'Forgive me, M'*sieu*, but from what are you running away?'

J.H.

A WALK AROUND THE BLOCK

RICHARD MABEY

It is becoming hard these days to justify the pleasures of simply going for a walk. In a world of sponsored hikes and mass pilgrimages strolling smacks of introspection, self-indulgence and an unhealthy lack of competitive drive. Ambling about with no badges of purposefulness – sloganed tee-shirts and dogs are the favourites – you are looked on as a figure of fun or, worse, of suspicion. Children clasp each others' hands as you approach. Long-distance yompers elbow you aside, a cissified obstacle not worthy of consideration. In America the physical act of walking itself is being systematically streamlined by the health industry, with prescribed garb, gaits and breathing patterns. Soon, no doubt, there will be customized mantras guaranteed to block out the distractions of the outside world. Going for a walk, one of the most civilized of pleasures precisely because it can be indulged in purely for its own sake, is now expected to *do* something, either for you or the world.

Yet in a roundabout and less transcendental way this has always been one of the aims of casual walking. 'Just off to stretch the legs,' we say, meaning, as everybody understands, the less mentionable intention of stretching (or relaxing) the mind. Kim Taplin, in her book *The English Path*, recalls the old Latin proverb *solvitur ambulando*, which roughly translates as 'sort it out by walking'. She points out the various connotations of *solvitur* – finding out, working out, unknotting, freeing – all good strolling agendas. It is the combination of gentle physical activity and close contact with the natural world that seems to do the trick. Even the basic business of navigating, of confronting traffic, weather and potholes in the lane, seems to help. It

may not be that calming, but it does bring you down to earth.

For Dr Johnson and George Borrow, both great wanderers in their time, making contact with the outside world took on a more literal meaning. Both were dogged by recurrent bouts of depression, and to keep some kind of link with reality they used to touch objects – trees especially – on their way. For William Hazlitt solitary walking was a great aid to contemplation, particularly amongst familiar surroundings. 'I can saunter for hours,' he wrote, 'bending my eye forward, stopping and turning to look back, thinking to strike off into some less trodden path, yet hesitating to quit the one I am on, afraid to snap the brittle threads of memory.'

These ritual qualities, the sense of marking out one's territory, seem to be an underlying part of the business of most strolling. We all have favourite times and occasions for going for a walk, and favourite well-trodden paths, too. Even away from home, a quick turn around the town is always more than just a way of working up an appetite. It is a kind of first-footing, a way of confirming your arrival and getting your bearings. It can also be an act of geographical courtesy, like sampling the local beer, and can give you the same quick savour of a place. In after-dinner constitutionals round hotel grounds I have heard nightingales in Suffolk and found rows of glow-worms along a Sussex drive. Whenever I go to the Yorkshire Dales in early summer, the village hay meadows on that first evening stroll seem to have a burnished newness, a compactness, that later, more far-flung tramps can never quite recapture.

But dawdling on foreign territory is when you

can look most conspicuously odd and out of place. One Easter in Suffolk, I broke a car journey to take an airing along a footpath that wound invitingly towards a copse in the middle of a barley field. It was an ancient track, banked and ditched, and I rather hoped there might be oxlips in the wood. I left the path, climbed a gate, and sure enough there were. But soon there was also an outraged farmer who had trailed me up the track. I don't think it was my minor act of trespass that had upset him, nor my feeble waving of the Ordnance Survey map as an excuse, so much as the sheer casualness of my arrival.

'You've got a car,' he shouted, 'you could have come to the farm and asked.' It was a reminder about the original purpose of footpaths that I have never forgotten.

You are on somewhat surer ground on your home patch, and here the routes can become ritualistic as well as the strolling habit. There are about half a dozen walks near my home in the Chilterns that I am repeatedly drawn back to. One, a mile out and back along a canal towpath, is really a walk of convenience, since it starts just a hundred yards from my door. Another, a short but sinuous tour of a famous wood of gnarled pollards called Frithsden Beeches, is a guaranteed cure for introspection. Beechwoods are conventionally likened to cathedrals, places for quiet meditation. Not this one. At all times and seasons it is a turmoil of gale-strewn trunks, grotesque natural gargoyles and fleeting patterns of light and shade.

But I suspect the reasons I am habituated to two other walks are more complicated. Although one is a half-hour hilltop stroll just a few hundred yards from my home, and the other a two-hour river valley circuit 10 miles away, they have a lot in common. Both are circular routes. Both repeatedly change their perspective, winding in and out of woods, round dog-legs, and opening up sudden views and hidden glades.

I began making the nearer walk when I was a young teenager. I was obsessed with bird watching at the time and this short lap was a condensed tour of all our best local habitats. For the first few hundred yards it followed a lane, past fields which were haunted by grey partridges and sometimes a barn owl. Then it struck off left into a thin strip of common woodland where the first chiffchaffs always appeared, and where, if you were lucky, you might glimpse redstarts on migration. Here and there, through gaps in the trees, you could gaze down into the valley of a winterbourne, a 'woe-water' that was supposed to flow only in times of trouble or war. There were owls down there, too, and wild mushrooms.

Later my weekly – daily, sometimes – trudges round this circuit took on a more intense, contemplative character. I would follow not just the basic route, but my own previous footsteps: along the right of the lane, hugging close to the dense blackthorn, cutting off the corner by the sentinel beech, turning for home along the field edge, not on the footpath just a few feet below. At one point I would always stop and gaze in something close to rapture at the vista that rolled away to the south, 2 miles of hills, copses, chalk scrub and green lanes, with the silver thread of the winterbourne knitting them together until it vanished in the distant heat haze.

In my fervent adolescent years that walk became a bench-mark, an arena in which I tested out experiences that seemed important to me. It was a path to take girlfriends along (and, absurdly, to try and escape from them). I revised for exams on it, chanting the elements in the Periodic Table in time with the passing trees. Occasionally, when birdsong was over for the year, I would take a portable radio with me, to listen to the carols from Kings College on Christmas Eve, and in one preposterous act of romantic overload, to a broadcast of Beethoven's Pastoral Symphony on Midsummer Eve, a true promenade concert.

I was, I can see now, beating the bounds, checking out both my personal parish and the shifts in my feelings about it. It says something about the character and stability of this corner of the Chilterns that after thirty years it can still cast a healing spell over me.

Grimes Ditch, an ancient banked and ditched track in the Chiltern Hills near Naphill Common in Buckinghamshire. Beechwoods, like cathedrals, are marvellous places for quiet contemplation.

But when I fear this domestic circuit won't work, or just want something on a grander scale, I opt for the further walk, down in the valley of the Chess. This is about as far as I would drive just for a stroll, yet, in contrast to my home patch, it has a distinctly southern feel. Bluebells flower sooner and swallows arrive earlier. There is a luxuriance of bloom and hedgerow that reminds you of Samuel Palmer's Kent landscapes. My walk passes through a line of riverside water meadows, sudsy with meadowsweet, where I once saw six cuckoos together in a single field. Then it crosses the river, climbs a little and returns along the foot of an airy beech hanger. The beeches are regularly blown down and with each new gap (and new diversion in the footpath) there are startling new views of the woodlands on the scarp ridge to the

ABOVE: Fleeting patterns of light and shade on a beech tree's weathered trunk.

RIGHT: Dappled light in autumn beechwoods.

north. They are cherry woods, for the most part, cloaked with white blossom in April, and later ringed by it, when the petals fall and settle round their rims.

There is a flamboyant, southerly feel about the people here, too. It is a popular walk, strewn with picnickers and paraders when the weather is fine. One regular plods the circuit in climbing boots, carrying a small dog in his arms. Another photographs the wild flowers on his knees, as if in reverent astonishment that they should open in his presence. Two others I have never glimpsed, but their polished champagne glasses are hidden high in the cruck of a riverside oak.

Can regular walking round a familiar beat influence one's thinking, become a kind of ingrained memory track that can be replayed at will? It can

certainly affect the way one writes. Even a short walk can provide a writer with a ready-made narrative structure just as effectively as a grand tour. Yet what is intriguing is how often the *styles* of walking find their way directly into the styles of written accounts. One critic, for instance, has suggested that W. H. Hudson's rambling prose 'perfectly echoed the long, slow unhurried tramping of his feet as he roamed through the gentle southern counties each summer.' Hudson, though, was essentially a tourist, and for me his long-distance ramblings about England echo more with the footsteps of the patronizing snooper. Far better, and closer to catching the feel of everyday meandering, is middle-period Richard Jefferies, when he was producing a mass of effervescent journalism for the new urban audience. The essays in collections like *Round About a Great Estate* (1880) are addressed directly to his audience. 'If you should happen to be walking . . .' many of them seem to begin. It is quite infectious. The reader is taken by the hand and *led*.

John Clare, by contrast, seems barely to consider his readers at all. He is caught up in the immediacy of the moment, or perhaps the remembered immediacy of his childhood, and his many poems which are based on favourite local walks conjure up the image of a boy darting with barely controllable excitement from one side of the road to the other:

> When jumping time away on old cross berry way
> And eating awes like sugar plumbs ere they had lost the may
> And skipping like a leveret before the break of day
> On the rolly poly up and down of pleasant Swordy well . . .

There are many others. John Cowper Powys's recollection of the 'sunken treasure' of his favourite field-path routes. John Bunyan's gossipy account of his *Pilgrim's Progress*, which mirrors his own wanderings about the Bedfordshire fields and up into the Chiltern heights. But the patron poet of strollers is William Cowper. After his first mental breakdown in the 1760s, Cowper went to live with friends in the quiet Buckinghamshire parish of Olney. Like many before him he tried to keep his melancholy under control by busying himself in active, domestic routines – gardening, walking, looking after his pet hares, and in something close to communion with the physical details of his small universe. 'The very stones in the garden-walls are my intimate acquaintances,' he wrote in a letter in 1783.

All this is reflected in his Olney poetry, which pays unfashionably vivid attention to the minute, living detail of the natural world. But it is the structure of his poetry, especially his masterwork *The Task*, that breaks most graphically from the taste for carefully constructed landscape des-criptions, and which owes most to his habit of walking. Much of *The Task* is not ordered to any particular design but offers scenes, observations, reflections exactly as they might be encountered on a stroll. Scale and perspective are repeatedly changing, so that one moment a wild flower is in focus, the next a whole cycle of work in a distant field. One passage in *The Task*, where Cowper is playing games with his own shadow, is a perfect evocation of the state of mind of the habitual walker. It captures not just the idiosyncratic view-point of the stroller, but, with the lightest of wry humour, hints at the one danger that lurks on the path: the possibility that the rhythmic step and familiar route may become so hypnotic that far from escaping your self, you become utterly absorbed in it:

> Mine, spindling into longitude immense,
> In spite of gravity and sage remark
> That I myself am but a fleeting shade,
> Provokes me to a smile. With eye askance
> I view the muscular proportion'd limb
> Transform'd to a lean shank. The shapeless pair,
> As they design'd to mock me, at my side
> Take step for step; and, as I near approach
> The cottage, walk along the plaster'd wall,
> Prepost'rous sight! the legs without the man.

Cattle grazing in the watermeadows beside the river Chess near Latimer in Buckinghamshire. The Chess valley has a distinctly southerly feel.

FACING UP TO REALITIES

On the white-papered wall above the desk where I am sitting writing this hangs a watercolour of a wild place known to countless thousands of walkers, a place comparable in quite different ways with the sodden crest of Kinder Scout and the fire-scarred face of the Cuillins. The place is a small road that winds up towards Malham in the Pennines. But here no close-up of the Cove, that cliff of mountain limestone, pitted like an old cheese by the pitons of rope hangers, nor nearby Gordale Scar where a torrent pumps oxygen into the youthful Aire by somersaulting down from the wreck of a spectacular cave. My picture is of a place I have known for over sixty years.

There is a tree, probably a wych elm, growing through the roof of a ruined cottage. This dwelling might have been built, block upon block, by Malham villagers who had heard from the carrier only a few days earlier that their king, Charles II, had fled to France after his defeat at Worcester by a Huntingdon Puritan who, before his conversion, confessed to having been the chief of sinners. Flowers which grow there are the pink primrose, Alpine penny-cress, spring sandwort and Jacob's ladder which makes a blue haze among the grey rubble. There is a swastika of walls to the lower left which seems undecided about where to go until, after hard-fought contest, it sweeps down Mastiles Lane, marking the old boundaries of the sheep walks of the Cistercians who built incomparable temples to God by inspired distinction between prayer, labour and what could be safely invested in wool. There is also a dominant tree in a halo of storm-wrack which is of the very stuff of the art of my good friend, David Bellamy.

The beginning of our friendship is a private matter marked by the picture I have tried, perhaps unsuccessfully, to describe. But I know him to have outstanding gifts which, unlike most artists, he is prepared to discuss in his endless search for capturing the indefinable. Five minutes after this picture was hastily sketched and its colour values put to good-quality cartridge paper, a torrential drenching swept down from Fountains Fell and in what follows we are the benefactors of how he can presage and turn to marvellous account the sort of weather most of us try to avoid.

J.H.

WILD
WEATHER SKETCHING

DAVID BELLAMY

The prospect of painting a delicate water-colour during a storm in intensely cold conditions and force ten winds at 3,000 feet is in all senses of the word elemental. However, despite the title, it is not my intention to attract a host of all-weather madcap artists to highly exposed regions. I am more concerned about pointing out the potentialities and showing how many of the problems can be overcome. Sketching and walking are two highly compatible pursuits. Walking is among the best ways of finding subjects and the effort involved in getting somewhere ought to supply enough warmth to enable you to sit down and sketch for a little while even on icy days in the Scottish Highlands. Sketching also provides an excuse to take a rest from the hard slog of mountain climbing.

Taking home a pictorial record of a trip, if only a sketch, is an attractive idea for the walker who has not tried it before. More personal than a photograph, it brings back all the memories of the walk: even the atmosphere and smells. With many of nature's most expressive moods occurring during bad weather, it seems a shame not to take advantage of the drama and put them on record. Nature is full of unexpected and occasionally violent surprises which can be appreciated only if we get out and observe them at first hand. As Boudin put it, 'Three strokes of the brush after nature are worth more than two days of labouring at the easel.'

Mild, warm weather is comfortable for sketching, but we limit ourselves drastically by waiting only for hot summer days. Bad weather has certain attractions: rain freshens up the landscape making colours more intense and vibrant; mist and haze simplify shapes and colours, often hiding irrelevant detail; angry skies can provide complete and dramatic subjects in themselves. A flask of hot soup helps morale, but if you are right-handed keep it on your left side – otherwise the brush often ends up in the soup. Even winter has many advantages that outweigh the obvious drawbacks. The sun is lower, giving longer shadows and greater contrast throughout the day. There is more variety in colour than in summer. Snow brings quite different opportunities and of course there are no midges or nettles to annoy us. Nothing is worse than having to scratch, dance and hop about as I have done during a midge attack when sketching in the Rhinogs.

Before tackling technical problems it's necessary to consider what it is you hope to achieve. Some may want to produce a sort of pictorial diary of a backpacking trip in a finely bound sketchbook, recording figures and references to almost everything including blisters; others may simply feel the need to make one stop during a day's tramp to produce a finished painting, whilst still others may wish to make rapid pencil sketches in a tatty little pad or on the back of their YHA membership card to be reproduced later as massive oil paintings.

It may well be, though, that at this stage you haven't any definite views on how you would like to approach sketching in the great outdoors and are more concerned about those awful people who descend on the unfortunate artist sitting nervously at his little easel. But be reassured: this can be fun. People on the whole tend to make kind and encouraging remarks about even the most appalling paintings. Children are always full

'A lull before the storm on Sgurr Fiona. Massive swirling clouds on the right-hand side of the painting help to balance the composition, otherwise the eye would "fall out" of the picture down the mountain's right-hand ridge.'

of praise and often much better behaved than adults: on one occasion whilst I painted Aira Force in the Lake District about thirty school children filed politely past behind me, followed by their teachers who stopped bang in front of my nose, totally blocking my view even though there were acres of room on either side. If you want to discourage viewers put yourself up against a wall, on a narrow ledge, in the middle of a stream, or lay an upturned cap on the ground with some coppers in it. Even so you can't avoid the occasional voyeur who will stop at nothing to look at what you are doing. You have the feeling that even water-cannon wouldn't shift that chap. But luckily he is a rarity. Mind you, I always find that when I'm sitting out in a blizzard people tend to keep well clear.

If you haven't tried sketching before I recommend buying only a pad of good-quality cartridge paper about 15×20 centimetres (6×8 inches) plus a selection of pencils graded from 2B to 4B. These, together with a sharp knife to maintain a good point, will be enough to start with. There is no need for an expensive outlay. A wide range of sketchbooks is available, from the humblest cartridge pad to tinted papers and attractively bound books. The sketchpad can be kept in pocket or mapcase and quickly brought into action. Viewers often don't realize you are sketching when you are working with just a pencil and pad, so it's a good way for the timid to begin. Skulking behind a wall when sketching 'into wind' I was once mistaken for a prying government official.

Alternatives to pencil are charcoal, conte crayon, and pens. Charcoal of course tends to be messy, but has a delightful softness, and large areas of tone can be applied quickly. A damp rag for cleaning hands and a fixative spray to stop the finished work rubbing are useful additions. Conte crayon, a hard chalk, comes in pencil and chalk form, in black, white, sanguine and sepia. It is useful for producing quick monochrome studies, and is best fixed like charcoal. Pens come in such a wide variety these days that I would say experiment with them until you find those that best suit your temperament. They are extremely effective if you wish to rescue a watercolour sketch that has gone wrong. Personally, I rarely use a pen as it is

ABOVE: 'A snowstorm in Westerdale on the North York Moors. The snow wasn't sticking on the ground but even so it was pretty wild while it lasted and I tried to convey the feeling of violent wind.'

RIGHT: 'Whernside from Ingleborough. Gusts of wind made me "reshape" parts of the hill as blobs of paint fell on to the paper where they shouldn't have. The sky excited me, however, as a snowstorm swept across the fell.'

not accommodating in wet weather. The final straw came one day while I was crouching under a massive boulder to sketch the Devil's Kitchen in Cwm Idwal. A trickle of water dripped off the boulder and caused a direct hit on the nib of my pen, turning what I had done into a sort of blot test used by psychoanalysts.

Eventually you might consider using colour. A full-scale oil-painting kit is scarcely practicable for those wishing to cover any distance on foot, and carrying a wet canvas across sodden moorland in a powerful gale is like trying to waltz with a live octopus. Soft pastels provide an excellent sketching medium, with beautiful, rich colours. However, you need to take quite a range of them with you in order to capture the colours since pastels don't mix in the way that paints do. As with charcoal a damp rag and fixative is helpful and it's best to use tinted paper of the Ingres type, though an ordinary cheap scrapbook will do if it is only for sketching. With pastels a pad is best as loose paper will rub laterally, causing much of the pastel to be smudged or dislodged from the paper. Unfortunately rain plays havoc with pastels.

To my way of thinking watercolour is best if you wish to sketch in colour. Paradoxically, it is perhaps easier to represent rain or snowstorms in watercolour than in pencil, though it isn't easy to carry it out. I like to use watercolours as often as possible, because it's the best way to put across the atmosphere of a place. Even if the colour is washed off enough usually remains to provide a useful guide. It normally dries fairly quickly out-doors, especially if you use a good-quality smooth cartridge or watercolour paper. The latter comes in various weights with a ROUGH surface, a NOT surface (not very rough) or a HOT PRESSED (smooth) surface. The ROUGH and NOT varieties take slightly longer to dry but on hot days they come into their own. The Winsor & Newton 'Cotman' paper is excellent for watercolour sketching, holding washes well, with an interesting surface texture.

Only a few colours are needed, as mixing colours should be encouraged. I recommend French Ultramarine, Burnt Umber, Lemon Yellow, New Gamboge, Payne's Gray, Raw Umber, Raw Sienna, Burnt Sienna, Bright Red and Viridian for

a start. Take three or four brushes: a 1-centimetre or 2-centimetre (½-inch or 1-inch) flat, a number five or six round and a number one or two rigger are fine for sketching. Red sable brushes are the best for watercolour, but they are the most expensive. There are quite a number of synthetic brushes on the market today which are very good. I find the Sceptre range from Winsor & Newton and the Prolene range by Pro Arte particularly good, long-lasting and with a good point which does not go limp when wet.

I keep brushes and pencils in an old plastic foam bath container, the cap of which unscrews to provide a water receptacle for sketching. Pads and paper are protected by a heavy duty plastic envelope large enough to take a variety of sizes. Even with this protection I sometimes find that after a week of continuous rain in the wilds the pages become saturated and stick together, forming beautiful patterns across the sketches. These items I keep in the rucksack with reserve brushes kept separately in case the brush container rolls over a precipice.

But this doesn't give you an all-weather system.

Rain and snow have no aesthetic pretensions. My secret here is the use of water-soluble pencils. These are often dismissed as child's playthings. They are no substitute for watercolour, but they do have their own delightful characteristics and provide an ideal sketching medium. Unlike ordinary pencils they are very effective when the weather turns nasty: essential weaponry in the mists of the Western Highlands. Make a start with four colours: black, blue, brown and green. They can be used in a number of ways, on their own or combined with watercolour washes. I much prefer to use the pencils with watercolour, first laying a watercolour wash on the paper, keeping it wet and immediately starting to work into the wet wash with a watercolour pencil. This has the advantage that you don't have to stop working to allow the wash to dry, thus speeding up the sketching process. I simply draw the features of the scene as though starting with a normal pencil. The black or brown pencil is best for this, although the blue one is excellent for rendering the outline of distant hills, automatically giving a feeling of recession. The pencils can also be used by dipping them into water and then drawing, but this needs constant dipping and the softness of the pencils means a lot of sharpening is necessary. Tones can be obtained by rubbing the pencil over the appropriate area and then brushing water across it; if you want to do this it is worth extending the range of colours you carry. I would recommend the Rexel Derwent Watercolour pencils as they have an excellent range of colours and are softer than others on the market. They can produce subtle gradations without necessarily leaving the original pencil marks on the paper.

Having assembled the materials I suggest that when planning your route on a map you give some thought to the possibility of subjects. While many scenes appear naturally unheralded, a little thought when reading the map can help enormously in locating others. This could even be geared to pubs along the way, providing a diversion for your companions while you stay to sketch the building, as I did in the Peak District one summer. It certainly loosened up my work, some say improved it. On a circular walk consider the best

direction in which to travel, bearing in mind the time of day in relation to light on the subject. For instance, very early morning is the best time to sketch Llyn-y-Cae on Cader Idris, when the sun – if it comes out – will be falling across the crags beyond the lake. Think too about approaching a mountain by the path alongside a stream rather than, say, an alternative path higher up, as usually the stream would make a superb lead-in to the finished painting, for example in Coire Ardair on Creag Meagaidh. Many of these tactics are learnt with experience. When on the move imagine you are being tailed by Red Indians. You are continually looking around you, scanning the scenery for possible subjects.

At last we are out in the great outdoors, sketchbook to hand and a scene in front of us. Where do we start? Look at the subject. What excites you most about it? Perhaps it is the light, the texture of stonework, or even shadows cast across a bank of snow. Move around and consider the best viewpoint; don't take the first one offered. Don't try to put too much in. Keep it simple. To begin with

'This view of a Lakeland stream was done entirely with watercolour pencils.'

'The Brecon Beacons from the Hay road. Snow began to sweep across the peaks and I only just had time to paint them in before the weather completely blotted them out.'

work only in ordinary pencil. Start with that part of the scene that first excited you and work outwards from that centre of interest. Forget about perspective and concentrate simply on producing as close a likeness to the original scene as you can. Look hard at the subject before committing pencil to paper: observation is the key to success and with patience Mother Nature will teach you a great deal about herself. Observe both shapes and tonal relationships – the differences in the darkness or lightness of an object when set against the adjacent part of the scene. Forget that your mind tells you that the cottage roof is black because it has been painted black, for if it is wet and the sun is shining on it the roof might well be the lightest part of the subject.

Normally the subject will show a varying amount of recession, technically known as aerial perspective. To create this feeling of depth or three-dimensional quality in a painting we need to be aware that as objects recede into the distance they appear colder (bluer); they are less dark in tone and less detail is visible. There will always be exceptions to this, but in the main it holds true. Therefore when painting a scene depicting a series of hills gradually getting closer, paint in the distant ones first with a pale tone. When this is dry paint the next closest hill slightly darker, and so on until the work is complete. Although there can be exceptions in watercolour, work in the light parts first, gradually introducing the darker areas. To ensure foreground objects stand out against a distant background make them more intense in tone. By introducing figures or animals a sense of scale can be achieved.

Strong wind is perhaps the worst element in which to sketch, but ample supplies of bulldog clips and elastic bands ensure that there is less chance of tearing sketchpads, or finding your almost-complete work of art face down in a muddy puddle. Wind can be portrayed by emphasizing bent trees and grasses, bent figures and wild diagonal clouds across the sky. The water-colourist David Cox was supreme in depicting windy, rainswept landscapes and his work is worth studying for this aspect alone. Rain can be annoying, but the work can be shielded by the body to a certain extent. Some artists use umbrellas but I regard them as a liability, and can imagine the sort of comments from others if I used one on the north ridge of Crib Goch. With watercolour pencils there is no need to go to great lengths to protect the work. To indicate rain with watercolour, use plenty of water in the sky and allow the washes to flow by holding the sketch at a steep angle.

Provided a suitable subject presents itself, painting in mist can be rewarding. There is greater unity as tones and colours are simplified. By ensuring that there is a prominent foreground feature – such as a tree, wall, gatepost or similar solid object – the work will have a feeling of depth as other features recede into the mist and simply become blurred areas of tone. This is best achieved in watercolour by laying an overall wash of light colour and while this is still wet introducing a darker colour into the wash to create a soft, fuzzy outline. Mist can also be quite exasperating: one February afternoon in the Cairngorms I walked some 4 miles across deep snow to sketch Coire an Lochain. The icy blue lochan looked inviting, pictorially that is. Alas, I had hardly begun the sketch when a thick mist swept down from the cliffs above and my subject vanished completely. On icy days gin is an excellent anti-freeze – for the water you are using for painting, I hasten to add.

It is worth asking yourself why are you sketching. If it is to learn how to draw or paint a certain object then a detailed study may be called for: you then have a reference sketch to take home. Perhaps you are happy with your rendering of trees, say, and simply want to take home a compositional sketch so that you can produce a full painting when you return. In this case you will not need so much detail, but will want to record the relationships of the various constituents of the scene. Or maybe you are just fascinated in capturing the atmosphere of the place. This is something best left until you have had more practice at sketching. In some ways it is interesting to make

'Hard Tarn, which is tucked away in the remotest recesses of Nethermost Cove in the Lake District. I did this quick watercolour sketch in light rain, and it demonstrates the loose application of colour washes. The rapid downward strokes of the brush are clearly visible and certain areas have been left white where they catch the light. Spots of rain have spattered the sketch, in some ways adding to its charm.'

'Storm, Sail Laith. This shows a blizzard about to arrive and the clouds torn asunder by strong gusts. The effect is heightened by using rough paper.' (From the collection of Mr and Mrs E. M. Trent.)

David Bellamy

small watercolours in discomfort as this demands quick, decisive action to get down the essentials. As it is a sketch and not a finished painting it can be tackled with much greater confidence. At times it will result in a glorious mess, but you will have learned a great deal. This is an ideal way to achieve spontaneity, the hallmark of a good watercolour. Naturally, while gaining experience, it is advisable to work in good weather until the rudiments have been mastered, otherwise sketching can be akin to an SAS training exercise. Don't expect to achieve a masterpiece during the first week, but by taking things a step at a time you will soon notice a gradual improvement in your work. You might even consider attending one of the many excellent painting courses held in various parts of the country, and there are several books on the subject of producing finished paintings from original sketches.

What can one do with companions when you wish to capture a scene? This is rather tricky, especially when they murmur mutinously as you sit sketching in a ferocious blizzard, totally oblivious of their stamping feet. The problem can be eased if you try to arrange for lunch breaks or rests to fall in places where you want to sketch. As you speed up your technique the situation improves, but it still needs to be handled tactfully. I find now that the boot is on the other foot. When Catherine, my six-year-old daughter, comes out walking she often insists on stopping to sketch, and her old dad must grin and bear it.

Sketching outdoors is one of the most therapeutic pursuits and a gloriously uninhibited form of expression. Don't allow yourself to be bogged down by rules, just get out and enjoy yourself. With any luck you will have some really dreadful weather in which to capture those incredibly atmospheric scenes. The seeds of enchantment and inspiration that spawn landscape art are within us all and it is when sitting amidst the natural environment that we are at our most receptive, though this might not be readily apparent as you sink slowly into a bog, sketching, as I did one wild wet day in the Preseli Hills. There is an urge to seek out the beautiful, the picturesque, and once smitten by the sketching virus there is no reversing the process. You are hooked for life.

THE THREATENED WILDERNESS

For thousands of years the battle between tropical air and air chilled in the polar sea has been repeatedly fought out over Southern England. In few places are the harbingers of storms from the Atlantic more evident and more ominous than among the granite tors that jut out from the rolling downs of Dartmoor. As among mountains when cloud layers move in different directions, you can predict their coming and are obliged to make a run for it. The wettest places are in the vicinity of Princetown which lies at the head of valleys running southwest towards Plymouth, but almost anywhere on that great moor you need not travel far to hear the music of streamlets.

With its oceans of clement air and water vapour, sculptured rock standing on debris called clitter, a variety of valleys which have never felt the cutting edge of the last great ice invasion, an abundant flora and fauna despite much starved soil, there could be no finer place anywhere in England for a National Park but, as T. S. Eliot put it in a different setting, '. . . Between the idea and the reality . . . Between the motion and the act . . . Falls the Shadow.' Although this Tom Tiddler's ground has been exploited by the Crown, by the gentry, by the unscrupulous rich and the unscrupulous poor for hundreds of years, the much-loved wilderness is now threatened as never before by faceless officialdom thirsty for water which, like tree-pulp, can be sold. It is physically blasted by the seemingly unshiftable, conscience-bereft military; it is sliced up by bypass-makers ever in the van of Progress. The peculiarity of Dartmoor's exploitation lies not so much in its magnitude as in its fearful variety. Almost every page of a newspaper contains a piece on a National Park, 'a large tract of land kept for public benefit.' Not one youngster in the tens of thousands who delight in Dartmoor ponies nuzzling up to them for proffered reward can be aware that they may next encounter the little horses in a tin of catmeat.

I have walked the breadth of the great moor in a nine-tenths' white-out, making appalling errors, missing the North Teign river, stumbling into Cranmere Pool and striking East Dart head which led me to Chagford by way of Wistman's Wood, but I love her still as I do my Lady Sylvia Sayer, foremost among her honourable defenders. I have, perhaps, set the scene badly for one of her astute captains, Brian Le Messurier, who works for the National Trust as a countryside interpreter. He will tell you in some detail what I am incompetent to offer in the way of instruction.

J.H.

WALKING ON DARTMOOR

BRIAN LE MESSURIER

In the spring of the year more walkers are humping rucksacks across Dartmoor's undulating skylines than at any other season. This is the training period for the Ten Tors Expedition when hundreds of young people are preparing for the largest annual mass-start two-day walk in England. The brighter weather and longer days also bring out the letter-boxers, those earnest, eager searchers who set off into the remoter parts of the moor to locate the hundreds of unofficial 'post boxes' to add to their collection of impressions of the rubber stamps they find there.

These recent developments reflect what people expect from the Darmoor National Park in the way of recreation, challenge and emotional satisfaction. Perhaps it is a desire to get back to basics, and see how our forefathers lived in their primitive longhouses and, even earlier, in those small ruined circular huts which are so abundant here.

Walking is really the only way to enjoy Dartmoor. There are many excellent riding establishments, but the pedestrian can penetrate places where horses are defeated: on rocky hill slopes, over boggy ground and along public footpaths. The only advantage of riding is that over good level ground the animal can move much quicker than a walker.

Dartmoor lacks dangerous cliffs, crags and escarpments. Our landscapes are horizontal rather than vertical. Even the bogs which enliven lurid Dartmoor literature from *The Hound of the Baskervilles* onwards are more imaginary than real, and no walker in daylight is likely to be troubled by more than wet feet and legs. The main risk on Dartmoor as on other British uplands is from the weather, particularly when both cold and wet.

Add a confusing mist and the stranger's cup of unhappiness is full.

To these natural hazards the ruthless Army has installed firing ranges across many thousands of acres on the finest sweep of northern Dartmoor. This has created not only noise, damage, disturbance and a legacy of unexploded missiles in the peat but the public is excluded for many days every year.

Much of this National Park is owned by Prince Charles, the present Duke of Cornwall, but the policy of the Duchy is that it '. . . would in fact be very pleased if at any stage the military are able to withdraw. Its position however remains as it has done for some years in that so long as the government of the day requires the Dartmoor training area it will continue to lease it to them in the national interest.'

This position is not accepted by the Dartmoor Preservation Association (founded 1883) which has been lobbying for the removal of *all* live firing and damaging training from the moor since the Services consolidated their wartime ranges after World War Two. (A smaller range existed south of Okehampton for many years previously.) The leading figure in this campaign is Lady Sylvia Sayer, a redoubtable fighter for National Park principles, and although the Ministry of Defence (MOD) remains entrenched, persistent pressure has produced concessions over the years, and we hope for more to come.

It is obvious of course that the weather and the Dartmoor firing programme must be considered before setting off into northern Dartmoor, but there are plenty of places to walk on the edge of the moor where they are not so important.

Local people have their preferred destinations. Plymothians are fortunate as the National Park runs up to the city boundary. Where the Plym is joined by the river Meavy at Shaugh Bridge a splendid circular walk can be enjoyed. Start by walking up through beautiful oak woods and using a long-disused quarry incline until at the top of the Dewerstone you realize how high you have climbed. This is one of the few places all around the edge of the moor where the scenery approaches the vertical, and is a well-known climbing crag. Now head north-east across the open moor to Cadover Bridge, visiting Bronze Age antiquities on the way, and return to Shaugh Bridge along the other side of the Plym using the Pipe Track, a path on top of a broken china clay conduit.

On eastern Dartmoor, Lustleigh Cleave was a favourite walking area in the 1930s when two-coach trains puffed up the Moretonhampstead branch line stopping at Lustleigh, and there was a tea room at Hammerslake for visitors to the Cleave. Motorists can now penetrate further on to the moor but if they have come to walk, passing by Lustleigh Cleave means they will miss a few square miles well provided with rights of way and richly endowed with granite crags.

If you are from Torquay or Newton Abbot the distant hump of Hay Tor beckons you out to see it at close quarters. A road passes nearby, and there

LEFT: *Dartmoor's undulating skylines.*

ABOVE: *Grimspound settlement, one of the many Bronze Age antiquities to be found on Dartmoor.*

are many other characteristic tors not far away. The Hay Tor granite tramway, of which more in a moment or two, is a popular walking route.

Chagford on the north-eastern rim of the moor became a holiday centre in late Victorian times and has built on this reputation. Opinions differ as to whether it is a village or a town, but it has such an assortment of good shops that you must judge for yourself. Should you arrive there unprepared and undecided whether you are going to walk, ride or fish there are shops – one of them on three floors – ready to kit you out from bobble hat to commando soles.

Dartmoor's two main wilderness areas are north and south of Princetown, and the highest and most extensive is the northern one. The heart of this plateau is Cut Hill – 1,980 feet above sea level. This is not the highest point on Dartmoor: High Willhays, Yes Tor and Hangingstone Hill can claim superiority, but for remoteness from so-called civilization, Cut Hill stands aloof and supreme. It is also further from a road than anywhere else south of Northumberland. The nearest point to which an ordinary vehicle can be driven is the Army road 3 miles to the north at Okement Hill, such is the extent of military incursion.

Within 2½ miles of Cut Hill eight rivers rise, some flowing north to the Bristol Channel, the others south to the English Channel. River heads on this high boggy plateau are bleak secret places.

Water oozes from the peat, the trickles coalesce, becoming murky, sluggish streams, until they leave the highest ground by tumbling over rocks for the first time to become sherry-tinted rills eager to grow and reach adulthood in the middle reaches lower down.

Cut Hill's rounded bosomy shape is hardly photogenic but, when viewed from a distance, it has a special kind of magnetism which draws the visitor back there time and time again. Its slopes are seamed and riven by gullies and groughs of the kind familiar to *aficionados* of Kinder Scout. The harsh climate has penetrated the unstable peat and washed it away over several acres north of the summit forming a moon landscape punctuated by decaying peat hags.

The hill got its name from medieval cattle drovers who, wishing to drive their animals over the watershed to the north of the summit, dug a pass across the interfluve, a 'cut' still marked on its western side by small upstanding stones. Frank Phillpotts, a keen hunt follower, used this method ninety years ago when he had a number of 'passes' driven through the blanket peat bog of northern Dartmoor for hunting and cattle-men. He linked clearings in the peat rather like the way in which de Lesseps joined up the Bitter Lakes to make the Suez Canal. These useful routes across difficult terrain were unmapped until I looked into their

history and plotted them in 1964. They now appear on Ordnance Survey maps. One of them, the North West Passage, winding up the southern slopes of Cut Hill, is marked at each end by memorial stones and has cairns along its length. Although Phillpotts didn't have walkers in mind when he created the peat passes, they are the people who use them most today.

About half a mile to the west of Cut Hill and slightly lower is Fur Tor, the most remote tor on Dartmoor. This granite pile crowns a spur overlooking the magnificent basin of the upper Tavy, and is a popular focal point for walkers. Whereas the summit of Cut Hill is a low peaty mound with no convenient shelter, one can always get out of the wind or rain at Fur Tor. Another attraction here is a 'letter box' and visitors' book. This Dartmoor custom began in the middle of the last century at Cranmere Pool, a couple of miles to the north astride the headwaters of the West Okement. In those days men in dark suits and bowler hats and women in long skirts left their visiting cards in some convenient receptacle, and the practice of leaving self-addressed postcards for

RIGHT: *Widecombe-in-the-Moor.*

BELOW: *Hay Tor on Dartmoor. From a distance the hump beckons you out to see it at close quarters.*

the next visitor to mail started when postcards became fashionable.

For many years there has been a stone cupboard at Cranmere Pool and a copper box at Fur Tor. A recent book about the hobby of letter boxing suggests that there may be up to a thousand boxes on the moor at any one time, but they don't advertise their presence. The observant visitor learns to recognize the signs: the imprints of moulded rubber soles, discarded cigarette ends and ring pulls tend to give away the plastic boxes concealed under nearby boulders.

The southern wilderness is lower and smaller but bleaker, with fewer landmarks. The southern moor's equivalent of Cranmere is Duck's Pool, a more satisfying destination since it means you are in for a hard slog to reach it. Cranmere Pool is only a mile from the Army road at Okement Hill. Duck's Pool is worth a visit to see the small memorial plaque to William Crossing (1847–1928), renowned for his *Guide to Dartmoor* which was first published in 1909. I had the honour to be asked to write the introduction to the reprint in 1965 and that has been in print ever since. He wrote other Dartmoor books, some recently reprinted, and his reputation as a reliable scribe and guide has never been higher.

By a quirk of history the whole of central Dartmoor is in the parish of Lydford which meant that parishioners had to make lengthy journeys across the moor for church affairs and to do suit and service at the manor courts. By a dispensation granted in 1260 the inhabitants of certain tenements farthest from Lydford were allowed to use Widecombe church for most purposes, so from that date the route over western Dartmoor became less used. It is still a public right of way known as the Lich Way, *lich* being Saxon for corpse, an echo of one of its former uses as a funerary track. In 1969 the closure of a section near Willsworthy was applied for, and the 1260 document was produced in court as evidence of past use. The application was refused.

Running across southern Dartmoor is the Abbots' Way, believed by some to be a link between Buckfast Abbey on the east of the moor and Buckland and Tavistock Abbeys on the west. Other authorities say that the line of medieval stone crosses a little to the north displays in its obvious piety a more logical route between monastic centres. Whichever course is the true one – and it is doubtful if we shall ever know – both routes are a delight to walk over as they lead across expansive moorland of primeval character.

Threading through the tumbled eastern foothills of high Dartmoor is a sinuous path known as the Mariners' Way. Tradition – or perhaps folklore – relates that several hundred years ago sailors passing between the thriving Devon ports of Dartmouth (in the south) and Bideford (in the north) used this route. Certainly an 11-mile succession of footpaths exists from north of Throwleigh almost to Widecombe. I am especially fond of the Mariners' Way as it was a favourite route long before the Dartmoor National Park Authority stiled, signposted and waymarked it. Not that I would wish these aids away. The path crosses streams by stone clapper bridges and stepping stones, and many of the stiles are of the old 'wood and stone' kind. Even the gateposts are worth looking at as they are often adapted from the slotted type. The walker passes ash houses – small buildings where the domestic ashes were stored for later use as fertilizers – a stone cross, old buildings, a castle, two churches and much superb scenery.

A small part of the Mariners' Way is traversed by the Two Moors Way, a long-distance route 103 miles from Ivybridge on the southern extremity of Dartmoor, across mid-Devon and Exmoor to Lynmouth near the North Devon coast. This proposal for a long-distance bridleway was put forward in 1965 but, amended over the years, it took its present form in the mid 1970s.

In these few examples I hope I have given sufficient evidence of the enjoyment to be gained by walking some of the moor's old paths. Crossing's *Guide to Dartmoor* and Eric Hemery's *Walking Dartmoor's Ancient Tracks* will give plenty of ideas for other paths. The point is that the Dartmoor walker is not confined to fixed routes.

Dartmoor's outstanding merit is its sense of freedom – which is why the prison is such an anachronism – and its protectors jealously guard the *de facto*, customary or traditional 'right' of access which exists over so much of the moor. Since 1985 and the passing of the Dartmoor

Commons Act public access on foot and horse-back to 90,000 acres of common land has been legalized. Access legislation is only part of the package: regulation of grazing is the other component.

What is the future for walking on Dartmoor? It looks favourable. For example the Plym can now be followed upstream from Plymouth to Dartmoor on one side of the river or the other. And on eastern Dartmoor the fascinating track of the Hay Tor granite tramway – where stone-carrying trucks ran on 'rails' of continuous granite setts from the open moor down to the Stover Canal in the Bovey valley – has become a route for walkers. It is called Templer Way and is named after the builder of the tramway in 1820. Collaboration between the National Park Authority and the South West Water Authority has produced a variety of walking routes through the plantations round Fernworthy, Kennick, Tottiford and

Trenchford reservoirs, especially enjoyable in the winter.

There are places I would dearly love to see opened up for walkers and among them are riverside paths through Buckland Woods and Holne Chase. Another outstanding excursion would be to follow the river Dart from sea to source. Consider the rewards: a river trip from Dartmouth to Totnes, then the Dart Valley Steam Railway from Totnes to Buckfastleigh, followed by a most wonderful walk on one bank or the other up to Dartmeet. Here the routes would diverge with one path going up the East and the other up the West Dart. Now there's a foray to really fire the imagination.

A stone clapper bridge over the Dart at Dartmeet.

THE GREAT ROLLER-COASTER

If there's one prospect of Britain I care for only slightly more than the view from the back bedroom window of a good pub when another long trail is over, it's an hour spent poring over a huge relief map of the kind you can find at the front of a modern atlas.

It all looks so deceptively simple. The lowlands are painted in a rather awful aniline green with heavily shadowed hills mostly to the west, ranging in symbolic height from a sort of episcopal purple to ominous grey and black. If to this prospect of delectable mountains bereft of boulders, black flies, downpours, dullness, foul peat, floods and fog the cartographer has added some attractive-looking little roads as a carrot for the over-cautious, delay departure for a few days and get in touch with somebody who really knows what you are likely to be up against. Such a person is Hugh Westacott who has trodden every foot of the way and gone back to see if there aren't easier and more inviting ways of getting round several dispiriting prospects.

As for myself, until I trod the north coast of Cornwall from Land's End to Watergate Bay at the beginning of *Journey Through Britain*, I had merely sampled Devon and Dorset more as a naturalist and antiquarian than a serious walker. The Isle of Purbeck abounds in fossilized treasure. In Lulworth Cove the late Sir Mortimer Wheeler discovered trenches from which the earliest known inhabitants thereabouts were slowly driven back, furlong by furlong, by the Beaker People, a race of ruthless pastoralists, but you risk a serious brush with tank brigade commanders if you poke about among those wildly contorted Upper Jurassic rocks. The Portland quarries, a little to the west, are the matrix of London and you may see where the fabric of St Paul's and other famous churches was dug out in solid blocks. Among much else in the cliffs of Lyme Regis are the fossils of those enormous marine lizards, the ichthyosaurs. The first was found in 1828 by an eleven-year-old girl, Mary Anning, to whom for this and subsequent discoveries a window was dedicated in the local parish church. By the time this extraordinarily intelligent fisherman's daughter achieved middle age she was a local heroine and on Christian name terms with some learned old Fellows of the Royal Society.

If to all this you add the mating call of red-billed choughs from the roofs of sea-caves (a sound rather like a broody hen, *kwuk-kwuk-kwuk*); if you're interested in the folk names for sea pink or thrift (cliff rose and *Tammon* in Celtic Cornish); and the reliability of lugworms in sensing whether wet sand is safe or subject to muddy depressions, you may get a glimmering of what I'm about when mere walking becomes tedious and your fellow travellers are collecting trail-badges, local bric-a-brac or perfumed information from the seaside Information Centres. But to do all this you must be constantly surprised by the unobvious and that comes from solid ground work.

Britain tails off into the south-west peninsula which, somewhat improperly, ends nominally and physically at Land's End in Penrith. It should have been the head of the Lizard that lies between the coves of Mullion and Coverack, half a day's sailing just round the corner. That relief map I've referred to shows darkish blobs that represent, successively from east to west, Dartmoor, Bodmin Moor and the wind-swept points of Penrith. Geologically speaking the peninsula is built out of Devonian rock injected with what became granite and even older fire-formed strata, the pre-Cambrian series. But unless you happen to be a geologist, this is dull stuff by comparison with the magnificent relics of prehistoric man who built tombs and temples with a solemn and heavy hand.

Quit the coast awhile and walk in a generous curve between Cape Cornwall and Zennor, named after a saintly woman. You will discover some of our finest, our earliest known monuments around Carn Kenidjack and Woon Gumpus Common which sound like part of an incantation. Stare at them awhile. They are the mute witnesses of our ancestors.

And now we must rejoin a professional guide.

J.H.

THE SOUTH-WEST PENINSULA PATH

HUGH WESTACOTT

The South-west Peninsula Path, usually known more mellifluously as the South-west Way, runs for approximately 600 miles – nobody knows its exact length – from Minehead in Somerset, via Land's End, to South Haven Point at the southern entrance to Poole Harbour. For much of the way the path follows the route that was, until 1913, patrolled daily by the coastguard and for most of its length the wayfarer can see, hear and smell the ever-present ocean. Because of its length, for administrative reasons and for the sake of convenience the South-west Way has been divided into sections, each corresponding with the local authority responsible for the path. The constituent parts are the Somerset and North Devon Coast Path, the Cornish Coast Path, the South Devon Coast Path and the Dorset Coast Path.

Each of the individual paths has its own particular charm and character which will be described later but, taken as a whole, for my taste, the South-west Way is not only the longest but also the most beautiful and interesting of all British long-distance paths. This large statement needs only a little justification. The scenery is remarkably varied, and in places spectacular, ranging from wild moorland in north Devon, the iron-bound granite cliffs of north Cornwall, the enchanting fishing coves of south Cornwall, the warm red cliffs, verdant valleys and estuaries of south Devon and the chalk headlands of Dorset. From every promontory and in every bay and cove there is some new delight awaiting discovery.

But it is the sea in all its moods that gives the path its special character. A change of wind can turn a placid seascape into a stormy scene with angry waves jostling each other, gnawing and fretting against the cliffs and hurling themselves furiously on to the beach. The constantly changing cloud pattern causes the quality of light to alter by the minute, sometimes bringing dramatic changes to the colours in the sea. I have sat on the cliffs watching the sea darken from light greens and blues through deeper shades and indigo until it was almost black.

Throughout the length of the path, but especially in Cornwall, there are numerous lifeboat stations, shipping markers, memorials and graves which serve as constant reminders of the influence of the sea. The most conspicuous are the lighthouses and lifeboat stations, many of which were established in the nineteenth century in an attempt to provide some protection to mariners in these dangerous waters. These are open to the public and wayfarers may like to visit at least one example of each to learn something of their work. The lifeboat stations are particularly moving with their simple plaques recording the names of the vessels wrecked and the number of lives saved which give only a hint of the desperate sea conditions into which the heroic volunteers of the Lifeboat Service have launched their boats to go to the rescue of fellow mariners. My favourites are at Sennen Cove, the Lizard, where in stormy weather the lifeboat hurtles down a steep ramp into a boiling sea, and Mousehole for whom the whole nation mourned a few years ago when the crew was lost after the boat capsized and was wrecked.

The spectacular scenery of Combe Martin Bay.

Long before the establishment of Trinity House, lanterns were hung in conspicuous church towers such as St Aldhelm's near Worth Matravers in Dorset. The many tall white lighthouses sited on lonely headlands throughout the south-west actually enhance the beauty of the scene and many, like those on the Foreland, at Hartland Point, at Tater Du and Start Point, make an interesting focal point in photographs. There are numerous marks and crosses erected by philanthropists and charities as aids to navigation with particularly striking examples on Dodman Point and Gribben Head and there are several mysterious white pillars, exactly one nautical mile apart, which were erected by the Navy for use in warship speed trials. At Loe Bar is a memorial to Henry Trengrouse (1772–1854) erected on the very site where he watched helplessly as the frigate H.M.S. *Anson* was wrecked with the loss of one hundred lives, inspiring him to invent a rocket apparatus to shoot lines aboard disabled vessels. In St Keverne's churchyard there is the mass grave of more than two hundred victims of the liner *Mohun* which foundered on the Manacles and at East Man near Swanage are the graves of one hundred and sixty-eight passengers who perished when the East Indiaman *Halsewell* was wrecked in 1786.

There are still many coastguard lookouts along the route but in these days of radar and other modern electronic navigational aids many are manned only occasionally. It is pleasant to get a friendly wave from a coastguard maintaining his lonely vigil but it is likely to be an augury of a change in the weather because he is probably on foul-weather watch.

Along the southern coastline smuggling was rife until well into the nineteenth century and it was considered an honourable calling to obtain duty-free brandy for the parson and baccy for the clerk. Yet, despite Kipling's romantic poem, it was often a blood-stained trade with running fights between well-organized gangs and the 'revenue men'. In the eighteenth century Prussia Cove was actually fortified with a battery of guns by a local smuggler seeking to protect his interests. There is an interesting museum of smuggling at Polperro.

Smuggling was real enough but the tales told by the gadzooks and prithee school of historical novelists of wreckers deliberately luring mariners to

their doom by displaying misleading lights are not only wholly fictitious but a shameful canard on the local fishermen who often made heroic efforts at rescue. The stories have gained currency because of a tradition of the sea that the cargo of a wrecked ship becomes the property of anyone who can salvage it.

Those who know the south-west only through the windscreen of a car or from lazing on its crowded beaches would be amazed to discover how empty walkers find this path; even in the height of summer it is possible to walk for miles without seeing a soul save for the occasional sailor or fisherman out to sea. Every so often crowds are met when it is necessary to descend from the cliffs and cross a beach but fortunately most people are like sheep and do not stray far from the sand-fringed shore, happy to leave mile after mile of glorious unspoiled coastal scenery to those, like us, with sufficient wit and energy to use their own two feet.

The scenery alone makes the South-west Way a joyous venture but the pleasure can be increased by those with the forethought to do some back-ground reading before they set out on their long

march. These 600 miles are redolent of history and it is well worth having some understanding of the events of the last three thousand years since the Phoenicians first came to Cornwall for tin and the Iron Age promontory forts, tumuli, barrows and stone circles were built by our prehistoric forbears.

Dorset, Devon and Cornwall enjoy some of the mildest and balmiest weather in Britain but, despite the better-than-average chance of sunshine, this is not an easy route to walk. Except for the fortunate few, its very length precludes the possibility of completing the entire route in one expedition and most people spread their journey over several years. It is very strenuous with numerous exceptionally steep climbs from beach to cliff-top, often repeated many times over a short distance, making a 12-mile walk a very hard day. The walker caught in a gale on the more exposed parts of the cliffs will quickly learn that it can be a hazardous route; more than once I have been forced inland to escape the violence of a storm and the risk of being blown into the sea.

The South-west Way is rich in wildlife. Along the whole of the route the walker's senses are

LEFT: *The lighthouse on Devon's Hartland Point.*

RIGHT: *Bude in Cornwall.*

quickened by a riot of flowers blooming on the cliffs which provide a habitat safe from the baleful effects of herbicides. Birdlife, too, is plentiful with ravens, kestrels and many varieties of seabirds including oystercatchers, cormorants and the comical puffin. I have seen seals and porpoises swimming off the Cornish coast; adders, grass snakes, foxes, red deer and many varieties of butterfly may also be encountered.

Even an experienced map-reader walking the South-west Way will welcome the aid of a guidebook. There are so many tidal estuaries which have to be forded, seasonal ferries, diversions due to cliff falls and artillery ranges open only at certain times that up-to-date information is essential. Furthermore, stretches of the path are still incomplete with new sections being opened

almost annually. The latest available information is published in *The South-west Way: the complete guide to Great Britain's longest footpath*. Despite its misleading subtitle, this is not a guidebook but an annual handbook published by the South-west Way Association in conjunction with Devon Books. It is an engagingly eccentric publication anonymously written in a strange literary style, larded with pithy comments that sometimes obscure its real meaning. The South-west Way Association is a local pressure group which has fought long and hard for the establishment of a coastal footpath and all who walk the route owe it their gratitude. Unfortunately, the Association seems limited in its viewpoint. The handbook fails, for instance, to mention the splendid, officially designated, alternative inland route

The harbour at Clovelly. This village is one of the highlights of the Coast Path.

between West Bexington and Osmington Mills in Dorset, presumably because it does not actually follow the coast.

The Somerset and North Devon Coast Path

This section of the path runs for just over 100 miles from Minehead in Somerset to Marsland Mouth on the Devon/Cornwall county boundary although most walkers, unless being collected by car, will continue for another 9 miles to Bude. It is the only part of the entire route which has no estuaries to ford, no gunnery ranges and only one seasonal ferry which is fairly easy to circumvent if not operating. The latest information about the state of the path is necessary because there have been several recent diversions from the original route and many miles of new route between

Barnstaple and Instow, using an abandoned railway line, have been opened.

The first part of the route runs through the Exmoor National Park and is characterized by rough moorland and deep wooded valleys. Wordsworth and Coleridge walked this way in 1797 and Coleridge composed the fragment *Kubla Khan* at a farm in Culbone but his poetic inspiration was lost when a man from Porlock knocked on his door. This is the very edge of the Doone country and graves bearing that dreaded name may be seen in Countisbury churchyard a short distance from the path. The scenery between Woody Bay and Combe Martin is as spectacular as any to be found between Minehead and Poole and walkers are unlikely to forget either the views or the 1,000-foot climb to the summit of Great Hangman. Once clear of Ilfracombe there is again much good walking, although the areas around Woolacombe and Croyde Bay have been spoiled by unsightly development. In fine weather there are good views of Lundy Island and the distant Welsh coast. The section between the Taw and Torridge estuaries, once busy with shipping plying to the Americas, is one of the dullest sections of the route but the walking is fast and easy along an old railway line.

Westward Ho!, named after Charles Kingsley's fiercely Protestant novel, was where the young Rudyard Kipling attended the old United Services College and immortalized his schooldays in *Stalky and Co.* From here to Bude the going is good with the highlights being the beautiful village of Clovelly, especially if seen out of season or early in the morning, Hartland Point and the wonderful section between Marsland Mouth and Crooklets. It is worth making a diversion to Morwenstow to see the church and rectory where the eccentric rector and poet, the Reverend R. S. Hawker, was the incumbent for forty-one years until his death-bed conversion to Roman Catholicism in 1875. His cliff-top hut, where he used to meditate, is close to the path and is now in the loving care of the National Trust.

The Cornish Coast Path

This section of the South-west Way begins at the Devon/Cornwall county boundary at Marsland Mouth but, as this is not accessible by public transport, most wayfarers will start their walk from Bude. It runs for 290 miles to Cremyll just across the Tamar from Plymouth. For most of the way the path follows the tops of granite cliffs with, here and there, outcrops of other igneous rocks. The tilting of the land has left the north Cornish coast with very few harbours, and being exposed to the prevailing wind and the long Atlantic rollers so beloved by surfers, it is much bleaker than the more picturesque south Cornwall which has an abundance of delightful little fishing coves.

This is the country of Arthurian romance, the lost land of Lyonesse and Celtic saints who, according to the legends, crossed from Ireland on mill-stones and leaves. It also has a history of appalling shipwrecks. Until quite recently, Cornwall was of considerable industrial importance especially for its deposits of copper, tin and china clay and, to a lesser extent, for lead and silver. Relics of industrial activity can be seen at Bude with its unusual inclined-plane canal where barges were hauled up on wheels rather than floated in locks; in the gaunt ruins of the engine houses which powered the pumps and hoists of the deep tin mines found on many sections of the Cornish coast; and at Hayle, which once had a thriving copper mining and smelting industry using Welsh coal brought in by boat. Falmouth has a beautiful harbour and is still a major port and around St Austell and Par are the unsightly remains of china clay workings.

Fishing used to be extremely important but the once-thriving pilchard industry died out when the fish took to deeper water and the huge shoals, for which a specially employed man known as a huer watched on the tall cliffs, are now only memories, together with the remains of pilchard cellars where the fish were salted and smoked. It is in Cornwall that the influence of the sea is most nearly felt, for these fang-like cliffs have been the

ABOVE: *Falmouth has a beautiful harbour and is still a thriving port.*

RIGHT: *St Ives in Cornwall, long favoured by painters, potters and sculptors because of the fine quality of Cornish light.*

grave of many a fine ship. Vessels from all over the world bound for Bristol, London and the south coast ports all made their landfall at Land's End which, like much of the southern coastline of Cornwall, is surrounded by dangerous reefs.

A few sections of the Coast Path in Cornwall are not worth walking. These include the stretches around Hayle from Gwithin to St Ives (but on no account miss St Ives itself), Mousehole to Penzance and Charlestown to Par. There is something to be said for completing the walk at Looe to avoid a long stretch of road walking before reaching Cremyll, although this means missing the fine views from Rame Head and Penlee Point at the very end of the path.

There are a number of ferries and estuaries on the route but only one that can cause serious difficulty. There is no regular ferry service between St Mawes and Place Manor but there exists an alternative to taking a taxi or walking some distance along a busy main road. I have used this diversion on several occasions whilst leading my walking

tours and can recommend it as a pleasant walk though, of course, it cannot compare with the official route around St Anthony. From St Mawes pier turn west and walk past the castle, then follow a coastal path overlooking the Carrick Roads to St Just in Roseland. Turn east mostly along footpaths to the A3078 which should be followed to Trethern Mill, then immediately turn east along paths and lanes to rejoin the coastal path just north of Portscatho.

The wonderful quality of Cornish light kept free of atmospheric pollution by the prevailing south-westerly winds has attracted many artists to Cornwall. At Newlyn, on the south coast, Walter Langley, Edward Harris and T. C. Gotch formed a colony of 'open air' painters, influenced by the Barbizon school, which flourished from the 1880s until about 1930, and picturesque St Ives on the north coast has for long been favoured by painters, potters and sculptors of whom Barbara Hepworth and Bernard Leach are the best known.

The South Devon Coast Path

Once across the Tamar the South-west Way assumes a quite different character. Gone are the granite cliffs, to be replaced by old red sandstone which gives the cliffs of South Devon their characteristic colour, but it is no less beautiful and the wood-fringed estuaries of the Yealm, Erme, Avon, Salcombe Harbour and the Dart are remarkably unspoiled. The soil is exceptionally rich, making South Devon one of the most fertile parts of England: a land of lotus eaters, of air heavy with the murmur of bees searching for nectar among the many sweet-scented flowers and of warm sunshine on wave-dappled sandy beaches.

Most of Plymouth was destroyed by Hitler's airmen and the only part that survived relatively intact is the Barbican. The city, on Plymouth Sound, is full of naval history and it is worth taking the harbour cruise that leaves from near the Mayflower Steps. It was from here that Sir Humphrey Gilbert sailed for Newfoundland in 1583 and the Pilgrim Fathers set out for America in 1620. During the hour-long cruise visitors will see a section of the first stone-built Eddystone lighthouse, the Citadel, the Hoe, where Drake is reputed to have been playing bowls when the Armada was

Kingswear, Devon. It is best to cross from Dartmouth to Kingswear by ferry.

recently opened, splendid section of coast path from Kingswear to Brixham and then proceed to Exmouth by bus and train.

If the ferry across the Yealm operates at all it does so during the high season and the only reasonable alternative is to avoid this section and start the walk at Noss Mayo. There is no ferry over the river Erme but it can usually be waded at low tide. The future of the ferry between Starcross and Exmouth is uncertain, but the river Exe can always be crossed by making a long diversion by train or bus via Exeter.

Noss Mayo, Salcombe and Dartmouth are enchanting places and the coast path which links them is often breathtakingly beautiful. Square-rigged sail-training ships are occasionally to be seen in these waters. One of the most moving and beautiful sights I have ever witnessed was when walking into Dartmouth one evening and watching a tall ship stealing under topsails across the water and hearing a shouted command which sent the cadets racing up the ratlines on to the spars to clew up the sails when the anchor dropped.

The route from Exmouth is strenuous, especially between Sidmouth and the delightful fishing village of Beer where we leave the old red sandstone for the chalk cliffs which continue as far east as Dover. Between Seaton and Lyme Regis the path runs through the National Nature Reserve of the Landslip which, although of considerable interest to naturalists, is a dull section for walkers as there are no views. Over the years portions of the cliffs have dropped into the sea. The biggest fall occurred on Christmas Eve 1839 when 20 acres slipped with a mighty roar to form an island a mile long and 60 feet high which has gradually been dispersed by the sea.

We cross the Devon/Dorset boundary somewhere in the Landslip but it is no hardship to continue for a short distance to the charming little town of Lyme Regis. Jane Austen was a frequent visitor here and set scenes from *Persuasion* on the Cobb, which is the name given to the picturesque and ancient harbour. Scenes from John Fowles' *The French Lieutenant's Woman* are also set here.

sighted in 1588, and the modern naval dockyards.

Unfortunately, the 144 miles between Plymouth and Lyme Regis are difficult going and the 30 miles between Brixham and Exmouth are so urbanized as to be not worth walking. Indeed, I recommend taking the bus from Torcross to Stoke Fleming to avoid 6 miles of main road walking, then following the excellent coast path into Dartmouth, crossing to Kingswear by ferry and catching the steam-hauled, privately owned Torbay and Dartmouth Railway to Paignton where connections can be made to Exeter and Exmouth. Others may prefer to walk along the

The Dorset Coast Path

The Dorset Coast Path runs for 73 miles but is only 65 miles in length if you take the alternative inland route from Lyme Regis to South Haven Point on the edge of Poole Harbour. It, too, has its own distinctive character cast by the friable chalk cliffs which the path follows for the whole of the way. There are no ferries or estuaries and the only serious problem is the artillery range on one of the loveliest sections of the route between Lulworth Cove and Kimmeridge. This is normally open for about forty-six of the fifty-two weekends in the year, at Easter and during the month of August, but is likely to be closed at all other times so it is important to time your arrival correctly to avoid a 9-mile detour along roads.

The Dorset Coast Path is the only section of the whole South-west Way where an official alternative route is provided. It runs for 16 miles from West Bexington to Osmington Mills, following a high-level route on the downs with splendid views over the sea. This section is littered with prehistoric remains including hill forts, tumuli, barrows and a stone circle and the magnificent fort of Maiden Castle is visible a mile off the path. It is an instructive lesson in landscape history to sit with a pair of field glasses and a map on the escarpment of Wears Hill and trace the various stages of agricultural development around Abbotsbury from the Iron Age through the Saxon and medieval periods to the agricultural revolution in the eighteenth century and the present day. Another advantage of the inland route is that it is more interesting than the miserable section around Weymouth, which is the only part of the Dorset coastal route not worth walking.

In Dorset the influence of the sea is less apparent than in Devon and Cornwall because fewer people have ever made their living from it. Apart from Weymouth, which is both a naval base and a commercial port, and the tiny harbours of Lyme Regis and West Bay, there are no safe anchorages for craft of any size along this coast. Walkers cannot fail to be impressed by Chesil Beach, an 18-mile long, 50-feet high and 200-feet wide natural barrier of pebbles thrown up over the centuries by the sea. The currents and tides seem to grade the pebbles according to size so that the largest are only found at one end. The chalk cliffs support an entirely different flora from that seen on other sections of the South-west Way. Gone are the ubiquitous sea pinks and in their place are large clumps of the striking blue viper's bugloss which contrast so well with the stark white cliffs and the short, green velvety turf.

At the remote hamlet of Kimmeridge are found black oil-bearing shales which the Romans worked into bracelets, rings and necklaces. Oil companies have been granted exploration and drilling licences and a number of nodding donkeys can be seen pumping the life blood of modern industry into storage tanks. Fortunately the effect on the environment has been minimized by screening the installations with trees.

Some of the steepest hills on the whole South-west Way are on the coastal path through Dorset, contrasting with two absolutely flat sections, one

of 24 miles between Burton Bradstock and Over-combe and the other of 4 miles right at the end of the path, an anti-climax after much strenuous walking.

We have now reached the end of our long trek round England's south-west peninsula. American clients sometimes ask me to recommend my favourite sections, a question which I always find very difficult to answer. If pressed, I admit that the parts of this marvellous coastline that I love best are the sections between Minehead and Combe Martin; Westward Ho! and Bude; Millhook to Newquay; St Ives to Penzance; from the Lizard peninsula to Mevagissey; Par to Looe; between Noss Mayo and Torcross; Budleigh Salterton to Beer; and, in Dorset, the inland section from West Bexington to Osmington Mills and the final coastal stretch to Swanage. But my advice is to go and see for yourself which you like best.

ABOVE: *The dramatic old red sandstone cliffs at Sidmouth in east Devon.*

LEFT: *The magnificent hill fort at Maiden Castle in Dorset. It is visible from the Coast Path a mile away.*

SOME ASPECTS OF THE PRINCIPALITY

Of all the mountain ranges of Britain, the great mass of Snowdon with its satellites Carnedd Dafydd and the Glyders stand highest in my imagination and remain there, untrodden, unsullied at least by me since the project put forward by an old friend, the late Elwyn Jones of the BBC Documentary Department, that I should walk around and across Wales in the footsteps of George Borrow. This scheme fell apart after I had done quite a lot of homework on Borrow's *Wild Wales*. My second-hand Everyman edition of that work had been painfully edited by a Welsh-speaking reader who with subtly poisoned irony had pulled much of it to pieces with interpolations and footnotes in faded red ink. Whereas the author had subtitled his great autobiographical work *Lavengro* with the words 'The Scholar, the Gypsy, the Priest', my unknown annotator cast doubts on his scholarship, his sense of direction and priest-craft with marginal notes.

When Borrow wrote that such and such a hamlet stood, let us say, twelve miles to the north-east of somewhere else, his critic crossed it out and wrote 'five miles to the north-west' and gave *his* interpretation of what the names in *cymric* really meant in the language of thick-tongued Saxons. George Borrow could have been right or wrong. His enormous gift for dialogue intrigues me; in a few casually deceptive sentences he cloaks quite ordinary situations in Borrovian magic, but when I traced his route on up-to-date maps I soon realized that many of his tracks are now busy roads. These are not for me, so the project fell through. But South Wales now, there's a different matter.

My younger brother, an historian, has a house high above Symonds Yat with enormous views of the Black Mountains and Brecon Beacons to the west which we have walked together. I know the Gower Peninsula fairly well and have ventured several times into the Cambrian Mountains north of Carmarthen. But how best can the whole Principality be viewed? The answer is only in several volumes. The best we can do is to box some of it in. David Bellamy, our weather-defying water-colourist, will look at the Pembrokeshire Path; Showell Styles, a poet at heart, will give us intimate glimpses of North Wales; Stephen Pern will essay Offa's Dyke in his own inimitable way and Brian Ford, a scientist, author, broadcaster, pianist and man of many parts will tell us of his home country, South Wales.

J.H.

WALKING IN SOUTH WALES

BRIAN J. FORD

Walking takes you back to a time that was. The car insulates you, keeps you from the people, ensnares you in a contrived confinement that shields out the culture as you speed through the land. Bikes whizz you past the people too, and do not take you into gullies or alleyways where life goes on. But walking is a baptism; an immersion in culture that washes over you like a reviving stream. And walking in South Wales takes you into a different world. For Wales is not England, and the Welsh are not English. There are social and cultural differences that it takes time to appreciate. But understand the differences and contentment swiftly follows.

The Welsh language is around, too, largely because of a movement in the 1970s that insisted it took its place in the modern shape of Europe. Nowadays there are assuredly many people who speak the tongue, although of course there are more who speak French. What really matters is not how many people speak Welsh, but how many cannot speak English. There is nobody now who fits that category.

So take Welsh as it should be: as an historic and fascinating reminder of the original tongue of the ancient British. Learn some of the root terms, like *pen* – head, or *bont* – bridge. It isn't true that the language is bereft of vowels, just that 'w' is pronounced -oo- just as it is in English (try it in wind, or weary, and the -oo- works as well as the 'w' sound). The double L is sometimes said as 'thl', but that's a bastard pronunciation. It is done with the edges of the tongue curled up as though you had eaten sharp gooseberries and any native will show you how to say that.

And a personal rule of thumb is that the 'y' and the 'u' are pronounced like each other. So the Welsh for Wales, *cymru*, is not said 'sim-roo' at all, but 'cum-ree'. Don't dismiss that as a strange convention; we do the same in English with the 'u' in busy, after all. And now you'll know how to ask the way to Ynysybwl, and what Pen-y-bont really means.

Cardiff is Europe's most unappreciated city, and when I first saw her in spring-like garb with flowering cherry and nodding narcissus blooms I found it a revelation. Cardiff was built as a whole, and has carefully contrived green vents between the buildings. From the town house in which I have had a home for nearly twenty years you can walk through parkland to the countryside, a bubbling brook by your hand, and from here radiate an endless combination of walking voyages.

And what variety! To the east of the city lies Dutch fenland, flat as a bowl of custard, drained by reens and protected by a dyke from the sea. To the south lie the lias cliffs and the sandy bays; to the west are the rolling meadows of the vale, whilst to the north are the steep-sided valleys and the mountains of the Brecon Beacons. The climate is mild and balmy; indeed my youngest daughter was five before she saw snow lying in the garden at home. It is wet, too, even though Cardiff – facing east, and lying to the west (not the north) of Bristol, contrary to what it is tempting to imagine – is in a partial rain shadow. So the plant life is rich, especially the ferns which rely on moisture during the critical sexual phase of the life-cycle.

Nestling under the dripping cliffs of Aberthaw are graceful growths of the maidenhair fern, in one of its few habitats. Hidden among the grass on Sully Island sprouts the adder's tongue, now a

scarce species; whilst it is the desert-like sand dunes at Merthyr Mawr that reveal the strange moonwort, an unfernlike fern with rounded sporangia looking like baubles. Floating on the channels of freshwater in the low-lying fens are misty masses of azolla, which sinks to the mud during winter and rises each spring like a bouyant mossy messenger from a lost world beneath. And the sea spleenwort hangs to the cliffs on Sully Island, just a few miles south of Cardiff, to remind you how near the open sea you truly are. At the river Hepste you will find the fine leaves, just a single cell thick, that are characteristic of the filmy ferns; while the regal osmunda, largest fern of all in Britain, still stands proud and erect in several secret sites.

Walk to the north of Cardiff, down the far side of the Wenallt, hop across the stream and swing on the great hanging growths of clematis that wait, like jungle creepers, for your visit. Break off a 3-inch stick and smoke it as you walk. You pass the crumbling old limestone walls that marked farms of an earlier era, and soon strike out through forests of larch and beech, birds bellowing, branches quivering, foxes nipping smartly away and magpies quarrelling over who saw you first . . . until suddenly you spy Castell Coch, the red castle, known for its tapering turrets as the parachutists' nightmare and famous on TV screens as Colditz. It is a fairy castle, less than a century old and built as a folly, but a familiar sight to the motorist who strikes out north in a parallel path to the one you are taking.

But while the motorist knows the castle as a pinnacle of a landmark, hanging in the clouds above the motorway, you find it this sunny morning lying away beneath your feet. Your path brings you out above Castell Coch, and sets it into a truer perspective as your head points up to the north and the challenge of yet greater heights. And just above Pontypridd, on the hillside that rises steeply away to the east, is a long slope where you can see straight up to the summit of the Brecon Beacons to the north, and right across to

Looking towards the Brecon Beacons in Powys. The highest point is a fraction too low to qualify as a mountain.

the Quantock and Mendip hills to the south, with the silver sliver of the Severn like a brook between you.

It is the glacial nature of the South Wales valleys that provides instant access from the urban to the rural. The lines of terraced houses, lying like lollipop sticks scattered on a wrinkled hearthrug, are only yards from the steep green valley sides and the rounded tops of the hills are never far away. Afforestation with unnatural stands of larch can make the journey less open than it was, but north of the valleys lie the still and serene lakes of the Pontsticill and Talybont reservoirs. With woodland slanting suddenly into the water the area has the peacefulness of the Austrian Tyrol and much of the grandeur, too.

Yet this is certainly Wales, with the mystic aura of an age of the bards hanging in the air. The hills around Cefn-Coed-y-Cymmer are legendary 'magic mushroom' territory; have been perhaps for centuries, and assuredly are today. In the hills above the waters of the Brecon Beacons you can find a chance to rest your feet and cheat a while, for the Pontsticill Mountain Railway will carry you a few miles for a couple of pounds and then set you down on the line of the track they hope to lay over the next few years, soundly en route for Pen-y-fan and the roof of the district.

This is the pinnacle of the Brecon Beacons, and gives a view that stretches way up to North Wales and towards Snowdonia, they say, on a clear day; whilst to the south lies the streak of the Bristol Channel and the hills beyond Bristol as a backdrop. At 2,907 feet it is a fraction less than the statutory 3,000 feet requirement needed for it to qualify as a mountain. But don't try to tell anyone that, or there will be trouble. Below you as you trudge downhill lie mountain streams, sparkling clear, with trout and crayfish in the water, and kingfishers flashing their iridescent way above it; sometimes the streams cascade through rapids or down veiled waterfalls of spectacular beauty. Above you lie the barren hillsides that are above the tree-line, and here you greet the occasional stand of thorn as a long-lost friend.

Barring your way to the north lies the Monmouthshire and Brecon canal, another popular way to save your feet for a while, cadging a lift on a

holiday narrow-boat and helping to earn your ride by manning the locks or the van-Gogh-style bridge at Talybont itself that nods slowly up and down like a donkey. Stone bridges carry you across the Usk, but the name of an old pub – The Old Ford Inn – reminds you that, in Welsh history, the bridge is a relatively recent arrival.

To the west of the Beacons, and as far from urbanity as one could wish to go, lies the area of the upper Neath. Here the seasoned hiker can explore the Hepste and the Mellte rivers, which tumble around rocks and cascade down waterfalls, vanishing into caves and then emerging back into the dappled sunlight like a biblical fountain struck anew from virgin rock. At one stage you walk behind the sheets of crystal water, peeking out as though from the windows of a glasshouse at the deep green valley beyond. At another you balance precariously across the edge of a waterfall, orchids and ferns awaiting you at journey's end.

But for much of the walk there is nothing but birdsong, the fresh splash of the stream and the muted softness of the verdant vegetation to occupy the mind.

One such valley runs up to what is now the Rhandir-mwyn reservoir. Just twenty years ago I spoke there with Miss Jane Jones, last of the line, with her halting English and steady gaze speaking of the invasion of the builders into her untouched corner of heaven. She showed me a long, thin dagger they'd kept for centuries, its blade razor-sharp, and triangular in cross-section.

'It was last used on the English in Abergavenny,' she said, 'where it slipped easily between the ribs.' To this day I remember her with sad affection, though I was glad enough when she went inside to put that knife away.

Up here in the pubs and shops the Welsh you hear is real enough. It remains as the daily language of commerce and social interaction, and a few words of your own – 'Bore da', rather than 'hello' – will convey a taste of respect for an ancient culture. The incidence of the language increases as you move away from the south-east of Wales, and in the mountains of Carmarthen (which still exist, even if not on maps) you will find a scattering of mills producing flour, woollens and mechanical power from the scattered streams sunk between rounded hills with steep sides that have the beauty of an idealized filmset and the transluscent light of unsullied woodland at its best.

The coracle has survived here too, on the river Teifi near Cenarth. An ancient craft, oval shaped and about 5 feet in length, it is fashioned from hazel twigs like a rounded canoe and was traditionally covered with animal hide. In that form it was described by the Roman chronicles, but it is now covered with tarpaulin instead. The little craft is propelled by a single paddle held under the arm and used to scull the coracle along, drawing it through the water rather than pushing it along as is the way with oars. The salmon fishers use this flimsy boat to this day to move quickly and safely around the river basins in pursuit of their quarry. A fortunate walker may be offered a lesson or two. Proficiency at propelling a coracle is a sure entry to the inner circle of the pub at lunch-time . . .

ABOVE: Coracle fishermen at Cilgerran in Dyfed. These ancient craft are propelled by a single paddle held under the arm.

LEFT: Castell Coch, the red castle, near Cardiff in South Glamorgan. Less than a century old, it was built as a folly.

There is a sense of isolation in this part of the world; farmsteads stand in open countryside with nothing else for miles. A coaching inn and the coach-house alongside stand in typical isolation 11 miles from Hwlffordd (Haverfordwest), 14 miles from Aberteifi (Cardigan) and 10½ miles from Arberth (Narberth), and offer a respite from the mountain winds. Settle in for a gossip at the New Inn and you'll hear of the topless barmaids and the mysterious fire that destroyed the roof a few years back; and if you are really fortunate you may be invited to try the swimming pool at the rear. The landlady, Jane Wilson, speeds through the local lanes on a 1,000cc motorcycle and in 1987 served bed and breakfast for £8.00 a night.

As you approach the Preseli Mountains herds of Friesian cattle stand scattered on the green slopes, like self-propelled chessmen with a built-in board; and then there are the mountains themselves, little known outside the area and with a

bleak barrenness like a slice of the Beacons trans-planted. The peaks of the hills in this area lay above the glaciation and show to this day the jagged-tooth roughness of the original mountain peaks, in contrast to the rounded softness of the summits of lower hills which were polished by the ice and subdued by its relentless progress.

And everywhere there are castles. We passed above Castell Coch at the beginning of this explo-ration, and we all know of Caerphilly castle with its vast area second only, I believe, to Windsor itself in the whole of Europe. There are great castles at Carmarthen and Pembroke, and con-spicuous ones at Manorbier and Cardiff. But there is even a castle at Barry, perched above the entrance to Porthkerry. There is another at Merthyr Mawr, sheltered by sand dunes that look like a piece of the great sandy deserts of the Mid-dle East. Fonmon Castle, still a family home, is in a secluded part of the Vale of Glamorgan where you would least expect to find one; while there is a largely unknown castle perched high above

Cardiff. This one was a revelation even to my respected friend Wynford Vaughan Thomas, who knew almost all of them. It is called Castell Mor Craig, and stands away from metalled roads on a high point of Caerphilly Mountain. From the reg-ular profile of the remains I imagine it was never completed – but with its magnificent setting and the fine views it commands it could have become one of the most famous and well-sited castles of them all.

It is finds like this that can only be made by the walker, stepping away from the motorway and out into the open countryside. Walk along the coast heading south, then west, from the capital and you'll find Ranny Point, where the first messages were sent by radio across water by Marconi and Kemp in 1897. Bunkers in the brambles above St Mary's Well Bay mark the oldest surviving missile launching station, from the Second World War. Round the corner is Sully Island, half a mile long and half a mile offshore at high tide, little known and gloriously isolated. It is cut off for almost

RIGHT: *Mumbles Head on the Gower Peninsula. The Mumbles marks the gateway to this favoured area, which is ringed with sandy coves and fringed with sand dunes.*

LEFT: *Everywhere in South Wales there are castles . . . Caerphilly Castle's vast area is one of the largest in Europe.*

exactly six hours, and joined to the mainland for as long again; but check the time of the high tide for the causeway is cut at walking speed and it becomes a dangerous torrent within minutes. There is another castle at the far end of the island, as you might expect; this one dates from Saxon times and has been partly eroded by the sea.

There is a castle actually in the sea at Porthkerry, for it emerges only at the lowest ebb tides. Look for the lias cliffs too, for they still reveal plesiosaur skeletons when least expected and ammonites several feet across have been recovered in the past. Walks through the Vale of Glamorgan itself will reveal little villages, roads that descend to splash through fords like the one at Llancarfan above which we all danced one crazy night, dodging long-eared bats as they swooped for insects in the humid night air of a hot summer.

And then there is Gower. I once missed the same boat twice in this favoured part of the world. I planned to catch the boat to Ilfracombe to lunch with a friend, and arrived at the quayside in Swansea to find the boat just two yards from the jetty and only just out of reach. Sadly I went to telephone, but watched as I spoke on the phone as the boat crossed the bay towards Mumbles pier – and a glance at the time-table showed that it called there first, before crossing the channel! I sped round the bay, vaulted over the turnstiles, ran to the quayside . . . to find the boat, for the second time that day, just barely out of reach and gathering speed.

Mumbles marks the gateway to the Gower peninsula, ringed with beautiful sandy coves, fringed with sand-dunes and covered with elder and gorse – a favourite with me since it flowers in every month of the year, adding a dash of ochre yellow to the bare brown hillsides. Even in mid-winter you may bathe at Pwll-du, a remote little bay with nothing but a pebble footpath to lead the explorer onward. The roads on the Gower spread outwards and end nowhere, like the rimless spokes of a broken wheel, and it is here – with the ubiquitous Gower ponies and the madly wheeling skylark for company – that the walker finds his metier. From the wide expanse of Oxwich bay to the cool stands of Port Eynon (yes, a castle stands on the high ground between them); and from the vast stretch of golden sand across Rhossili to the beauteous sculptural headland of Worms Head; round to the great mudflats where the cockle women of Pen-clawdd still cling to the vestiges of a traditional way of life; this is a world of its own. Rolling moor alternates with scrubby dune, the reedy curlew vies with the shelduck for your attention, and the whole peninsula lies just a short distance from Swansea with its railway station and bustling city life.

The Gower ends at Loughor – and again there is a castle there too, just to mark the fact. Just as the English settled in western Pembrokeshire and left behind an English accent and English place names – Templeton, Cresswell and Honey-borough lying a little to the west of Llanteg, Llwyn-y-brain and Llanfallteg – so there are a few English names in Gower; the walker may find Freedown and Fairyhill, Cockstreet and Harding Down, to match Bryn-afel and Bach-y-cochs to the east. There is even a Cheriton on the Gower, matching the Cheriton between Milton and Sageston in Pembrokeshire, and the family of Cheriton Bishop, Cheriton Cross and Cheriton Fitzpaine in Devon (and yes, there is a Cheriton in Hampshire, not far from where I went to boarding school, and another in Kent). So know that you are walking in the footsteps of other travellers from earlier ages.

They came and found a restful home in a different land, establishing a life and a name in a new nation. And so may you find respite, too; whether it is a short-term immersion, like a dip in the sea, or a long-term affair, akin to the baptism with a new way of life, is entirely up to you. In either event, enjoy the walk, for Wales is a land to savour and the Welsh are a people to meet.

Rhossili, looking towards the beauteous sculptural headland of Worm's Head. The Gower Peninsula is a world of its own, a haven for walkers.

The Spirit of Dyfed

The presiding spirit of a place, the *genius loci*, can be awesome, unutterably aloof as I once saw him on Yr-Wyddfa, the summit of Snowdon, between the Crib Goch and Crib y Ddysgl when a light powdering of snow emphasized the synclinal folds of his toga. In Glen Dessary, that rift on the rim of Lochaber, he lingers on amidst desolation. In fourteen days of hard going I never saw a wilder glen. It looked as if, during a violent spasm, a cathedral had collapsed.

He may dwell in those quietest of places at the heart of our North Yorkshire moors or among the reeds of Hornsea Mere in Holderness. In Pembrokeshire with its inlets and outlets, its vistas and scattering of visitors, the sea-wrack and thundering spume, I have encountered him on the basaltic cliffs of Skomer Island where I stared '. . . above the screaming, growling, groaning proletariat of sea-fowl on The Wick: there a pair of peregrines had their eyrie and when not stooping after puffin or razorbill, jackdaw or meadow-pipit they would stand motionless for hours, surveying the multitudinous life of the cliff with cold indifference.' Those words were written nearly forty years ago by Ronald Lockley, distinguished naturalist and founder of the Skokholm Bird Observatory who about that time explored what eventually became the Pembrokeshire Coast Path.

I took my two young children, now married with children of their own, to Skomer off the southern hook of St Bride's Bay on what turned out to be a boisterous morning in May. A boatman picked us up at Martinshaven, the nearest beach on the mainland. At his first effort to shove us off, a big wave, a St Bride's special, lifted the bows to an alarming angle and my younger child – to my consternation and her delight – fell back into a pool of water in the bilge. We got away, eventually, into a see-saw sea and landed I've forgotten where and how except that her sister, not to be outdone, fell overboard.

Flaming gorse bloomed all around the innumerable tiny fields and stone boundaries from which the nesting storm petrels squealed and purred like cats. But the grand chorus, the continuo, came from the clamour of sea-fowl. When we arrived half a dozen naturalists were at work, including the late great James Fisher and Julian Huxley. We were told weird tales such as that of the peregrine falcon that flew down to its eyrie with a decapitated jackdaw which had been ringed. That avian Spitfire tore off a leg and proffered it, still ringed, to a chick who steadfastly refused it. Eventually, in one gulp, she swallowed it herself. We saw weird sights such as short-eared owls looping the loop in broad daylight at a height of about 500 feet on courtship flights, calling *boo-boo-boo* a dozen times or more.

Solva in Dyfed.

   The island is scarcely 2 miles across its widest diameter, the one from Saunders Fist to Little Sound. I went back to grey Skomer on several occasions and to her smaller and lower sister island of Skokholm which is entirely composed of warm-coloured old red sandstone and to that Atlantic seal nursery, Ramsey Island, sanctified by the bones of ten thousand saints, but in memory nothing can match that first sight of The Wick, high home of the Spirit of Dyfed and Lord of the far-flung sea-fowl. It pleases me to report that nobody can say where his children the wave-skimming storm petrels go for the greater part of the year, that is from September to the following May.

   Dyfed abounds in dolmens, Iron Age forts and Norman castle mounds. To get a picture of those turbulent times read the *Itinerary* of Girald de Barri, one of the most formidable of the Giraldines. A grandson of Girald of Windsor and the Princess Nest, this zealous churchman bargained with popes and marched the length of Wales in the Company of the Knights of the True Cross, a noble band heaven-bent on recruiting bowmen for the third Crusade. Since there are two or three guides to the whole length of the Pembrokeshire Way – of which the best is the one I referred to on page 95 by Adam Nicolson – I have suggested to David Bellamy that he should write about what areas immediately catch the eye of an artist.

J.H.

THE PEMBROKESHIRE COAST PATH

DAVID BELLAMY

Pembrokeshire, according to Giraldus Cambrensis, the twelfth-century priest of mixed Norman and Welsh descent, is the finest part of all Wales. As this most vivid and witty of medieval historians was both a native and much given to exaggeration, some might dispute this statement, but undeniably the county can claim outstanding scenery. Thanks to sensitive national park management it remains largely unspoilt. Marloes Sands, Lydstep Caverns, Newport Bay and Dinas Head are all natural beauties, and the harbours at Lower Fishguard, Solva and Porthgain still retain an air of past glories. Other places of particular interest are the great castle of Pembroke with its towering keep, Manorbier Castle where Giraldus was born, the twelfth-century cathedral and Bishop's Palace at St Davids, and the tiny chapel wedged in the cliffs at St Govan's.

The Pembrokeshire Coast Path, the third long-distance footpath to be created and which was opened in 1970, runs from Amroth, not far from Tenby in the south to St Dogmaels in the north of the county, a distance of 181 miles. Although the coast is unquestionably wild and rugged, it is not dangerous if care is taken and walkers know what they are up against. This is especially apparent where the path has been torn away in a cliff fall. The power of erosion is forcefully illustrated at St Govan's in the south of the county where massive blocks the size of a barn have slid away from the cliffs and now lie below, pounded by the sea. When sketching on the coast my biggest problem is to remain alert to incoming tides whilst absorbed in what I'm doing. I failed to do so on one occasion below the intimidating cliffs at St Govan's when it seemed as if my palette had made

a bid for freedom for it suddenly floated past, caught by the rising tide. Within minutes my trainers were full of sea water and I had to beat a hasty retreat across huge boulders. It is easy to see why the coast rescue services are kept busy during the tourist season.

Coming from Pembrokeshire, I have seen the county in all its humours, and although I'm deeply attached to several places along the coast, the St David's Peninsula is the one I return to most. Unlike much of the coast path, this is one of the few places where it's not difficult to work out a circular walk, returning to the starting point by cutting across the neck of the headland. While other circular walks can be devised only the Dale – Marloes Peninsula and Strumble Head – rival St David's in providing a natural route. To dedicated walkers any length of road to be covered is anathema. However, in many of the back lanes of Pembrokeshire the going is between hedgerows which in spring are radiant with masses of primroses, campion, celandines and soft green mosses.

Cyclopean rock scenery, rock arches, caves, sandy beaches; a landscape dotted with stunted cottages, their slurried roofs designed to resist the fierce Atlantic gales, these are all part of the St David's Peninsula. It is mostly founded on hard igneous rock, more resistant to the sea than that of St Bride's Bay. In addition the area has a number of rocky outcrops that tower above the landscape to give it a distinctly different character to the

The tiny chapel wedged in the cliffs at St Govan's. 'The power of erosion is forcefully illustrated here – massive blocks of stone have slid away from the rocks and now lie below, pounded by the sea.'

Marloes Beach, a place of great natural beauty.

David Bellamy

south of the county. It also shelters delightful little places such as Solva and Abereiddi. In general the climate is mild and I recall sitting on Manorbier beach one December night without a jacket sketching by moonlight, and also the exhilarating, almost magical sound and smell of the sea beneath the stars.

The walk I shall describe runs from Solva to Abereiddi. It has the advantage of prevailing winds at the back of you for much of the way and splendid views ahead towards Carn Llidi, Penbiri and Strumble Head. Route finding on this part of the coast is hardly a problem: just follow the sea. The going is fairly easy under foot. Of numerous ways of returning to Solva from Abereiddi, the most direct is through Carnhedryn Uchaf and Middle Mill, the latter a charming little hamlet. The total distance is about 26 miles, most of it along the coast path. Alternatively the walk can be started at St David's, from where it is easy to reach Caerfai Bay or St Non's Bay, breaking off at Penbiri or other points along the route. St David's makes an excellent base and there is a youth hostel below the southern aspect of Carn Llidi, north of the village.

Solva is a place in which to linger. Hemmed in by the steep valley sides, it abounds in odd corners where those engaged in sketching and other furtive pursuits can escape from the curious. Many of the buildings date back to the smuggling era. It has been suggested that the Vikings called the place Solva in honour of one of the fairest of their princesses and I am prepared to accept this romantic belief. It is not easy to leave the balmy atmosphere of the harbour on a warm summer day and climb high above the drowned valley but as you follow the rim seawards, the view is dramatic. Despite its hazardous entrance, Solva, the finest natural harbour in St Bride's Bay, used to be a thriving commercial port for lime and coal with no less than nine warehouses jostling for space on the small quay. The lime kilns remain a prominent feature.

Above the harbour entrance the path turns westwards. Out at sea are a group of rocks with Black Scar, the westernmost, appearing like the sinister shape of a submarine at dusk. Here the cliffs are truly wild and sensational, though not as jagged as they are further west. The sea seems a long way below. Turning any corner you are impelled to look down, and at Porth Llong can be seen the gaunt wreck of a tug, stranded and firmly perched on the rocks below a great cirque of cliffs. This was one of three Greek tugs which, in late October 1981, were bound from Liverpool to Piraeus. Two of the vessels were unmanned. They were being towed by the third and when the propeller of the lead tug was fouled by the tow rope, gale force winds and heavy seas began to force them towards the treacherous coastline. Eventually all three were thrown on to the rocks, a testimony to the savage nature of this beautiful but dangerous coast. The crew were all rescued by an RAF helicopter and the St David's lifeboat. One of my friends has the curious job of scrambling on to this wreck at the dead of night when the tide is low to sit in eerie isolation awaiting a rescue party. He runs the adventure school at Twr-y-Felin, in St David's, and the courses there include simulated coastal rescues. As may be imagined he makes sure that his students are pretty well trained before putting his own safety in their hands!

The Pembrokeshire coast has seen many wrecks and it was reputed that in the eighteenth century many ships were beguiled there by the diabolical trade of setting up false lights. Cargoes were then swiftly disposed of, at times even with the assistance of local gentry and customs officers. There is a tale that, during a church service, news came through of a shipwreck nearby. The parson enjoined his congregation to show temperance before he asked for a head start in the race to the stricken vessel.

However, this coastline has also witnessed many heroic rescues. The seventeenth-century pirate Bartholemew Roberts, or Black Bart, was born not far from the St David's Peninsula at Little Newcastle. He was among the first to hoist the 'Jolly Roger' and once siezed a treasure-laden vessel within sight of forty Portuguese men o' war. When about to engage in battle he would appear on deck dressed in a crimson coat and accompanied by a band.

St David's Head still seems far away. The views across St Bride's Bay on a clear day are extensive: the great arc of coastline culminating in the dis-

tant outline of Skomer Island lying off the end of the mainland. Skomer is one of the finest seabird islands in Europe. The path descends to Caerbwdi Bay, a bouldery cove with fantastic rock formations. To the westward side impressive cliffs rise high above the sea, leaning at a steep angle, and hewn like slates. Much of the stone used to build St David's Cathedral was quarried both there and in neighbouring Caerfai Bay. This is a delectable spot, often deserted even on the best of days.

Beyond Caerbwdi the cliffs become steeper towards the headland. Because adjacent Caerfai Bay can be reached by road, its small sandy beach and varicoloured pebbles attract quite a number of holiday makers. It is easy to see why the coast path was originally thought to be only 168 miles long, when a later survey revealed the true distance to be 181 miles. Calculating the mileage with so many in and outs, ups and downs, must have been a very considerable task.

At St Non's Bay sharp upthrusting rocks pierce the waves in strong definite lines. Scrambling about among them for the best view of a cavern or group of rocks recalls youthful delights. What marvellous subjects for sketching or painting they make, especially when sharply angled sunlight falls across the scene. White gulls are caught against dark backgrounds as foaming waves explode on solid rock, the power of the sea apparent even on a calm day. In these timeless places hours pass unheeded when sketching.

Non was the mother of St David who, according to legend, was born here during a violent storm. At the same time the stone against which Non leaned split and the imprint of her hands was left there for all time. What now remains of St Non's Chapel is the lower parts of the walls. Whole volumes of legends are associated with St David and it has to be faced that he was not always on good terms with his neighbours as an encounter with the Irish chieftain Boia reveals. That man's wife, fed up with her holy companions, decided to taunt the monks by compelling her maids to use lewd words and play immodest sports wholly unclothed. But St David stood firm and soon had his brethren hard at work to dissipate their feelings of lust.

At Trwyncynddeiriog – and what other mass of

rock can boast such a grand-sounding name? – immense sharp rocky buttresses form solid bulwarks against the sea. In places massive overhangs and caves have been created where the action of the water has eroded even these mighty pillars. Here nature is raw and unforgiving, where Atlantic gales seem to vent their full fury on a defiant coast. The varying rock strata, and, at times, striking changes in colours with purples, greys, greens, ochres and red Cambrian rocks beggar simple description.

Porthclais, formerly the port of St David's, puts you in mind of a small fjord, perhaps best seen in midsummer when small pleasure boats bob about in the choppy water beside the ancient and battered quay. Almost everything, even the ancient stone steps, are draped in glistening seaweed. Here, where the river Alun meets the sea, the blessed St David or Dewi, reputedly the son of a Cardigan chieftain, was baptized, and here the Norsemen landed time after time to ransack the cathedral city. At this point the path takes one of its tortuous turns inland, with views across the inlet to typical Pembrokeshire cottages hugging the brim and framed by the sculptured and stunted trees, a feature of this wind-thrashed landscape. Sadly, these traditional dwellings are gradually disappearing.

After Porthclais the drop to the sea is precipitous. A little way out a monstrous rock arch soars out of the sea, leaning at a seemingly impossible angle, way below the path: one almost expects mermaids to appear. How odd it looks. It would be ideal if it were possible to explore the amazing rock architecture at sea level, for in some ways coastal walking can be frustrating when the only viewpoint is from the cliff top. It must have been terrifying suddenly to witness a Viking long ship skim round these rocks as it sped in to Porthclais intent on pillage, burning and rape.

'The dramatic rock arch at St Non's Bay. Here, sharp upthrusting rocks pierce the waves in strong definite lines.'

As you approach Porthlysgi Bay, named, it is thought, from some Irish pirate, the serrated south end of Ramsey Island appears and the sea ahead is ruffled by the strong currents flowing out of the Sound. The scenery becomes distinctly wilder. Nowhere along the whole coastal path is the sense of remoteness greater. Here the sea fowl take over. The air is full of gulls, their cries competing with the sound of surf. Here surely is the home of the great Kraken and other monsters, and as the sea thunders and smokes it gives a serpent-like motion to the rocks. You are now seeing the Pembrokeshire Coast Path at its wildest, and on a really rough day, at its most awesome. But the going is still easy underfoot.

As you turn northwards beside Ramsey Sound the sea below runs fiercely, especially at the narrows between island and mainland. Here, at low tide, the Bitches stick out of the water like a half-submerged man trap. A castle on the outermost rock would surely have been one of the most romantic of sites, though probably of little military value. What better place for sirens to lure mariners to their doom! The legend is that the Bitches were created when St Justinian, tiring of life on the mainland, retired to Ramsey, but the coming of visitors interfered with his vigils and he prayed for the causeway to be destroyed. In some miraculous way this was done and all that remained was the wave-worn reef we see there today.

In common with most of the Pembrokeshire off-shore islands, Ramsey is rich in bird life with clamorous kittiwakes, fulmars, shags, choughs, razorbills and guillemots, there in abundance. Unfortunately, the clown-faced puffins seem to have fled when rats were accidentally introduced from the mainland. They can be found on Skomer, however, which in company with Skokholm harbours the world's largest concentration of shearwaters, but these are nocturnal birds and rarely seen by day.

Once more the craggy eminence of Carn Llidi comes into view, this time towering high above St David's lifeboat station at St Justinian's. Here, in early spring, I found much new walling had been carried out, beautifully done with clods of turf and earth placed in between stones, and more turf laid on top. By late May or June grasses and small flow-

ers will adorn the stones – an artist's delight, and so typical of this part of the county. The waller obviously took great pride in his work, which can't have been easy since winds on some of the wilder days on this very tip of west Wales are strong enough to knock you over.

Drop down to the south end of Whitesand Bay at Porthselau and you have a breath-taking view of Carn Llidi where the angular rocks seem to have been arranged for the inspiration of artists. Turner came here in 1795 and sketched St David's Head. His watercolour depicts fishermen in Lilliputian scale to accentuate the size of the rocks. This wild coastline intrigued him and he made several studies of the Bishops and Clerks, as well as Ramsey Island. If the tide has retreated you can walk along the beach, otherwise continue along the path above. Not far from the glorious

'*Carn Llidi from Porthselau. Drop down to the south end of Whitesand Bay and you have a breath-taking view of Carn Llidi, where the angular rocks seem to have been arranged for the inspiration of artists.*'

beach of Whitesand Bay with its large car park stands the site of a chapel dedicated to St Patrick who set sail for Ireland from that shrine. Some think that he may have been a Pembrokeshire man.

At St David's Head stands an Iron Age fortress and burial chamber, Arthur's Quoit. A single pillar supports the capstone, said to have been tossed there by King Arthur from a nearby hilltop. Late one December I received such a ferocious battering from the wind that my ears tingled for hours and it was difficult to co-ordinate a pencil with the right part of the sketchpad. Then begins the final tramp along the jagged northern coastline. Before reaching the inlet of Gesail-fawr, however, a path leads away to the right, to the summit of Carn Llidi, an interesting diversion from the walk. At nearly 600 feet the views are superb and on a very

clear day may produce a glimpse of Ireland.

The switchback nature of the path continues, with a sharp descent before the long climb past the north face of Penbiri where the easy scramble makes a pleasant change from the slog, slog, slog of pathway walking.

Back on the main tracks there are distant views of Strumble Head and its lighthouse which gleams in the sun like a space rocket on its launching pad. After the tortured looking rocks of Porth Tre-wen there is Abereiddi with a cluster of cottages and its black, sandy beach, reputed to have been a landing place for smugglers' illicit cargoes during the eighteenth century. Slate was quarried here until the turn of the present century and carried to Porthgain by a tramway along the coast. It is a place to savour at all times of the year before you return to your starting point across the peninsula.

Master of Unorthodoxy

Although I sometimes go considerably out of my way to avoid walkers in the open air, it follows that as an author, a hungry reader and occasional reviewer, I have met most of the best in print and not a few of the worst in a variety of conditions. We are all of us prone to encounters with amiable eccentrics but, offhand, I can think of none with better claim to the title phrase I have borrowed from one of his extremely amusing books: *The Beach of Morning,** a gallivant from Lake Chad in Northern Nigeria. The author is Stephen Pern, a truly prodigious walker who is more than slightly off his chump. We have twice crossed each others' footprints, swopped drinks, discussed God, Man and the Cosmos and, late at night, argued about what the hell we were really up to.

After his fledgling years on a Sussex dairy farm, I heard from his publisher that he had walked not just up to but right round an East African lake I called the Jade Sea. We may forget – which isn't at all easy – that he had been in the Parachute Regiment and had, later, hopscotched across several borders in West Africa. By far his most spectacular achievement has been on the crest of the Great Divide, that well over 2,000-ft long and uncommonly high watershed between Mexico and Canada. By comparison, Offa's Dyke, the Mercian ditch between Saxon England and very Welsh Wales is small beer in the well-stocked cellars of Stephen's memories. But walks are what you bring to them as much as exported capital. Certainly he is unlikely to go back there because, to quote him again, 'It is more fun to launch new ships than to winch up what has sunk,' an example of undiluted Pernod.

One of his peculiarities and what so often endears him to me is his vulgarity intermixed with verbal jewellery. I'm unable to paraphrase, briefly, how at speed on his motorbike he was grossly interfered with by his pillion passenger who, up to that point, he didn't know was a notable and distinctly unorthodox Kanuri whore. He is at one with Blake in believing that . . .

> Mutual Forgiveness of Each Vice
> Such are the Gates of Paradise.

Not long afterwards we have him wading through wave-breathing water. I don't think it really matters where. Sometimes a wave would catch his legs 'but seawater dries so fast in all the walking, all the going and the not-arriving. "Walking where?" I wondered and the geckoes sang at midnight. "Where?" the

---

* Hodder & Stoughton (1983).

Pen-y-ghent.

little lizards asked. The word made walls for caves, and lids for graves and waves rolled questionless across the night.'

In its way, Offa's Dyke teases the imagination as much as any better known ancient monument. In his *National Trust Book of Long Walks*,* that most enjoyable record of a lover's journeying, Adam Nicolson tells us that we 'are walking down the hazy edge of two things in conflict . . . (yet) this is not an edge, but the heart of things. History's detritus is only a tide-mark, made irrelevant in 1282 when Edward I conquered Wales.' Many years ago, before much was signposted, I got lost several times by following previously undiscovered dykes (or maybe they were irrigation ditches) and struck off east from Knighton into Housman country glad, nevertheless, that I had wandered through thickly wooded, friendly and curiously deserted Radnor.

J.H.

* Weidenfeld and Nicolson, 1981 with photographs by Charlie Waite.

OFFA'S DYKE PATH

STEPHEN PERN

Was it an ichthyosaurus that first crawled out of the sea? At any rate I felt like one. Having crossed the Severn bridge on foot I'd puddled down to the estuary shore in pursuit of the retreating tide. What I wanted was an inauguration, a boot-tip in the water before setting off – sea to sea – for Liverpool Bay, but what I got was an all-over coating of slime and a lengthy detour to a laundry. So much for day Number One – a.m.: fell in the mud; p.m.: watched breeches spin dry. Offa's Dyke Path wasn't quite the romp I'd expected.

But the cleansing operation did give me time out in Chepstow, the 'Welcome to Wales' sign down by the Wye, a public two fingers at the Norman castle. The townsfolk seemed a virile lot – urgent graffiti in the public loo and, despite passing shoppers, a Cortina rocking vigorously in the car park. Such is the stuff of long-distance hiking – by their litter bins (always full) and their phone booths (never empty) ye shall know them.

Sliding noiselessly from my nylon sheets I rose to greet the dawn. It was nowhere to be seen but the High Street was bustling and my breakfast already congealed. Eating it was a mistake. For the first mile out of town I could hardly move; for the next five I was starving. But enough of breakfasts and bedsheets. I'd shrugged off bungalows, milkmen and dogs and was looking down on the Wye, on textbook meanders cut through limestone cliffs, on small boats turtled in the mud. An unlikely gorge – fat water, no rapids, jackdaws and seagulls sharing the same loops of sky.

Why were they doing that? If only old Robbo or Miss Points of fond memory were here to tell me. But the years pass and even geography masters and biology mistresses move on; he, bless his soul, to a Cumberland graveyard; she to the Canadian prairies. On this walk, though, age had its advantages; the trail for the first 30 miles at least was less a wild courtship of fell, field and sky than a meditative stroll with the past.

In its initial stretches the Dyke Path almost had me drugged, the very trees – the unfurling beeches, the towering limes – transports of unusual delight. At any moment I might see Maid Marion tied to a trunk, a corrupt prior wobbling past. A Mercian might pop up with a sign reading 'Keep Off the Dyke'. A thousand years had been stuffed, willy-nilly, into some kind of internal scanner: Celt, Saxon, the Norman invasion not just facts on this walk but real memories, engaging not just interest but emotion. I found myself taking sides as I sauntered along, working out military training rotas, dividing lands between imaginary sons, though the excuse for the walk, Offa's Dyke itself, had me stumped.

Being a Norman was no problem at all. I could see at a glance what their castles were for but the Mercians were an enigma, their earthwork, the greatest in western Europe, now neither small enough to ignore nor large enough to defend. Twelve hundred years on and its 80 broken miles are often no more than a hedge line, here a sheep-nibbled hump through a field, there a ribbon of gorse, though on the wooded cliffs above the Wye the Dyke remains an imposing eyebrow, always commanding views to the west, brooding perhaps

The Norman castle at Chepstow in Gwent.

on the foundations of a nation, a badger-haunted dream of times before England began. William Wordsworth, whacking out the good lines above Tintern Abbey, may well have used it as a desk.

Right now the Abbey ruins were surrounded, trapped against the river by coaches in fresh spring warpaint. Descending, I imagined charred bodies of monks and horribly whooping grannies, but Henry VIII took care of the brothers and the grannies were all pooped: it was a very hot day. I lay on my back with a choc ice or two playing a form of Pooh sticks with the pattern of stone against sky. By closing one eye I could move it all left, by closing the other it moved right. Routine stuff for a twelfth-century mason but to me the tracery was exquisite.

So were the wild cherry trees, periwigs of blossom dusting the slopes, spring still just a tear on the twig. Everything seemed so young. Even the nettles could be stroked without getting stung, the exposed geology of the Wye gorge now quilted by tumbling farms. In the Bush Inn at Redbridge the talk was of recoil-less shotguns; a little further on of dog trials and sheep.

I didn't exactly meet Janet Reed, we just happened to be in the same field, me ostensibly eating a Mars bar, she puppeteering with sheep, at least that's what it looked like for the half hour or so that I watched her. She could do anything with them. She had them bunched up, she spread them all out, she ran them through a maze of propped gates. And all she had was a dog. She, and the dog, were practising for the British Championships. Walking down into Monmouth I wished I could do something like that, dance a tango, play the flute, whatever . . .

More stone walls, another castle – I was getting fed up with history by now, but the following morning my interest was revived by arrow slits in the barns. In Monmouth I'd taken my second B and B of the trip and come on through fields yellow with oil seed rape, counting the sweeps a tractor had made spraying the young wheatfield nearby. Lulled by this somewhat lifeless scene, a sudden 'oink' pumped me straight in the heart. It was only a pig crashed out in the hedge but as unexpected these days as a footpad. The next thing I saw was a buzzard, prematurely, I felt, as

wild country – in the shape of the Black Mountains – was still 10 miles ahead. When I reached it that evening I saw why the buzzard had left. Hang-gliding is something else I'd like to try, but not in the crowded airspace of the Hatterall Ridge. The coloured sails looked like far-off confetti, disappearing as I climbed the hill. Where had they all gone for the night? Down to the main road probably.

I woke at five-thirty, grabbed my socks from a fleece-hung fence and set off. This was more like it! Not a single castle all day, at least not one I felt guilty about missing. To my left there was Llanthony Priory, down in the vale of Ewyas, but I wasn't about to drop 1,200 feet to see it, and in any case I was frightened of becoming a hermit. Something about the place seems to affect the soul – one of the marcher lords wound up here as an Anchorite when he should have been repressing the Welsh, and further up the valley, at

LEFT: *Offa's Dyke Path near Chepstow.*　　　ABOVE: *Tintern Abbey. The tracery is exquisite!*

Capel-y-ffin, were even stranger goings-on, a bisexual community the guidebook said, with 'its own particular rights and rituals'. It didn't occur to me for several days that most communities are bisexual anyway, and I hurried primly forward. A short distance on I ran into a couple of hill ponies. More of the rights and rituals, I thought, though which was which I couldn't tell. While 'Right', an ungainly mare, did a sugar-begging act from the front, her partner crept to the rear. They had obviously done this before. 'Ritual' knew exactly where to take the first bite – right in the goodies pocket of my rucksack. I swung round as the ripping sound reached my ears, brandishing a switch of heather. Evil little bog-trotters.

It wasn't my rucksack's day. Having descended from the dizzy height of 2,306 feet, the highest point on the 176-mile trail, I rolled down Hay Bluff and into Hay-on-Wye itself where I met a woodcarver and was invited to stay for the night.

The woodcarver had a dog. The dog either had an incontinence problem or hated rucksacks, or both. Matters came to a head some time in the night and despite disinfectant and a sinkful of suds I left town with a social liability on my back. Hay, incidentally, is where old books go to die. Even the cinema has been converted to a sort of rest home, the hopeless cases outside in the rain at around a quid for a dozen, the rest inside on miles and miles of shelving. The interest lay not so much between the covers – most volumes were highly forgettable – as on them: 'To A from B, Xmas '49'; 'Never say die, Yours, Roger'. It was mild eavesdropping really. I wondered who Roger was for miles.

Strange miles – not England but not really Wales, the hills and valleys cobbled together, almost conspiratorial in their efforts to grass over the past. Between Hay and Montgomery – 45 miles – the landscape was of dingles and dells; of

shrunken hamlets – a chapel, a church; of far-away noises; of buzzards and sheep; of scores settled long, long ago, England becoming Wales and vice versa. To anyone but an islander border zones must be commonplace, but I found this loose handshake between Saxon and Celt disconcerting. I needed a definite boundary, something I could actually stand on. So had the eighth-century Mercians, which is why, according to Dr David Hall, their king had commanded the Dyke.

'Biggest bluff in history,' said the don from his perch on the bank. 'You can't really attack or defend it. It isn't a fort, it simply concentrates the mind. Must've given the Welsh one hell of a shock.'

'Why?'

'Logistics,' said Dr Hall. 'It was built near enough overnight. Offa had roughly 250,000 men at his disposal. Let's say he transmuted their taxes one year to a short period of direct labour. OK, season one he sends out survey parties. They mark the line, apportion work through administrative units. The next spring – wham! – a blast of concentrated effort, co-ordinated all the way. Eighty miles is just under half a million feet. Divide by 250,000 and allowing for variables each bloke digs, say, 4 feet of dyke – two weeks' work at most for a fit churl with a mattock. Some gangs do better than others, hence the variable dimensions; some don't link up too well which accounts for a few of the kinks. Manpower and blisters – Offa got

ABOVE: *Gorse bushes lining a Shropshire stretch of Offa's Dyke Path.*

LEFT: *The Black Mountains, Powys.*

101

his dyke built about as fast as you'll walk it.'

Faster probably. I was feeling unaccountably tired. Perhaps the weekend break I'd had with friends outside Knighton was taking its toll. The Dyke remained unsympathetic, galloping up Panpunton Hill with the exuberance of a red setter. I half expected it to be chasing the sheep at the top. By mid-afternoon I was creased, and, thinking how much like wooden cowbells the local rivers all sounded – the Unk, the Lugg and the Clun – I lay down and fell fast asleep. You can do that in south-western Shropshire. You won't get stared at or run over. A vehicle that does more than twenty around here is a wasted resource, overtaking largely unknown. If you must have wheels, get a tractor – it'll block the lanes nicely and give you splendid views over the hedges – though I woke that afternoon to the sight of four people travelling towards me on their knees.

They were obviously botanists.

'Taste this,' suggested Tom Davis.

'It's grass,' I said. 'And uncooked.'

'Try it.'

Thus I discovered sweet vernal, perhaps the best chew in the land. Smoked honeysuckle is the closest description I can give it. Clun Forest (not a real one) was full of places like this – a travel writer's nightmare – so instantly private, hidden and remote that one's instinct was to say nothing about them.

Next day I reached Montgomery. I was, as ever in these small border towns, nonplussed. Where was the traffic? The standard Department of the Environment eyesore? English county towns are so often centres of loin-girding that places like Montgomery – completely unswamped – can be quite disorienting. What else was missing here? It wasn't till I'd left that I realized there hadn't been any suburbs, that the whole place, not a quarter mile through, had been green to its elegant door. It's curious how subconscious knowledge like this sometimes strikes you.

Twelve miles north of Montgomery – tediously flat most of the way – I reached a lock on the Shropshire Union Canal. I sat on a bollard, lit up a fag, and watched bits of willow fluff on the water. They hardly moved. Until that moment I'd never bothered to watch the way that canals don't flow.

London 160 mls., B^{ps} Castle 8½ – the milestones on the towpath made me feel a bit like Dick Whittington, except that my rucksack still smelt of dog pee. I left it outside the Lion Hotel, Llanymynech and went in for lunch. 'Drink in Wales, Dine in England', the sign said. The Powys/Shropshire border runs straight through the bar.

Two more lumps of upland and 60 miles to go: I wound up and out of the Vale of Montgomery and camped that night on a golf course. A dragon appeared to have captured the village of Llanyblodwel below. Half sigh, half roar, I heard it rising through the mist, saw propane burners flare briefly and a yellow pear drop in the evening sky. It drifted slowly away to the west. The company of Thunder and Colt, in nearby Oswestry, make a hundred hot-air balloons a year.

I could have done with one myself. The countryside was knee-deep in dung. The lapwings loved it, peewitting in a frenzy over the freshly spread fields. They were probably hunting grubs for their chicks though the hooded crows still seemed to be house-building, annoying the few ponies I'd seen for the last of their winter fur.

I was about to moult slightly too. I'd been walking for eleven days by this time but had scarcely reached the Hundred Years War – the fairy-tale

LEFT: *The castle and town of Montgomery from the churchyard.*

RIGHT: *Chirk Castle in Clwyd, north of Oswestry.*

outlines of Chirk Castle to my right, the restful hum of afternoon milking to my left. Medieval England, with the convenience of electricity, seemed reassuringly intact, so to say that the sight of Cefn-mawr was a shock is something of an understatement. I just stood in the middle of a field with my mouth open. Then I remembered old Robbo. We'd printed 'MINERALS' and 'CHEMICALS' over our sketch maps of this area. Spreading across the hillside ahead I saw what 'CHEMICALS' actually meant. Grime, dereliction, pale, hard-pressed women, men wedded to chip shops and pubs.

The Dyke Path swings within a stone's throw of all this before crossing the Dee via Telford's cast-iron aqueduct and heading upstream for Llangollen. As an argument for the creation of long-distance footpaths the past few miles could not have been more eloquent.

I'd played hopscotch with the border since Monmouth, but the last 40 miles of Offa's Dyke Path were unequivocally Welsh: Mrs Maureen Jones, for example, at Llangollen Post Office, just off to America with the local choir. This was still spring, but in summer the world comes to Llangollen, even if it has to hitchhike. Choirs to the first International Musical Eisteddfod here actually sang their way across war-shattered

France. 'That it was possible,' wrote the Eisteddfod committee chairman, 'for such an event to take place at all within two years of the end of hostilities was, to say the least, impressive, but that it should occur on an improvised stage, in a canvas auditorium, erected on the Recreation Ground of a small town in North Wales was perhaps something of a miracle.'

A miracle repeated every July since, though the fact that the Eisteddfod is now one of Europe's leading festivals is probably the least of its qualities, the hype so much froth on the Dee. Llangollen is a humbling town. You didn't really come here to win, one felt, you came simply to take part.

Which is more or less what I felt about Offa's Dyke Path itself. Despite the last swooping miles over the Clwydian Hills, it isn't the ruggedest of footpaths. The Iron Age forts between Llangollen and the holiday resort of Prestatyn are impressive but not over-large, the heather not impassably deep. This had been a walk with time, not against it, the last few hundred yards past 'Clwyd Cream Ices' to the sea not a triumph but a privilege.

SOME THOUGHTS ON SNOWDONIA

If I'd had an inkling about how much that most companionable of writers, Showell Styles, knows about walking in North Wales I might have taken up Elwyn Jones's suggestion that I should retrace George Borrow's famous journey; but, as I have related, it came to nothing and it was a down-at-soul fellow who turned his back on the Pass of Llanberis dominated, I recall, by the A4086. A pity this since, although I know very little about Snowdonia, I have thought about great Yr Wyddfa and his companions for as long as I can remember. At a time when I must have been in short pants I heard in a lecture by the late William Pearsall, one of the Founding Fathers of what was then the new science of ecology, that when the range was shoved out of the sea some six hundred million years ago, the principal peaks were twice the present height of Mount Everest.

Amidst sounds of gulps all round, he rapidly drew the folds of the summit of Snowdon on the blackboard and pointed out that they were depressed or valley-shaped. In geological language they were synclinal, wholly unlike the upfolds of the Pennines which are anti-clinal. By extrapolating the lines of those folds, Pearsall's tutors had worked out the height of the original volcanic mass. All that we see today are the baked and fossilized stumps of the sea floor which, but for the roof of lava almost wholly gone, would have been eroded and much flattened ages ago.

Pearsall's lecture was followed by one of his distinguished colleagues, Walter Garstang, who related how very early forms of life such as trilobites were given a tremendous evolutionary push by that same period of volcanic activity. As stratographic mnemonics for dullards such as myself he put his theories into verse form and I still remember one that began:

> Ere Snowdon raised his lofty head
> Above the Cambrian Sea,
> King Paradoxus called his sons
> And many sons had he . . .

It went on for a dozen or more verses to show how the descendants of a group of highly adaptable marine trilobites, the Paradoxides, were first to leap ashore. It intrigues me to think that it might have been in the Devil's Kitchen, now a great chasm on Glyder Fawr and one of the last known resorts of one of the rarest plants in Britain, the beautiful snow-white Snowdon lily *Lloydia serotina*. This plant was named in honour of the first man to find it, Edward Lloyd, towards the end of the seventeenth century. But a slight shadow falls across these recollections.

Pen-yr-Ole-Wen, Snowdonia.

Not 100 miles from Llanberis, looking pretty scruffy on an abortive TV try-out, I strayed into a humble tavern and greeted the locals who promptly switched from English to Welsh which, from glances and chuckles, I took to be uncomplimentary. I related this to Elwyn Jones who spoke only Welsh until he achieved long pants and later lectured in that language to the elite of *Plaid Cymru*. A year or two later while working on some television programme largely based on Snowdonia, he went into that tavern and said nothing until the same thing happened to him. Whereupon, since, as he put it, 'they were speaking pidgin Welsh badly,' in the controlled voice of a BBC commentator he verbally re-enacted in their own language something close to what happened there about six hundred million years ago. He blew his top.

J.H.

WALKING IN NORTH WALES

SHOWELL STYLES

On a March day of dense freezing mist my compass brought me to the summit cairn on Foel Fras, northernmost of the Welsh three-thousanders. A folded scrap of paper wedged among the icicles on the cairn caught my eye; I pulled it out and found that it was addressed to Peter Pan. The scribbled note said that the writer had arrived there on top of Bera Bach with no tea left in the thermos and knew now how Scott must have felt. It was signed 'Mary'. Though I hadn't much hope of encountering the addressee I buttoned the note into my anorak pocket and continued my traverse of the Carneddau. When I got down to Ogwen the note had disappeared.

This is the sort of weird inconsequence that tends to happen to walkers on the Carneddau, where without doubt some aftermath of Welsh wizardry lingers on. Typical of these mountains is Mary's conviction that she was on Bera Bach, a minor summit a mile and a half west of Foel Fras, but the frequency with which walkers get lost on this broad east ridge isn't the only oddity of the Carnedd range. Enchantment of a less recondite sort attends the grand walk over the five 3,000-foot tops from Aber on the north coast of Wales to Llyn Ogwen at the foot of Tryfan. It's a main highway of walkers (not to mention fell-runners) but full of compensatory delights, especially if you choose a clear day in autumn and come down to Ogwen by the east ridge of Pen yr Ole Wen – *not* by the eroded 'path' descending on the south.

Erosion and over-population are problems on the North Wales ridge traverses which are the choicest and best-known walking routes. Both can be dodged by using the map to plan cross-routes; the Carneddau, for example, can be fully and more peacefully savoured by a west-to-east crossing from Bethesda up long, lonely Cwm Llafar to Yr Elen and over to the Conwy Valley by way of Cwm Eigiau. If losing the Outdoor Pursuit crowds is compensation enough for losing the high tops, there is very pretty walking to be had in the quiet countryside east of the lower Conwy, where behind the untidy fringe of the north coast resorts three charming rivers – Dulas, Elwy, and Aled – wind their way down from the Hiraethog moors.

Most walkers, however, come to North Wales to walk on its mountains, and the long ridge of the Glyder that confronts you when you arrive at the southern end of the Carnedd range invites another end-to-end traverse. From Capel Curig over Glyder Fach and Glyder Fawr, Y Garn, Foel Goch, and Elidir Fawr down to Nant Peris gives a magnificent hill walk for a long summer's day, with spiky rocks and piled boulders to contrast with the eerie-misty hogsback of the Carneddau. The classic ridge route hereabouts is the scramble up the North Ridge of Tryfan and the Bristly Ridge of Glyder Fach, with descent by the Devil's Kitchen path or the Gribin Ridge; but this is not strictly a walk and in winter or spring can become the sort of place characterized in the old mountaineering ditty, where

> More safety we all of us find –
> True climbers and shoddy –
> In absence of body
> Than ever in presence of mind.

Across the A4085 from the Glyder rises Moel Siabod, with a scrambly way up on the south, an

An aerial view of Llyn Mymbyr, Capel Curig, in Gwynedd, North Wales.

easier walk on the north from Plas-y-Brenin, and superb summit views. A modest walker with no summit ambitions could have a worthwhile day and see a good deal of these mountains by starting from Penmachno 3 miles off the A5, crossing to Dolwyddelan and thence over the toes of Siabod to Capel Curig, all on ancient trackways with – usually – little or no foot traffic.

All this time Snowdon has loomed on the horizon, its summit cone of Yr Wyddfa just visible from the Carneddau, splendidly poised above its craggy cwms when seen from the Glyder, displaying its peerless Horseshoe to the viewer on Moel Siabod's cairn. Alas, poor Snowdon! Since George Borrow, ascending by the Llanberis Path with his step-daughter, noted 'groups of people or single individuals going up or descending the path as far as the eye could reach,' Snowdon has been degraded by sheer weight of numbers. Its most popular paths are metalled pavements or fenced alleyways, their steep places buttressed by netted cubes of rocks. According to a recent survey 1,500 walkers and 1,000 train passengers reach Snow-

don summit on a fine day in summer, and during the peak period from 1.30 p.m. to 3 p.m. the summit may have over 1,000 people on it at any one time. The Crib Goch 'knife-edge' of the Horseshoe used to be classed as an easy rock climb; yet so many walkers use it nowadays that in August you have to queue up to get along it. In spite of all this, however, the highest mountain in England and Wales remains an irresistible magnet for hill walkers.

There are two ways I've discovered of experiencing the old magic of Snowdon. One is to start at daybreak by the path from Rhyd-ddu (the least spoiled) so as to be on top before the first train arrives there, and descend to starting point using the Snowdon Ranger path. The other, the Girdle of Snowdon, is for the walker-scrambler. It starts from Rhyd-ddu and circles Snowdon summit clockwise on a radius of 1½ miles, crossing the six

ridges and dipping into and out of the six cwms, and since you merely step across the tourist routes as you come to them you see little of the mountain's desecration and much of its vast store of untouched scenery and solitude. It's a long day of walking for a fast goer and more satisfying if done in a leisurely way with a bivouac in, say, Cwm Glas.

Looking westward from the Rhyd-ddu path up Snowdon you see the bold outline of the Nantlle Ridge between you and the sea. This is a very popular ridge walk – deservedly so, especially if it's continued over Mynydd Craig Cwm Silin or along its base to look at the famous Great Slab – but its popularity has led to the conversion of one steep but easy slope into a hellish declivity of fine shale that gives a timorous walker sore fingertips.

On the other side of Cwm Pennant from these Nantlle hills the shorter Moel Hebog range has no such horrors. It can be traversed from Beddgelert – Moel Lefn, Moel yr Ogof, Moel Hebog – after a preliminary purgatory of forestry roads. For unfortunately on all the hill slopes hereabouts the Dark Peril has crept year by year closer to the ridges and will creep closer yet; the Snowdonia National Park Authority has no power to stop it. A good many people like trees. But forestry means dead trees as well as live ones, and a first sight of a felled area, which looks like old film of the Somme battlefields, would persuade anyone that forestry and natural beauty can't live together.

Westward again from these conifer-cursed hills the peninsula of Lleyn reaches far out into the Irish Sea, and here there is any amount of good and unfrequented walking of the field-path-and-stile sort. To walk the coastline of Lleyn, as I did once, is enlightening; there are still, after all, beauty spots unadvertised and footpaths unpopulous in North Wales. Across Cardigan Bay from the peninsula the notched blue palisade of the Meirionnydd hills stretches away southward to where Cader Idris dips a long arm into the sea. Behind this Rhinog palisade lies hill country of a different nature from Snowdonia proper.

Double-peaked Arenig Fawr lords it over this 300 square miles of hill and moor between the Rhinog and the heathery humps of the Berwyns, a walker's mountain with an easy route from Llyn Arenig Fawr to the top. All the rest is countryside for the man or woman more interested in exploring a beautiful region on foot than in clambering over crags. The scenery is softer than in Snowdonia and so, quite often, is the underfoot going; the ardent bog trotter would be in his element on a walk across the Migneint, north of Arenig, and could rely on keeping his boots well soaked if he continued it westward to Ffestiniog and the Moelwyn group.

Cnicht and the two Moelwyn tops provide a horseshoe walk which includes only the mildest of scrambling and can be done leisurely in five or six hours. Longer and more demanding is the Seven

RIGHT: An aerial view of Snowdonia.

LEFT: The Llanberis pass near Snowdon.

LEFT: *The humps of the Berwyns, looking from the Tanat Valley.*

RIGHT: *Cader Idris. The best walks are the ascent from the south into and out of Cwm Cau, and the descent on the north to Dolgellau.*

Summits walk, starting from Croesor and linking the seven tops over 2,000 feet, which gives panoramic views from the long crest that is the watershed between Cardigan Bay and Liverpool Bay. For the real wilds of Wales, though, you must look southward from the top of Moelwyn Bach to the Rhinog range 5 miles away.

Somehow, Rhinog (pronounced *Hrinnog*) seems just the right name for this broad broken wall of crag and heather fronting the sea between Glaslyn and Mawddach. Here are the oldest rocks, the Cambrian, their platform-like slabs scored by glaciers and their ridges carved into small sheer cliffs, the roughest and trickiest terrain to walk in that you could find south of the Scottish Border. For much of its 15-mile length the range is free from the stamped-out paths of the massed hill walkers and you need to use some hill sense, as well as map and compass, for your route-finding even on a clear day; given competence with these, the Rhinog, I think, is the place for the solitary wanderer to find content. Rhinog Fawr, in the centre of the range, could have a party or two on it in summer but you can often have the other parts of the ridge to yourself. And there is no place in Britain where you can so satisfactorily play the John Buchan hero hiding among rocks and heather if you should spot an oncoming gang when you're feeling disinclined to be sociable.

The Rhinog end-to-end is a fine walk. In my Alpine-climbing days I used to do it as a training walk and take 8 hours over it, which allowed one 15-minute halt for lunch. This was to misuse a glorious traverse which ought to be lingered over. A much better way is to camp or bivouac on the Bwlch Drws Ardudwy, which is about halfway, having started from Maentwrog at the northern end. The southern third of the range, properly called the Llawlech, drops straight down to Barmouth whence one can conveniently return to near starting point by train. On that last descent, unless you are sprinting to catch the train, you'll be halting continually for the splendid views of Cader Idris across the Mawddach Estuary.

For my taste the best walk on Cader Idris is the ascent from the south into and out of Cwm Cau – as impressive a cwm as any of Snowdon's – and the descent on the north to Dolgellau. Ten or fifteen years ago the descent route by the celebrated Fox's Path could have been recommended; today it's eroded to a dithery slithery slide on precipitous shale, and the all-too-obvious ordinary track is preferable. Cader is a very popular mountain, though it is not (as most people will tell you) the highest mountain south of Snowdon. That distinction belongs to Aran Fawddwy, 39 feet higher,

which you can see 10 miles away to the north-east when you have climbed the neat concrete steps on Cader's cairn.

Once the two Aran summits were the focal points of much very fine hill walking; they are so no longer. You can walk to both tops, but only by the least interesting route, plodding through mashed bog beside a wire fence. For this privilege the National Park Authority pays rent, on your behalf, to the hill farmers. If you approach the Arans from the east, their grandest side, you are liable to be shouted at, rounded up, and sent down in disgrace. All the same, I would chance this (though not with a large party) to complete my favourite long-distance walk.

Prestatyn is by no means my favourite seaside resort. But above it the humps and bumps of the Clwyd range start up to run southward, the first span of a bridge of hills that crosses North Wales from sea to sea and makes a natural high-level route for a walker. The map will show you how handily and with how few breaks the crests lead on: Clwyd, Llantisilio Mountain, Berwyns,

Vyrnwy Moors, Arans (where you dodge the farmers) and finally the whole length of the Cader Idris ridge to where it dips down to the sea at Llwyngwril.

When I walked it, using B & B's, I took ten days for the 128 miles; a backpacker might do it in one week but would be better advised to take two, lingering here and there to explore the unvisited side glens. For here, rather than in Snowdonia of the holiday hordes, the walker is likely to feel and breathe, with Gerard Manley Hopkins, 'All the air things wear that build this world of Wales.'

That special air, and the Wild Wales of a century ago, become each year more difficult to find and experience; there is a real danger that before very long they will be lost in the current lust for development – development of forestry and roads and tourist industry. The traveller on foot, if he plans his journeys wisely, can have his fill of wonder and wilderness still in North Wales. But if he were to ask 'When should I go there?' my answer would be, emphatically, *'Now!'*

AWAY FROM IT ALL

An old friend of mine who did his best to teach the elements of geography and science to classes of really tough kids at a school in a notorious Birmingham slum thought it might be a good idea to take the youngsters out on some field trips in the area which Geoff Allen will be describing. It didn't work out at all well. Like the young widow Ruth, the Moabite who, when she settled in Bethlehem to be near her mother-in-law, found herself, in that gripping biblical phrase, *in terra aliena*, in a totally strange land, the kids had no identification with what they were accustomed to.

Handy pieces of the Cambrian quartzite of the Lickey Hills were good to chuck at ducks. Rounded boulders from those most ancient of volcanoes which today are the Malvern Hills could be rolled down the slope, to the consternation of those trudging up. Instead of giving up the idea of field work, my friend then took his little terrors on a conducted tour of some of Birmingham's rubbish tips where butter-coloured ragworts, convolvulus and flaming willow-herbs sprouted through the familiar remains of bicycles, rusty dustbin lids, shattered chamber pots and mattresses reduced to springs and tattered fabric. The youngsters were fascinated. They wanted to know how the plants got there. They collected names and it wasn't long before many of them wanted to be out and away again.

It was this same friend who pointed out that Birmingham is a unique example of a large and quite hilly city that almost squats on a water-parting, the northern Trent and the Severn to the south. It was originally sited on relatively poor land as a meeting ground for farmers from the surrounding richer villages. In mid-glacial times it was covered by a huge lake many times larger than Windermere. This was caused by ice-blocked rivers constantly seeking new drainage channels of which today the Watford Gap on the M1 is an outstanding example. As my friend rightly put it, geography is everywhere.

Here we have the essentials of the topography of the Midlands. Though the country is undulating rather than flat, the heart of England is fundamentally a plain. To the west the limits are well defined by the edge of the Welsh massif provided by the Malvern and Abberley Hills, Wyre Forest and the Wrekin; in the north the plain wraps round the southern end of the Pennines. Many of the main features of the Midlands are surprisingly old. When we climb the Wrekin or one of the ridges of Charnwood Forest or even the little Lickey Hills or the Nuneaton ridge, here and there we notice shattered pre-Cambrian rocks peeping through the surface soil. They provide excellent road metal in parts of the country which require much and produce little.

J.H.

AROUND THE HEARTLAND

GEOFF ALLEN

It took an eighty-year-old Londoner to open my eyes to one of the most comprehensive views of the Midlands. We had loafed away a rainy morning reliving old holidays on the slide projector before the clouds cleared and the sun came out. So did our maps. 'I'd like to go there,' said Eddie, pointing – perversely, it seemed – at the middle of the industrial Black Country. His eye, however, sharpened by over sixty years of scanning Ordnance Survey maps, had focused on the Rowley Hills, 10 miles from Birmingham, a green oasis rising from a sprawl of heavy industry and suburbia to a height of 876 feet above sea level.

On that crystal-clear afternoon there were marvellous bird's-eye views of the Midlands' landscape from the two tops, Turner's Hill and Darby's Hill. Easily visible were the Malverns, the Clees, the Abberley Hills, the Wrekin and Cannock Chase; nearby Clent, with its proud cockscomb of trees, seemed barely a handshake away. What really startled me, however, was to see stretched along the distant south-western horizon, 55 miles away, the Black Mountains of South Wales.

But the Midlands, though rarely dead flat, is not a predominantly hilly area. Less apparent from our viewpoint were the lowland features that interest walkers: the quiet lanes, the canal towpaths, the river banks, the maze of field paths and the network of official and unofficial long-distance walks.

Let's start with the hills. The Lickeys, the Waseley Hills, Clent and Kinver Edge – each with its own distinctive character – have successfully hemmed in the south-westerly spread of Birmingham and the Black Country. For generations the stamping ground of West Midlanders, they are now country parks linked together by the North Worcestershire Path. A superb walk this. From Forhill – 2 miles south of Birmingham, and the middle of nowhere for walkers without a car – it pursues its hilly north-western course for 26 miles to Kinver Edge, where real long-distance enthusiasts can transfer to the Staffordshire Way for a further 95 miles' bash, but more of that later.

In the pre-motoring era, the Lickey Hills were the Hampstead Heath of Birmingham. On fine Sundays and Bank Holidays electric trams carried Brummies out there in their thousands (a few yards of tramline survive at Rednal bus terminus). Today the country park covers 524 acres and rises to almost 1,000 feet at the toposcope on the level plateau of Beacon Hill.

As an open public space the Waseley Hills are a modern creation, the original farmland having been acquired by the then Worcestershire County Council in 1971. Rather bare and breezy, their Windmill Hill toposcope invites the walker to peer westwards at the Abergavenny Sugar Loaf 57 miles away.

The Clent Hills are, happily, almost entirely owned by the National Trust. Walton Hill, the higher of their two main summits, attains 1,035 feet, and across the deep valley rather grandly called St Kenelm's Pass – after the boy king allegedly done to death hereabouts by his sister in Saxon times – the Four Stones crown a slightly lower hilltop. Any aura of prehistoric romance is spurious; a relic of the eighteenth-century mania for 'improving' landscapes, the stones were installed by a Lord Lyttelton of nearby Hagley Hall.

Rising gently from the east to about 540 feet, yet falling perpendicularly to the west, Kinver Edge is a giant inland cliff where 'cavemen' lived in sandstone rock houses until after the Second World War. The subsequent deterioration of these intriguing two-hundred-year-old dwellings has fortunately now been halted by their owners, the National Trust.

Moving west and crossing the Severn, we come to the Abberley Hills, 4 miles south-west of Stourport-on-Severn. Though they also fail to reach the 1,000-foot mark, the walking on their three tops – Abberley, Woodbury and Walsgrove – is delightful. In Abberley village is a charming little Norman chapel, handily opposite the Manor Arms, and a couple of miles away a wing of the vast, burnt-out Witley Court houses one of only two Baroque churches in England, the splendid St Michael's.

Still in Worcestershire, we find the Midlands' only approximation to a mountain range: the 8-mile long switchback of the Malvern Hills, rising dramatically from the Severn valley to 1,395 feet on Worcestershire Beacon. Erosion is a problem here. With over a million visitors annually, many of them storming the ancient hill fort at British Camp, the Malvern Hills Conservators have felt compelled to construct a surfaced path to the earthern ramparts. Environment-conscious walkers will concentrate on the more southerly, lower and less frequented hills of the chain.

Eastwards across the broad Severn valley rises the great dome of Bredon Hill. Though the summit plateau is largely under plough today, the earthworks of Kemerton Camp, an Iron Age hill fort dating from the two centuries before Christ, rise clearly from open grassland at its northern rim. The nearby stone tower, Parsons' Folly, is said to have been built to a height of 39 feet in the eighteenth century by a Mr Parsons of Kemerton Court, so that its top would be exactly 1,000 feet above sea level. There is splendid walking on the hill and round its necklace of lovely stone-built villages. Best recommended is the ramble from

The eight-mile long switchback of the ancient Malvern Hills, rising dramatically from the Severn Valley to 1,395 feet high on Worcestershire Beacon.

Parsons' Folly along the north-eastern escarpment to Ashton-under-Hill, with the delightful little Dumbleton Hills and the great wall of the Cotswolds rising ahead.

Swinging further east into south Warwickshire (known as the Feldon, to distinguish it from Shakespeare's Arden, which lies north of the River Avon), Brailes Hill, near Shipston-on-Stour, Edge Hill of Civil War fame and the nearby bulbous Burton Dassett Hills, north of Banbury, reward the climber with wide-ranging views. From the unpretentious little country park at Hartshill Hayes, near Nuneaton, one can look across the Anker valley and find relief from counting the forty churches, which the late Arthur Mee claimed were visible, by gazing at the distant hills and tors of Charnwood Forest in Leicestershire. Good walking is to be found there, too, south of Loughborough, on and around Beacon Hill and Barden Hill, near the county's only youth hostel, the simple-graded but comfortable Copt Oak. The Meltonian Marathon walk gathers in the highlights of the area in a single 26-mile canter, including the surprisingly wild 860 acres of Bradgate Deer Park at Newtown Linford.

At Cannock Chase in Staffordshire we find a

ABOVE: *The wide-ranging view from Edge Hill, of Civil War fame.*

RIGHT: *Clee Hill, in Shropshire.*

much larger surviving wilderness, though its 26 square miles of heath and forest constitute Britain's smallest Area of Outstanding Natural Beauty. The wide range of wildlife to be seen includes an ancient herd of fallow deer.

I've left until last the crowning glory of Midlands walking: the Shropshire hills. There, approaching the Welsh border, the rambler must change gear, both figuratively as he prepares to attack much bigger hills and often sartorially to cope with rougher, wilder, higher country. High, in this context, means 1,792 feet on Brown Clee Hill, the undoubted summit of the Midlands; its twin, Titterstone Clee, is about 40 feet lower. From these heights we can gaze westwards over Wenlock Edge to the tops that enclose Church Stretton: the Hope Bowdler hills, Caer Caradoc (decidedly a mini-mountain, though only 1,506 feet) and the vast, high, wild moorland, unfortunately tamed a little by narrow motor roads, of the Long Mynd.

Further west and just within England rise the Stiperstones, bleak and rocky underfoot, with great piled tors and an outlook clear across mid-Wales to Cader Idris and the Arans. 'Inviolable, taciturn, evil' – the adjectives bestowed by locally-born novelist Mary Webb early in the century still evoke this most atmospheric of hilltops.

Medieval Ludlow is a fine centre for Shropshire walking. South-west of it, amid lusher country, woody and steeply undulating, another ancient hill fort, Croft Ambrey, overlooks the National Trust's relatively modern (fifteenth century) Croft Castle.

It is difficult to walk in the Midlands today without becoming enmeshed in the thickening web of long-distance footpaths. The Staffordshire Way pursues a sinuous course from Mow Cop, a rocky hilltop north of Stoke-on-Trent, to Kinver Edge on the Hereford and Worcester county border. Also beginning in Staffordshire, the 80-mile Heart of England Way connects Cannock Chase with Chipping Campden. Alternatively the Cotswolds can be approached along the 42-mile Wychavon Way. Starting from Holt Fleet on the Severn near Droitwich, this interesting and varied route will take you over Bredon Hill before finishing at Winchcombe (unless you decide to

continue along the Cotswold Way, but that's another story).

The West Midland Way, described in a superior pocket-sized hardback guidebook, throws a 162-mile noose round the Birmingham and Black Country green belt. A more sinister looking hangman's noose dangles from the northern boundary of the map of Shropshire, from which the 172-mile Shropshire Way strikes south across the plain to Wem, before flinging a great circle round the scenically more interesting southern half of the county. Taking in the Long Mynd, the Stiperstones, the Clees and the free-standing Wrekin it returns to Wem, having passed near all seven of the county's youth hostels.

In this brisk round-up of the rambling high spots of the Midlands, I can mention only briefly another useful network: the towpaths of the canals that meander peacefully through the area. They would merit a chapter to themselves, as would the rivers (principally the Avon and the Severn, the second of which has public footpaths along its banks for most of its Midlands course). And in the innumerable rights-of-way shown on our Ordnance Survey maps there is a third network, available only to those willing to go out and walk. Yes, there's a lot more to be said about rambling in the Midlands than space here can accommodate.

The Stiperstones, bleak and rocky underfoot, with great piled tors and an outlook clear across mid-Wales.

THE CHARACTER OF
THE COTSWOLDS

Although Mark Richards, an extremely energetic farmer, says he developed a passion for the rugged landscapes of the north of England, his Cotswold upbringing brought home to him the subtle relationship between Man and his environment. The famous oolitic limestones of the Cotswolds have provided material for an industry which has flourished since Roman craftsmen built sumptuous villas from stone quarried in the vicinity of Bath. Varying in hues from pale grey to a rich golden honey tone, they have about them a gracious radiance which puts you in mind of bright sunshine on pale soil, trim villages and rich woodland.

By contrast those much older rocks, the carboniferous limestones of the Pennines, are what we associate with wind-thrashed mountain ash, low skies and the driving rain of the Yorkshire Dales. Both geological systems are derived from calcium carbonate and were once the floors of ancient seas, but whereas the Pennines are largely homogenous, the lop-sided scarp of the Cotswolds with a steep face on one side and a long steady descent on the other has been chemically transformed by subterranean pressures, heat and time into a rich variety of oolites with minute grains like the roe of a fish. Here is some of the finest building stone in Britain; here is a trail, the Cotswold Way, that extends from Bath to Chipping Campden, in distance just short of 100 miles, and here are opportunities for innumerable diversions on foot. Mark Richards writes with the authority of a pioneering pathfinder.

J.H.

COTSWOLD EDGE

MARK RICHARDS

Though I cannot really claim to be a true Cotsaller, a native of many generations standing, my Cotswold ancestry goes back to the turn of the century when my grandfather left Cornwall where his father had turned to farming when the bottom fell out of the tin industry. The Cotswold farm of my father's youth, high up on the wolds at Hawling, with its proper balance of livestock to arable land and workforce to acreage was a far cry from modern practice. In essence the wolds were still largely pastoral; the calcareous grasslands predominated and the soils were organically sound. Contemporary nonsense about growing continuous cereals and the consequent retreat of permanent pasturage to the rough banks at the valleys' heads and along the embayed scarp is a sad reflection on changing times. Economic pressures that created this monoculture have brought about change in the rural communities too, which were, until the last war, still deep in the service of agriculture. It is sad to see how so many villages now act as little more than comfortable 'green' dormitories to the great population centres.

The region fascinated me, but in my youth the edge of the Cotswold escarpment figured only as a sequence of steep hill roads for the family car to negotiate. Hill names such as Fish, Stanway, Sudeley, Cleeve, Chatcome Pitch and Crickley punctuated many a journey. Through adolescence the scarp emerged more coherently, when as a Young Farmer with a car of my own I attended events in the Vale and made occasional forays to Gloucester Market. When I joined the Cheltenham-based Gloucestershire Mountaineering Club in 1969, the coherence of the Cotswolds came home to me clearly while spending summer evenings planning weekends in the hills of Wales and the Lakes. It was then that I met Tony Drake, one of the Club's founding fathers, a shrewd lifetime fighter for public access to the Gloucestershire countryside. At that time he was deeply concerned with two of his own ideas for long-distance footpaths: the Cambrian Way, a difficult rough country walk across the roof of Wales, and the Cotswold Way.

Although the Cambrian Way fell foul of a farming lobby vehemently opposed to the creation of a 'Pennine Way' in Wales, the Cotswold Way, which was created in 1970, has flourished.

I mentioned earlier the vast acreage of corn that has blanketed so much of our ploughland, but it looks as if the tide has turned and the sheep are coming back. It is to be hoped that this will encourage the creation of many more trails. The adoption of target waymarks across corn fields might be an answer but as yet they are far from common. Much better for walkers to enjoy springy turf than to have to weave a tortuous course through a waving ocean of wheat, barley or, worse still, oil seed rape.

The Cotswold Way provides a superb range of scenery which should be energetically explored by those who are intent on getting away from the carefully plotted route. Despite the ingenious strategy that went into devising the escarpment trail I prefer the rolling countryside of the dip slopes and many of my own most enjoyable forays have been improvisations.

Langridge in Avon, at the southern end of the Cotswolds. The sheep are being brought back to many farms in this area, which improves routes for walkers.

The Cotswold scarp may be likened to the crest of a wave as it heaves up before it breaks on the shore. This comes from the tilting of the oolitic strata and the foundering of the capping rocks upon the beds of lias clay. The slopes have a hummocky and undulating countenance. A stroll along the brink of the scarp provides many long-range views beyond the Marlstone edge to the Forest of Dean, the distant Black Mountains, and further north, to the Malvern Hills.

The City of Bath has the patrician air of a fashionable suburb of the metropolis, emphasized by its M4 link with London. It is here, out of the depths of the Bristol Avon valley, that the escarpment trail begins, climbing on to the breezy plateau of Lansdown Hill. The edge is reached for the first time at Prospect Stile from where the view is southwards over Kelston Round Hill to the distant Mendip Hills. Lanes rising up from Kelston and North Stoke are recommended as alternative approaches to Prospect Stile and Little Down, an Iron Age hill fort resting on the westernmost spur of the entire escarpment. A prominent feature 6 miles to the west is Dundry Hill, an estranged outlier of the Cotswold Jurassic system, rising due south of Bristol. Further lanes lead up on to the plateau from Upton Cheyney ('the high farm on the oak island') climbing to Brockham End, a deep west-facing combe favoured as a site for a Roman villa.

There must have been numerous Roman farming estates along the southern sheltered reaches of the scarp; indeed it has been tentatively suggested that Dyrham, 6 miles north along the Cotswold Way from here derives its name from a Roman deer park still in existence in early Saxon times. Hanging Hill has nothing to do with gallows, despite the name of the lane that mounts its northern slope. Slaughter Lane, a reference to 'sloe berries', is a notable viewpoint revealing an 18-mile length of the Southwold scarp north to Stinchcome Hill.

View from the battlefields near Lansdown, Avon. The escarpment trail begins from the breezy plateau of Lansdown Hill.

The natural way off Lansdown Hill is followed by a minor road over Freezing Hill to Tog Hill. This road precisely defines the course of what archaeologists call the Jurassic Way, an ancient dry ridgeway route traceable from Bath along the spine of the limestone belt through Lincolnshire to the Humber. This old way regrettably plays little part in the modern pedestrian route which, for the main, holds to a (largely conjectured) line slightly back from the scarp.

The Cotswold Way, keeping to field paths and quiet lanes, enters Cold Ashton. Here, from the front of the splendid manor, Avon County Council's Limestone Link Path descends St Catherine's valley on its way to Shipham, thus forging a union with the West Mendip Way. Attractive footpaths can be followed east to Marshfield, a village of character, astride the old Bristol to London coaching road. It is noted for its Mummer's plays and, due to large deposits of fuller's earth, has an historic link with the cloth trade.

Continue along the scarp to Dyrham House, a superb National Trust property, before crossing Hinton Hill with its hill fort and the M4. The route slips through Tormarton and cuts across Dodington Park to reach Old Sodbury. The grand house, screened by mature trees, was created in Classical style for a dignitary of the West Indies; the park itself was landscaped by Lancelot 'Capability' Brown.

After climbing defiantly out of the Avon valley, the escarpment winds north in a more chastened mood. Nonetheless, over the centuries this stripling edge has attracted durable settlement, protected by shallow wooded combes and watered by constant springs. Although much has vanished, little communities such as Old Sodbury, Little Sodbury, Horton and Hawkesbury have survived as part of the fabric of the Southwolds.

For economic self-sufficiency during late Medieval times it was found necessary to supplement the export of a superior staple of wool by learning the fine weaving skills practised on the Continent – hence the adoption of St Adeline, patron saint of Flemish weavers, at Little Sodbury Church. Overseas craftsmen were welcomed into the area hence the common local surname of Fleming.

Bridleways may be followed due east to Great Badminton, home of the Dukes of Beaufort, and there is the opportunity of diverging to inspect both Horton Court and Hawkesbury Church where can be seen a plaque to the second Earl of Liverpool. This son of Baron Hawkesbury remains the longest-serving English Prime Minister. From 1812 he served for fifteen years, a precedent for the present lady incumbent to consider.

The nature of the scarp alters a great deal north of Hawkesbury Upton where a plateau top pond marks a pocket of fuller's earth. Hitherto the scarp has marched north unchallenged, a simple plateau edge falling into a clay vale, but here we find the first of numerous long wooded re-entrant valleys. Sheltering within one of them, the Kilcott, is Midger Wood Nature Reserve. It is also worth leaving the Cotswold Way to investigate the next valley, Ozleworth Bottom beyond Alderley. The church here, like the one at Avening just across the plateau, is set in a circular churchyard indicative of a pre-Christian site. Boxwell, home of the Huntleys for many centuries, is quite the most elusive of hideaways amid its surround of ageing box trees, and there is a fine view from the National Trust's Newark Park.

Although heights become commonplace further north, for the first time since Lansdown Hill the Way attains the 700-foot contour line on Tor Hill. It then descends into Tyley Bottom to Wotton-under-Edge, composed of a happy blend of vale and wold, which developed in the eighteenth century into a prosperous cloth-manufacturing centre. Beyond Westridge Wood the Way crosses Waterley Bottom to climb Stinchcombe Hill, a grand promenade peninsula from where the Berkeley Castle lowland and the silver ribbon of the Severn can be seen. My favourite scarpland view is from Drakestone Point: south to Nibley Knoll with the Tyndale Monument, and Brackenbury Ditches.

There is not much to be said for Dursley but the little hills of the Tableland are ample compensation, especially Cam Long Down, Uleybury, and the Uley amphitheatre, cradled in a bowl of beech woods. The scarp's leading edge on Frocester Hill offers breath-taking views towards Slimbridge on the Severn shore and the Forest of Dean.

We are now in the Golden Valley gap west of

'strutting' Stroud, and the path rises along a wooded ridge to the halfway mark of this 100-mile route at Haresfield Beacon promontory fort. From here the Cotswolds take on an even fairer face, the path crossing Rudge Hill, with its precious herb-rich grassland, to enter Painswick, the much-crowned queen of Cotswold villages. In Painswick are town houses with all the elegance of a wealth earned from the cloth trade and none of the vulgarity of the post-1800 industrial growth that eventually gripped Stroud.

The panorama from Painswick Beacon and the scarp beech woods embellish the Way north to the steep helter-skelter Double Gloucester Cheese run on Cooper's Hill and beyond to Birdlip Peak. The Painswick Stream valley offers a beautiful sheltered alternative advance via Tock-nells Court and Cranham. Equally rich scenery can be enjoyed by leaving the escarpment and exploring the headstreams of the Frome, the Toadsmoor Valley and the country in the vicinity of Sapperton.

Leaving motorists to marvel at their Barrow Wake viewpoint, walkers may care to inspect the Neolithic hill fort of Crickley, subject of much archaeological investigation. Twisting round on Shurdington Hill the Way briefly follows a former monastic droveway linking Badgeworth with the long-lost sheepwalks of Upper Coberley. It rounds the belvedere on Leckhampton Hill, with an unmatched bird's-eye view of Cheltenham. Note the Devil's Chimney, an intriguing quarry-man's folly. At Seven Springs rises the river Churn, longest and highest tributary feeder of Old Father Thames, and therefore in my opinion the true source. It is worth leaving the Edge to ramble either down the Churn and neighbouring Coln valleys or across the high wolds clothed in corn and copse.

Beyond the deep trench of the Chelt valley the Cotswold Way mounts on to Cleeve Common, the highest ground on the entire route and, by dint of its broad expanse of open country, a superb place to wander free. The view is tantalizing, particularly in the evening when a setting sun highlights the distant Black Mountains, the

FAR LEFT: *Early spring in Sapperton, east of 'strutting Stroud', in Gloucestershire.*

LEFT: *Thatched cottages in Chipping Campden. This graceful town is an appropriate place to end the journey along the Cotswold Edge.*

Malverns and Brown Clee Hill. We are now on the Northwolds, descending via Belas Knap long barrow to Sudeley Castle and Winchcombe, the royal seat of the Hwicce, rulers of the old kingdom of Mercia. Walkers can branch off the Cotswold route to follow the waymarked Wychavon Way, which treks northwards to the river Severn via Droitwich, with several ancient saltways. Since there is always keen pleasure in following ancient routes, try the Pilgrim's Way to Hailes Abbey. This was founded in 1246 for the Cistercian order by Richard Earl of Cornwall, younger brother of Henry III. Climb the scarp again to visit Beckbury hill fort and stroll along Campden Lane, thereby renewing acquaintance with the Jurassic Way last trod on Tog Hill, above Dyrham.

The hinterland of this wold's end are the original Cotswolds. Cutsdean is 'Cod's valley' and the surrounding former hill pastures now covered in corn 'Cod's wold'. The highest point in the parish at exactly 1,000 feet is Cutsdean Hill, where there is good evidence that this was the Mons Huuicciorum 'hill of the Hwicce' recorded in AD 780.

The Way slips down the scarp to visit the exquisite golden-stoned villages of Stanway and, more especially, Stanton, before switching once more to the high ground to approach Broadway, or you can make detours to Laverton, Buckland and Snowshill.

Though Broadway lies nominally in the vale shire of Worcester, it clearly belongs to the Cotswolds. Still a popular tourist centre it has been attracting visitors since the turn of the century. Most walkers will prefer to climb to Broadway Tower's crest for the sight of a noble scarp and fertile spreading vale. In the wooded combe to the south of the Tower is Kite's Nest, a farm unusual in that it is being run on a thoroughly organic basis. We can only hope that Richard Young's concepts will come to be more widely accepted, even if it means that wholesome food will cost a little more. Profits for future generations will depend on long-term improvements in the condition of the soil and a steady step-by-step return to broader-based farming.

For walkers the Cotswold Edge declines from the heady heights of Broadway Hill. Motorists can continue along the Jurassic hills via the A44 to Stow-on-the-Wold, advancing with the ancient ridgeway, then principally by minor road and byway to Edge Hill, and so on to Northants and ultimately the Lincolnshire Wolds.

Nearing the Rollright Stones the underlying rock takes on the rusty brown hue of an ironstone that has many admirers (me included), but it is not true-blooded Cotswold. The golden stone of the Cotswolds finds its final home and resting place in Chipping Campden and a 'History in Stone' is the town's proud motto. In medieval times it was also a market where huge quantities of wool were brought off the wolds and from as far away as the Welsh marches to be graded by staple merchants and despatched to Southampton bound for Italy and the Low Countries.

Today, resisting commercialism, Chipping Campden rests serene, elegant and graceful, tucked into a fold behind the scarp at the northern head of the Cotswolds and to descend there is like reaching the end of the rainbow. What more appropriate place to rest at the end of our journey?

Stanton is an exquisite golden-stoned Gloucestershire village at the northern end of the Cotswolds.

Some Notes About Loners

Although he's justified his attitude in his superbly well-written books, I value particularly a letter from Ronald Blythe which ends: 'Apart from the ineradicable joys of certain companionable walks, I recognize that these long and shapeless rambles of mine must have descended from some childhood longing for privacy. "Where have you been?" "Out."'

Ignoring the outright braggarts, most authors lead double lives. By far the majority are those prepared to publish most of the truth, smudging if not suppressing that quantum to their discredit, leaning perhaps on Dean Swift who, in *Thoughts on Religion*, wrote 'Violent zeal for truth hath an hundred to one odds to be either petulance, ambition or pride.' Then we come to the minority, those bare-bosom exhibitors who, like Augustine of Hippo, are lashed equally fiercely by Swift's dictum.

On the purely physical, not the spiritual, plane I recall late at night conversations on different occasions with two men I deeply respect for their character and capacity for derring-do, one of them a conqueror of Everest under appalling conditions and the other the most senior, certainly the most adventurous of African game wardens. He had, a day or two earlier, gained his pilot's licence for his first solo flight when, at maximum altitude before descent, his troublesome joystick detached itself from whatever joysticks are normally attached to. Concerned only that the plane didn't go into a tail spin, he somehow managed to float it down to the ground. With contrived nonchalance I asked him – as I had asked the mountaineer a year or two earlier – 'Have you ever been afraid?' And both men, who as far as I know were unacquainted with each other, paused before shaking their heads. Both, I discovered, were essentially loners.

As Ronald Blythe put it to me in another letter, 'I rarely carry a map or a watch and so, presumably, my walking, psychologically, has something to do with being a little outside place and time. Occasionally I get stranded or, that beautiful word, benighted. I don't much mind the weather but hate carrying a pack or indeed anything except a book, and wear jeans and a jersey.'

Bygone times and the places he selected for pilgrimages in *Divine Landscapes** have more than what Aldous Huxley called 'a numinous quality' since we are inspired to quest on our own. And for good reason because, as he says, 'There is scarcely a meadow or hill, let alone a village or town which cannot still be read in both metaphysical and material terms.' That book is above the desk on which I am writing and for me it could not be in a more useful place as I reach up for it when, all too often, the mind stales and the paragraph drafted in blobby Biro ink

Sunset in the Rhinog range, in the wilds of Wales.

looks unutterably banal. Bunyon's Bedfordshire, Julian's Norfolk, Wesley's Cornwall, these and a dozen more are All Saints, mostly uncanonized but worthy to be numbered among the throng celebrated on the first of November.

In a chapter entitled 'The Sacred Shore' he dwells with love on the imperishable memory of St Cedd as can be experienced by the perceptive on the uncommonly lonely Essex shore, especially in the vicinity of Bradwell where that pupil of Aidan of Iona built a gaunt chapel out of the stones of a Roman fort. The sounds there are only those of the sea, the fetch and swash of waves on pebbles. All life is symbolized by a solitary tern, hovering.

J.H.

*Viking, Penguin Books, 1986.

WITHIN WALKING DISTANCE

RONALD BLYTHE

I find it hard to explain myself when it comes to walking. All my life it has been my ordinary way of getting about on the home ground, this, due to the remoteness of the two small farmhouses in which I have lived in succession, spreading itself for 2 or 3 miles in every direction. Further than this I cycle or catch trains; on the home ground I walk. I have never been able to say like J. E. Morpurgo and all my family and friends that 'God would not have invented the automobile if he had intended me to walk' as cars were clearly never made for the likes of me. I hear myself saying, 'I don't drive' – never, 'I can't drive'. Nor do I add, 'I walk', for would not this imply a preference, a stand?

People occasionally tell me that my life would be transformed if I drove, forgetting how transformed it has been because I cannot. Thus I walk a mile or so daily to fetch the milk, and often late at night in the sharp air, and to the farm shop, and to the neighbours, and 2 miles to the pillar-box and however far it happens to be to one or other of the surrounding villages. And so I have done since a boy. There is a sensible school of opinion which says that if one doesn't drive, one should not dwell in my house, forgetting the dozen or more generations who dwelt in it before me and found it unexceptional to foot it in all directions. 'The time will come . . .' they warn. But then the time will come when their licences will not be renewed. It would be easier and praiseworthy, maybe, to be able to state that ages past I came out against the car for environmental reasons, but the truth is that I did not, and I no more know why I am a non-driver than why I am such a natural walker.

My walking, I find, falls into distinct categories.

When I am alone it is mainly confined to getting to and from the house for the usual domestic, professional and social purposes. When there are guests it expands into 'going for a walk', an entirely different business. Because so much walking is involved coping with each day's requirements, I rarely just go for a walk on my own – unless I am in an unfamiliar part of the country, or abroad, when the need to do so becomes a craving. City, coast or moor, the urge to explore on foot and in solitude can be overwhelming. My loner-walking prize experiences have been catholic to say the least. Huge hikes through New York and London, under-estimated tramps through North Cornwall, tentative travels across plains and in woodland, and always a private walk reconnaissance wherever I happen to be, if only for a day. Hazlitt was adamant about walking alone. For him conversation was an inside activity – 'I cannot see the wit of walking and talking at the same time.' I can – sometimes – with very particular companions. I can recall to this hour the dreadful exhaustion of the school-crocodile walk, and the mother, father, brothers and sisters' Sunday stroll, the slight sickness of bumping along together in the heat and 'keeping up'. By myself I would manage four times the distance and arrive back exhilarated and believing that I had found a way to live for ever.

So first, the necessary daily walking up the cart track to fetch milk and post letters, a climb out of

Old Suffolk farmhouse, thatched and half-timbered, at Purton Green.

130

the valley done at all hours from before breakfast to midnight. Long ago it was simply the way between two 100-acre farms, and the distinction between these ancient homesteads and their lands can still be discerned in spite of all the amalgamation and change which have been going on since the 1920s. This rough lane, getting on for almost a mile in length, is a ceaseless pleasure to me, even during the few days each year when it is blocked with snowdrifts and I have to take to the bitter high ground. The village says, 'It's another world down there!' And it is. It is what we in Suffolk used to call a 'Tye', a little farming community so distant from the village centre that it developed separately, building up over the generations, though without knowing it, its own ethos.

In Victorian times my family toiled away at Cuckoo Tye, a delectably situated farm on the high ground between Lavenham and Long Melford, whose spectacular churches dominated the blue distance. My own farmhouse, low-lying and secret, offers no such broad views, although the nut-walk does end in a huge open spread of river scenery which always comes as something of a shock. The barns and stackyard, now gone, would always have excluded this superb panorama which is half Suffolk and half Essex, so that the farmers from Bottengom's, my home, must always have had to walk a fair way to glimpse what existed just outside their own Tye.

It is no less of a shock to walk to the main road, the top, as we call it. There the scene is prodigious. Five miles into Suffolk with John Constable's Stoke-by-Nayland magenta on the horizon and, at night, the lights of the scattered cottages and great houses so numerous as to suggest a city. But there are no lights from the green hollow where I live, although I have left them burning and although there are many windows. The lie of the land, as much as its dense foliage, conceals all. The track is pitched a short way above a brook and below one of those vast East Anglian cornfields which were once ten fields. It has just had its tall centre ridge of grass sliced off to reveal its flint metalling, not to say smiles of relief on the faces of friends whose cars have had a bad time lately.

Parsons used to have something called a Sermon Walk, a long stretch of lawn for com-

posing on the hoof, and the track has, more than once, helped me to write. Although not if I self-consciously set out to think of what to write. *Solvitur ambulando* – you can sort it out by walking – only succeeds through a stealthy process of my going on one of my lengthy and endless errands to fetch this or that, and then falling into composition, as it were. But this good fortune seems to be a feature of the track.

The horses in the meadow on the brook side trot to the gate for a chat and a nose rub. Partridges, pheasants, rabbits and, now and then at dusk, a fox, scatter and disappear to take up panic stations in the ditch or wheat. After tea a chevron of geese whirrs and squawks its way from my neighbour's reservoir to the river, regular as clockwork. There are larks. When I pointed one of these out to an Australian friend, he stood stock still for several minutes as the high speck, almost motionless, cascaded its great song, and said, 'So *that's* a lark'. There used to be nightingales, especially on hot summer nights when the windows

LEFT: *Stoke by Nayland in Suffolk.*

RIGHT: *Vast East Anglian ploughed fields at Brantham.*

were wide and the piano was being played. Now and then there are children, their voices raised because tracks leading to nowhere, as it is locally thought, are uncertain and adventurous. Once I encountered, on a dreadful day of storms and cold, a rambling club with drenched maps and faces for which my track, as part of its itinerary, simply had to be taken, like some dose. But chiefly this is my solitary path, private, matter-of-fact, and yet fanciful. It is the one I have walked all my adult life, mostly to collect something very ordinary.

The walk taken to air the guests is superb and as one enters upon it directly from the garden its immediate effect on those who haven't previously accompanied me on it is gratifyingly apparent. As host, I am careful about what to provide: guidebook facts for those who like them, Hazlittian silences for those who need to hear their own inner commentary. The walk is actually two longish hikes in the form of a figure eight, so that when we reach the point where the circles join I can judge the walker's ability to make the big or small round. Having got into one's stride, not having far enough to go can be more wearing than making the full distance. I remember how, during childhood, having plagued to be given a picnic and the kind of appurtenances required for the breakfast to teatime tramp, we would sometimes come home about an hour later, to the obvious dismay of the grown-ups, who had their own plans

for what they called their 'bit of peace'. However, like all common walkers, or people who chiefly get about by using their feet, knowing that I can walk a very long way without tiring, and indeed without a thought of the mileage, I do recognize that many of my friends are not up to this, not even if they jog. Joggers, I find, are among the worst kind of walkers, having no notion of its reflective pace and drift. The punishing element being absent, they trudge by my side clearly foxed by effortlessness.

The top ring of the eight takes over where a high-banked footpath leads to the Stour, and the long way round, and a lane which looks just as it must have done in 1787 leads to a marshy wood and then out to Little Horkesley, a village whose recent phoenix-like experience lends it an intriguing quality. For its medieval church and its pub The Beehive were totally destroyed by bombs during the last war and yet stand there still, replacements clearly, yet with a strong feeling of the original buildings having risen up. The new church is charming and fresh as a daisy, full of cracked and scorched memorials, including three vast wooden Norman effigies, one with a black face from the bombing. Next to the church and also dragged back from oblivion is the beautiful house which grew out of the Cluniac Priory and all around is a landscape suggestive of the chase. After these sights the walk is no more than the

serpentine road home, dodging the neighbours' cars with their glimpses of waving hands and grins. Who was that? Who could tell? Only somebody who recognises people by the machines they drive. Soon we descend to the farmhouse in the quietness.

The long walk via the river would always be my preference. Water meadows, flint-packed earth, willow plantations and then the Bailey bridge across the Stour at Wiston, under which we used to swim. By the river, almost hidden by black-berry, teasel and nettle, is the towing path used by the barge horses which John Constable painted and, here and there, are the service canals cut by the Stour navigation company which his family helped to run. The river is actually the rich brown colour of the traditional landscape paintings which he detested, with dace and perch shooting through its currents, and with wicked pike lurking in its reeds. Kingfishers, too. A field or so along the opposite bank is the spartan house which Sir John Soane designed for a director of the Bank of England and then, straight ahead, a small apsed church with a weatherboarded bell turret and, inside, an exquisite sequence of wall paintings of the simplest kind and including one of St Francis preaching to the birds which is so near-contempo-rary that I have always wondered who it was who carried this story from Assisi to Suffolk within a decade of the saint's death. This totally Norman church is crammed with early Victorian mock-Norman furniture, although essentially most of it is what it was in the twelfth century.

The walk continues to the Bures–Nayland road, one of the most beautiful lanes in the Stour Valley and, for me, deeply significant, for it was here that two old friends, then young, John Nash and Adrian Bell, wrote and illustrated their book *Men and The Fields*, which describes this river-scape in the late thirties. We pass Creem's Farm, where Adrian wrote the words – and also his trilogy, *Corduroy*, *The Cherry Tree* and *Silver Ley* – and then The Thatch, where John spent the sum-

Typical Essex scenery, near Great Maplestead.

mer holidays from teaching in Oxford painting what was for both men a very special stretch of England. I can actually see the whole of this Nash–Bell territory from the garden but to wander the 3 or 4 miles through it is what provides the real vision. This is what I hospitably offer to those who accompany me on the long walk, with a running commentary, if they prefer it, tacitly if they do not. The valley is broad and shallow here, very hot in summer, so that the cows stand with their feet in the contributary streams and the oaks are blue with a kind of held-in heat. The river carries scents and bell music from far away in brief gusts and bursts, and in the winter a howling wind.

Halfway along there is a crossroads. Right to Arger Fen, declared by Oliver Rackham to be one of the most ecologically extraordinary sites in Europe, and our bluebell and blackberry-picking haunt as children. Left to Wormingford and home. More roadside canal diggings – the artist's uncles and aunts lived in this village and, of course, ran the waterway – and then the church on its knoll with its Norman tower made of Roman bricks and its heady views to the opposite height where St Edmund was crowned King of the East Angles, and from here the footpath home along a track where – and how can he be praised enough! – my farming neighbour has maintained not only the old path, but all its stiles. The changes pro-duced by the new agricultural policies to do with dairying and cereal growing are already very noticeable, and local conservationist replanting of hedges and trees is having such a swift influence that the anxieties of the 1960s are now barely imaginable. I am old enough to remember the Valley during the unparalleled splendours of its Depression, with the river solid with flowers and its pastures lush jungles, and its farms hanging by their finger-tips to fragile profits.

Along the footpath home I think of an elderly man who came to see me, or rather the room in my house where he was born. 'Did you walk to school from here?' 'No, I ran'. I told an old schoolfriend of his about the visit. She racked her brains for a glimpse of him and then said, 'Oh, yes, John! He was the boy who ran.'

THE WAY THINGS GO WRONG

As we ought to have learnt from The Preacher in *Ecclesiastes*, 'the race is not to the swift, nor the battle to the strong . . . time and chance happeneth to them all.' How often have we tried to cut off a corner, gone over the top instead of wisely clinging to the contours, ignored the notice that said 'Private', poured away a precious litre of water in an effort to economize on weight for that last vigorous 6 miles' stride out to where somebody had suggested we might reach hospitable quarters, only to find, too dark and too late, we had been beguiled yet again on to one of those paths not incompatible with that corner of hell which is paved with good intentions?

It's happened in more of those coniferous slums of the Forestry Commission than I care to think about. In the Cheviots I have no wish even to see Auchope Cairn again after that muddy and misbegotten effort to reach properly named Sourhope in the cloud that got there first and obstinately refused to go away. Drove roads in the West Highlands, especially in the vicinity of Glen Dessary, Carnach and Ben Mor Assynt, have a distressing tendency to disappear in critical places. But beyond our own incompetence we have small grounds for complaint or regret, and on most occasions everything appears glorious in the morning.

The exception that tests the rule sorely is on the face of it a curious one, since the Viking Way climbs up on to the crest of the Lincolnshire Wolds but in fancy rather than in fact it holds only to that portion which has not been commercially raped beyond recognition by wholly unscrupulous Euro-farmers backed by banks, pension funds and misnamed insurance agencies. As I wrote* after walking the easternmost length between the Humber and the Wash: 'By dumping barbed wire in critical places, by throwing signposts into ditches, by ploughing up age-old paths to within a few inches of stone-built walls, by shaking their fists at incursionists, the get-rich-quick farming community has reduced parts of what I trod into something resembling the thoroughfare of Carthage when Scipio Africanus had done with it. The farmers don't sow salt but Amazon M40 pelleted sugar-beet seed treated with organo-mercurial fungicide and methio-carb insecticide dressing probably has more serious long-term effects. In a vain effort to keep strictly to the path, it took me three hours to cover less than 6 linear miles. As Tibullus, that obstinate lover of nature, said, the first two leagues were beaten out with flails.'

Should anyone wonder why I have granted strictly limited space to a route still in need of radical surgery, it is that Lincolnshire's problems are echoed

*Journey Home, Constable, 1983.

136

Rolling downs in winter.

throughout the country to a lesser, certainly never greater degree, and no man in what Ptolemy referred to as *Lindum Colonia* is more competent to speak of its hurts than Brett Collier, Vice-President of the Lincolnshire and South Humberside Area of the Ramblers Association.

'But what's he know about *anything?*' asked a polished lout on behalf of the Country Landowners Association.

I shrugged my shoulders. 'Well, y'know,' I said, warming up to the opportunity, 'he's been a regular soldier with the rank of Major, a riveter in a Kawasaki shipyard, a coal miner in Nagasaki, a headmaster in Lancashire and Malaya, a teacher trainer in Kenya and a college tutor in Lincoln.' I had been waiting to say that for months. Time and chance happeneth to us all.

J.H.

LINCOLNSHIRE

BRETT COLLIER

'Dull, flat, uninteresting, isn't it?' people say on learning, half incredulously, that one comes from Lincolnshire and then they admit that they have never actually set foot in the county. To the south and east of Lincoln it is indeed true that the enormous saucer of the Fens which surround the Wash and extend into Cambridgeshire and Norfolk is uncommonly flat but it has a peculiar charm of its own due to its strangeness, its wide horizons and limitless sky.

It is not a county well known for its scenery, and indeed it is commonly supposed to have no scenery at all, but Lincolnshire is full of surprises, from one of England's loveliest cathedrals set high upon a hill to the Bluestone Heath Road, as fine a road as any in England for 14 miles over the Wolds, where nothing obstructs the enormous view eastwards across rolling fields and the rich farmlands of the Lincolnshire Fen with bold churches, whose spires and towers point to Heaven and speak of faith in God throughout the centuries.

Its relative geographical isolation sprang initially from the long North Sea coastline without any real navigable rivers except the indentations of the Humber and the Wash. Bounded on the north by the Humber and southwards by the band of swamp and marsh merging with the Fen, the old region of Lindsey might almost have been an island. Its situation mainly to the east of the great artery of Ermine Street that was built by the Ninth Legion to link London with York and its successor the Great North Road (today's A1) has tended to make the county something of a backwater beyond the mainstream of commercial activity. The direct northwards course of the Trent, one of England's largest rivers, on its way from Newark to fall into the estuary of the Humber has contributed to this isolation. The Romans raised banks against the sea and constructed canals and dykes to drain the Fens, many of which may still be seen today. After the Romans left it formed part of the kingdom of Mercia until the Danish invasions and by AD 886 the whole county had become part of Danelaw. The '-by' and '-thorpe' endings of village names are Danish in origin and they account for about a third of all the village names in the county. Lincolnshire received bad publicity from the choleric Henry VIII in 1536 when, irritated by the county's part in the disturbances accompanying the dissolution of the monasteries, he described the place as 'the most brute beastly of all Our Shires.'

Few outsiders are even aware of the 40-mile stretch of chalk uplands known as the Wolds that belie common belief that Lincolnshire is flat. These Wolds contain rolling, chalky downs, quiet streams and endless tiny sheltered hamlets hung with beechwoods on the slopes above their deep valleys. Tennyson was born in 1809 in the village of Somersby at the foot of the Wolds and his poems, like Lincolnshire, are full of sky, immense distances and details of nature acutely observed.

Calm and peace on this high wold
And on these dews that drench the furze,
And all the silvery gossamers
That twinkle into green and gold;
Calm and still on yon great plain
That sweeps with all its autumn bowers
And crowded farms and lessening towers,
To mingle with the bounding main.

In Memoriam

Lincoln, one of England's loveliest cathedrals, set high upon a hill.

One overworked cleric at South Ormesby, just over the hill from Somersby, has sixteen churches in his group of parishes half hidden in deep valleys, each parish with perhaps less than a dozen regulars. The 'county top' where the Coronation bonfire was lit at Normanby-le-Wold is just over 500 feet high and is on the route of one of the most attractive sections of the Viking Way, which runs from the Humber Bridge at Barton on Humber across Lincolnshire to end at Oakham in Rutland, once the county town of what used to be the smallest county in England. The Norsemen never actually used this as a route. It was created – with considerable difficulty – from existing public rights of way, apart from one section of disused railway line, but it cuts across an area once entirely under the domination of Danelaw, so the evocative title is not inappropriate. The next village along the Way from Normanby-le-Wold is Walesby where the Ramblers' Church nestles on a hillside with distant views of Lincoln Cathedral on its hilltop 20 miles to the south-west. Walesby Top Church – there are two – is on a medieval vil-

lage site and has a unique stained-glass window dedicated to wayfarers. Twice a year ramblers' services are held there and on each Trinity Sunday the church is crowded with rambling groups from most parts of the country.

The Lincolnshire Wolds consist of 40 miles of chalk uplands that stretch from the Humber almost to the coast and as far south as Horncastle and Market Rasen, most of which is included in an Area of Outstanding Natural Beauty. Lindsey Loop is a 100-mile figure-of-eight recreational route created by local ramblers through this Area of Outstanding Natural Beauty in order to link six ancient market towns in East and West Lindsey: Alford, Caistor, Horncastle, Louth, Market Rasen and Spilsby.

No crowded or eroded paths here, for one can often walk all day without meeting anyone except when passing through villages or perhaps wave to

a headphoned tractor driver busy ploughing out a headland across an already enormous field. The rain has made deep ravines which are rarely seen unless on foot or horseback, for the roads tend to follow the contours of the land. The walking isn't always easy, though, for many of the paths may be ploughed out and obstructed by crops so that even a competent map reader would have difficulty without a walk leaflet as a guide.

Marion Shoard's contention in her latest book *This Land is Our Land* that feudalism has survived to a far greater extent than is generally supposed is borne out by the domestic policies of Lincolnshire. Until 1986 a large map displayed in the main corridor of the County Council bore the legend 'Respectfully dedicated to the Nobility, Clergy and Gentry of the county'. This exaggerated regard for their ambitions and power comes out plainly in their conflict with people insisting on using public footpaths and bridleways. In April 1987 a Dunholme landowner set his dog on an elderly couple walking along a little-used path with the comment: 'I can do what I like on my own land.' The Earl of Yarborough decided to remain in Lincolnshire when the county boundaries were altered in 1974 and the upstart South Humberside was created. Today the county boundary goes round his estate.

On a map the Lincolnshire boundary looks distinctly odd but it clearly demonstrates the kind of power that, in the past, led to whole villages being moved out of sight of the Hall and it supports one of Marion Shoard's main themes. Recently a long-standing complaint against a particularly flagrant example of farming encroachment upon roadside verges brought the official response from the Highways Department '. . . historically the Authority has regarded this with non-disapproval.' The double negative means that they acquiesced in this kind of theft which explains why it's so prevalent. Lincolnshire is a Shire county probably unique in having no alternative base of power such as a university or large-scale industry and for far too long the squirearchy have dominated local policies, often to their own advantage. One District Councillor and Vice Chairman of the committee debating the issue of recognizing the creation of Lindsey Loop recreational path boldly

declared his belief as a landowner that: 'It is the policy of this Council not to interfere with the farming community.'

Although the 1986 Annual Report of Lincolnshire County Council blandly states: 'Farmers have increasingly co-operated by maintaining paths through standing crops' this is quite contrary to what we have discovered by monitoring the effects of the Countryside Commission's Ploughing Code distributed to all farmers in England and Wales during 1986 and the continued reliance of the Council upon so-called voluntary co-operation. The full extent of the problem of ploughed-out paths and crop obstruction is clear from up-to-date figures obtained from a county-wide survey. This showed that 96 cross-field paths in every hundred had been obstructed in one way or another. The majority of headland paths were also ploughed despite the fact that in a number of cases we had co-operated with the farming community and reluctantly accepted diversions on to headlands. We now discover that the Highway Authority has agreed to pay farmers annually, for all time, a small sum to maintain the headland path created, whereas the reinstatement of the

ABOVE: *North Kyme Fen, to the south-east of Lincoln.*

LEFT: *The Ramblers' Church at Walesby.*

LEFT: *The Lincolnshire Wolds, 40 miles of chalk uplands, most of which is included in an Area of Outstanding Natural Beauty.*

RIGHT: *The Church at Somersby in Lincolnshire, the village where Tennyson was born.*

former cross-field path used to fall on the farmer. This may explain the current avalanche of diversion applications on to headlands but it is stupidity for any council pleading lack of finance to deal effectively with field-path problems voluntarily to accept additional and unnecessary commitments. An important issue here is that complaints regarding ploughed-out paths may be submitted year after year without any effective enforcement action being taken to resolve the problem. Many such complaints are now ten years old, although a diversion application by the offender for the same path is dealt with at once. However, one non-NFU Lincolnshire farmer was actually fined for ploughing and cropping a cross-field path in March 1987, perhaps as a token gesture, for there must be hundreds more in the legal queue.

Because a 60-foot wide green lane that 'disappears' under the plough can quickly add more acres to grow the subsidized cereal crops we don't need, the Lincolnshire poacher of today is after bigger game than the odd hare. And the green lanes of Lincolnshire that frequently form the only sizable oasis of unfarmed land have never been more at risk than they are today. The inde-

terminate status of these lanes, particularly in Lindsey, where only one was ever officially registered as a Road Used as a Public Path, is a conservation disaster brought about by the political clout of landowners and the greed of the farming community.

Early in the 1950s, in the absence of clear criteria, the placing of public rights of way upon definitive maps was at best haphazard and at worst fraudulent. At a Department of the Environment Inquiry held at Saltfleetby in 1987 many people from the village spoke about using a green lane leading up to the churchyard since childhood but it was not placed upon the definitive map as a public right of way because 'everyone knew it was a lane and the hearse used to go up there.' Now, thirty years later, newcomers to the village have built a house and fenced off the lane because there was no documentary evidence of its true status.

Lincolnshire County Council claims that by using Manpower Service Scheme teams they have erected over 1,000 signposts and built 905 stiles during the twelve-month period to June 1986. It would be interesting to discover how many of those signposts are actually in place today and a

rough estimate is that at least a quarter of them are stolen or destroyed within six months. One signpost was discovered in a farm trailer at South Carlton twelve hours after it had been pounded in. Another set of direction signs has been removed on eight occasions even though the bolt threads were spoiled to prevent the nuts being taken off. A member of the Ramblers' Association who drives a lorry was told by a farmer customer: 'Here's a couple of quid. Knock down that footpath signpost on your way out.' He didn't touch it but the post wasn't there on his next visit.

Sir Marcus Kimball, MP, explained to members of the Standing Committee considering the details of the Wildlife and Countryside Bill in 1981: 'The Pony Club in my constituency has a most enjoyable battle with one specially active member of the Ramblers' Association who spends all his time putting up footpath signs. The members of the Pony Club find happy occupation in the summer going round taking them down again.' This was a Member of Parliament representing 'the people' at Westminster. At the time we were, quite legitimately, acting as 'agents of the County Council' and saving ratepayers' money in

erecting footpath and bridleway signposts without charge in the correct place and pointing in the right direction. Under cryptic influence the County Council soon refused to supply any more with the lame excuse that it might interfere with a gas main or electricity cable way out in the countryside. Sir Marcus Kimball (now Lord Kimball), an influential Scottish landowner and former president of the British Field Sports Society, has stated that there should be a shift from the notion of public footpaths and bridleways as rights to their being seen as privileges whose continued existence would depend upon the 'goodwill' of farmers and landowners. Another of his suggestions was that in the changing circumstances of farming today there could be a 'crop' of field paths with payment by so much a metre. No one asked how much should be repaid for these stretches of public paths that were already under crops.

Due to immense pressure by amenity groups and the general public plus the Ombudsman who found Lincolnshire County Council guilty of maladministration regarding the ploughing and cropping of an inter-village path, there has been reorganization of those representing the farmers.

It comes from the changing fortunes of agriculture and the belated recognition of the value of tourism in a rural area, including, of course, walking. Reorganization, yes. But not rebirth.

The County Council now assists farmers by assembling and installing 'stile kits' instead of fulfilling their statutory obligations. It is, however, extremely frustrating to find so often that beyond the new stile and signpost there is not the slightest indication of the line of the path through a crop. Lincolnshire's long-awaited Director of Recreational Services very soon recognized where the power lay when tackling the thorny problem of reinstating paths after ploughing by publicly announcing that 'Feet on paths are the best way to reinstate them.' This neatly absolves the County Council from taking any effective enforcement action, but it is a chick-and-egg situation for until a path is clearly defined on the ground most people will not have sufficient knowledge or confidence to use the public right of way and are reluctant to venture through any visible obstruction. The new Director states that most crops are not really an obstruction for one can walk through them, but walking through a cereal crop wet with dew or after a shower often means getting wet to the waist and when dry it is surprisingly dusty or dirty. In addition, there is no means of knowing how recently crops have been sprayed with a range of unpleasant chemicals. One woman who happened to be second in line when walking through a cereal crop later lost control of her car twice on her way home through unknowingly inhaling droplets stirred up by the person in front of her. She spent the next twenty-four hours ill in bed. The leader of the walk had a burning sensation for many hours and has not again worn shorts on a Lincolnshire trail.

Despite all Lincolnshire's field-path problems, however, a walk along the Wolds sections of the Viking Way or Lindsey Loop in whatever season of the year is likely to be a memorable experience.

Sheep grazing on the Lincolnshire Wolds.

THE PEAK DISTRICT

That large-scale relief map I've referred to more than once is particularly useful for showing us where, from all points of view, the Midlands retreat before the broken teeth of the Pennines and much that is associated with the North of England appears as the blunt end of a wedge driven between Manchester and Sheffield. These regional terms must be handled cautiously. The Greater Pennines or Pennine Upland are often referred to, wrongly, as 'a chain' whereas they scarcely form even a range. They are relatively simple in structure and homogenous in rock constituents; that is they are largely built out of those geological bed-fellows from the great Age of Coal, mountain limestone and millstone grit with a sprinkling of shales. The not-so-High Peak is flat-topped and used to be known as The Honour. William the Conqueror granted it to his bastard son, William Peveril, but the Peverils lost their Honour when they made a bad job of poisoning the Earl of Chester. The region is a small mineralized belt, rich in lead with a little silver, the product of some unseen igneous presence, still steaming quietly underground, hence the spa towns of Buxton and Matlock (there are five Matlocks) and the great houses of the well-lined gentry, Chatsworth, Haddon Hall, Hardwick, Bolsover, Kedleston and many more.

Roland Smith, our guide, is both a passionate and a prejudiced man. He is hugely prejudiced in favour of the Peak National Park where he is the Head of Information Services. He is both the Park Crier and the Park Shoulder always there to be leaned on. He is angry that the government can give more to one London theatre than it does to all ten parks. Since I am so fond of this irrepressible bog-trotter he will forgive me, I know, for pointing out that his gaunt bailiwick stands in the top north-western corner of Derbyshire, a cloud factory not far from Glossop and the Yorkshire border. The stone walls are grey, the houses are grey and the sheep are all grey. What then is there to commend itself to us about this odd county? First and foremost it breeds an heroic race, a stoic race that refuses to compromise with life.

Dissent, Nonconformity, Protestantism, these are the qualities that thrive in that forbidding climate. It is enough for a Derbyshire man that the Church is established for him to seek to disestablish it. As an occasional visiting foot-man I am tempted into those tiny limestone dales to the south that are almost invisible until you drop into them: Dovedale, Beresford Dale, Lathkill Dale, Millers Dale and Monsal Dale where the banks of streams are bedecked with butter-dock and musk, meadowsweet and hemp agrimony.

J.H.

BOG-TROTTING AND OTHER DELIGHTS

ROLAND SMITH

There's a special breed of walker curiously dedicated to the highest and wildest parts of the Peak District, the area accurately described on Ordnance Survey maps as 'the Dark Peak'. His distinguishing features are a scruffy, dog-eared anorak; baggy, heavily-patched trousers or breeches, and down-at-heel walking boots, usually covered by peat-grimed gaiters. A strange, almost fanatical gleam comes into his eye at the mention of the Marsden–Edale, the Four Inns, or the Derwent Watershed, and he'll become as lyrical as his blunt northern tongue allows about cloughs and groughs, hags and crags. He is affectionately known as a bog-trotter.

Not for him the gentle, chocolate-box charms of the limestone dales or the rolling, enclosed pastures of the White Peak further south. He shares his lonely habitat with the staccato bark of the red grouse, the elusive dash of the white mountain hare, and the mewing hawk, quartering the wild moorland sky.

The bog-trotter thrives on some of the most difficult and dangerous walking country in Britain: the peat moors and mosses of Kinder Scout, Bleaklow and Black Hill. The very ring of their names, stark and elemental, gives a clue to their nature. Most of the high moors of the Dark Peak are covered by a thick layer of peat, the heavily eroded remains of vegetation which failed to survive under extreme acid conditions. Occasionally you come across the bleached bole of some long-dead birch, poking out like an exposed skeleton from a bank of peat, a reminder of the tree cover which has gradually been felled, burned or cleared for grazing over a period of 10,000 years.

The drainage channels snaking through the peat in a crazy, compass-defying maze, are known as groughs ('gruffs'), and the steaming banks of peat which they have carved out are called hags. To walk, slither and slide across the groughs and hags of Kinder or Bleaklow is an experience unique in Britain, and as strenuous a test of stamina and navigation as you will find in our mountains. Cumbrians, Welshmen and Scots may scoff at the elevation of these modest 2,000-foot aspirants to mountain status, but make no mistake about it, these peaty plateaux have claimed the lives of many a 'mountaineer' who foolishly underestimated their rigour on the mere basis of their height above the sea.

It is the mark of a true bog-trotter to be able to walk quickly and safely across these brooding and often featureless moors, and quite incredible times and distances have been recorded. One of the most famous was Fred Heardman, bullet-headed landlord of the Nag's Head and Church Hotel at Edale, in the shadow of Kinder Scout. 'Bloody Bill the Bog-trotter,' as he was known, became a near-legendary figure among Peakland walkers. He inaugurated the 73-mile Colne–Rowsley walk and once trod barefoot from Langsett on the Sheffield fringe to Edale to win a bet of a pint of shandy. Well known as the cheery host of the two Edale pubs, Fred Heardman was the subject of many stories, some apocryphal. I recall one about that day when Fred threw two customers out of the Nag's Head when they were the worse for drink. Undeterred, they staggered down the road to the Church Hotel to continue their carousing. Imagine their surprise when none other than Fred popped up from behind the bar to greet them.

The classic Derwent Watershed, one of the stiffest bog-trots in the Pennines, was first achieved by a tall, long-legged Manchester businessman named Eustace Thomas with four friends, in 1918. They completed the gruelling 38 miles in 11½ hours. The route traditionally starts and finishes at the Yorkshire Bridge Inn, now sheltering beneath the grass-covered embankment of the Ladybower Reservoir above Bamford. It ascends the heather-covered slopes of Win Hill to its craggy pike, and one of the finest panoramic views in the Peak. Corn Law poet Ebenezer Elliott went a little over the top in his description of the view from here:

> King of the Peak! Win Hill! thou, throned and crowned,
> That reign'st o'er many a stream and many a vale!
> Star-loved and meteor-sought, and tempest-found!
> Proud centre of a mountain-circle, hail!

Local legend has the valley of the River Noe, entrance to the secret valley of Edale between Win Hill and Lose Hill, as the scene of a Dark Age battle. The winners of the bloody encounter camped on Win Hill, while the losers, needless to say, chose Lose Hill.

The shapely cone of Lose Hill dominates the Hope Valley, and is one of the few real peaks in the Peak District. Its summit is more correctly known as Ward's Piece, in memory of 'the King of the Clarion Ramblers', G. H. B. Ward. Bert Ward, socialist and philosopher, placed an advertisement in the *Sheffield Clarion* newspaper in 1900, saying he would be taking a walk round the Kinder Plateau the following Sunday, and appealing for any kindred spirits to join him. Thirteen people turned up on a lovely autumn morning – and the famous *Sheffield Clarion* Rambling Club was formed.

This remarkable organization became one of the foremost workers' Sunday rambling clubs in the north of England, and its annual handbooks,

edited and largely written by Ward himself, became classics in walking literature, much sought after today. Ward's catch-phrases, 'A Rambler made is a man improved' and 'The man who never was lost, never went very far' became the club mottoes, and his poetry, historical research and home-spun philosophy filled the handbook's pages year after year.

Leaders were exhorted: 'The ramble will be taken, wet or fine' and it was decreed that a 'whipper-in' must be appointed. Leaders were also expected to provide a reading or useful information on place names en route, and also 'to see that some song is sung upon the way.' Early handbooks included the lyrics of these songs to be sung in the open air, most of which were written by Ward.

The New Year Revellers' Ramble was the toughest of the lot, as Ward's instructions made clear: 'We go, wet or fine, snow or blow, and none but the bravest and fittest must attempt this walk. Those who are unwell, unfit, inexperienced, or insufficiently clad should consult their convenience, and that of their friends, by staying at home. Ladies, on this occasion, are also kindly requested not to attend.'

One of Ward's best-loved songs, 'Land of Moor and Heather' was composed in memory of the ramblers who had died in the Great War, and was sung to the tune of 'Land of Hope and Glory'.

> Dear Land of Moors, with Hope uncrown'd,
> Men wait thy freedom yet!
> On craggy brows, belov'd, renowned,
> Vile trespass boards are set.

Those stark lines refer to the fact that most of the Dark Peak at that time was forbidden country to the rambler, and many of the published walks in the *Clarion Handbooks* were deliberate trespasses over the sacred grouse moors of titled, usually absentee, landowners.

'Upon all this country lies a curse,' wrote Professor Cyril Joad in *The Untutored Townsman's Invasion of the Country*, 'the curse of the keeper.'

Although only 16 miles from the centres of the teeming cities of Sheffield and Manchester, the high Peakland moors were uncrossed by public paths and policed by stern-faced gamekeepers instructed to evict ramblers on sight. Sir Arthur

Near Padley Bridge in Derbyshire, looking across Burbage Brook to Carl Wark hill fort in Yorkshire.

LEFT: *Near Little Hucklow in Derbyshire's Peak District.*

BELOW: *Ladybower Reservoir above Bamford, where the classic Derwent Watershed bog-trot traditionally starts and finishes.*

Hobhouse, in the report which proposed the Peak as one of the first of our National Parks, complained: 'Many of the finest moorlands, where thousands wish to wander, are closed against "trespassers" and an altercation with a game-keeper may often mar a day's serenity.'

Mind you, many of those ramblers from Sheffield and Manchester way were not in the least intimidated by the keepers, and many actually enjoyed an encounter. Being young and fit, they could usually outrun a sweating, swearing game-keeper in a session of hide-and-seek across the groughs of Kinder or Bleaklow.

Jack Jordan, one of the original thirteen Clarion Ramblers, remembered one such encounter in the sixtieth anniversary *Handbook*. A group of walkers were standing on a forbidden hilltop when a keeper was seen running up towards them, obviously intent on turning them back. When he finally reached them, he was so out of breath he could hardly speak, and had to sit down to recover. One of the group went over to him and gravely called for a doctor. The 'doctor' came over and, poker-faced, examined the distressed keeper. After taking his pulse and asking a few questions, he advised him to walk slowly home, assuring him he would be all right if he took it steady. The frightened gamekeeper duly obliged. But on other occasions, ramblers were beaten up by stick-wielding keepers, and there were injuries on both sides.

By this time, as Professor Joad put it: 'Hiking had replaced beer as the shortest cut out of Manchester,' and thousands of ramblers from the depressed northern cities which surrounded the Peak flocked out at weekends and would not be denied what they saw as their right to roam the open moors.

A diminutive out-of-work mechanic from Manchester suddenly found himself at the centre of a much-publicized 'mass trespass' on the forbidden mountain of Kinder Scout in April, 1932. It was to be the first time that Benny Rothman, secretary of the Lancashire British Workers' Sports Federation, had ever set foot on Kinder, but he'd often looked longingly at the challenging crags from a distance. After a well-attended rally in a quarry near Hayfield, about 400 ramblers set off up William Clough for the plateau. As expected, they were intercepted by an army of keepers, and scuffles broke out. As a result, five ramblers were charged with riotous assembly and occasioning actual bodily harm (*not* trespass or damage) and were imprisoned for periods of between three and six months.

The so-called 'Battle of Kinder Scout' has entered walkers' mythology, but it was to be an important catalyst which eventually led to the creation of the Peak District as Britain's first National Park in 1951. Mass rallies of up to 10,000 ramblers, addressed by people like Professor Joad and Tom Stephenson, called for free access and National Parks, and it became a priority for the post-war Labour Government. Advised by Hobhouse that 'A National Park in the Peak District will not justify its name unless this problem (of access) is satisfactorily solved,' the newly formed Peak National Park authority made the negotiation of special access agreements with landowners an early task. Now 76 square miles of those battlegrounds of the twenties and thirties are covered

Wolfscote Dale in Derbyshire, the gentler side of the Peak District.

ABOVE: *Footpath sign on the Pennine Way.*

RIGHT: *Dovedale in Derbyshire.*

by these agreements, which allow free access throughout the year except when shooting is in progress.

Ewan McColl, Press Officer for the Mass Trespass, sang of the '. . . pleasure in dragging through peat bogs and bragging of all the fine walks that you know; There's even a measure of some kind of pleasure in wading through ten feet of snow' in his famous rallying song, 'The Manchester Rambler'. There was, and still is, a special kind of Spartan, invigorating beauty in these wild, high moors for the mill workers from the grimy industrial cities on either side. One guidebook author described Kinder Scout as 'a clean, bare antechamber to heaven', while another thought it 'one of the most silent places in the world'. Later, in more pragmatic mood, John Derry described Ashop Head as 'the most featureless, disconsolate, bog-quaking, ink-oozing moor you ever saw.'

The toughest, most stamina-sapping section of Tom Stephenson's great monument, the Pennine Way, slogs through this kind of country between Edale and Standedge. There are many stories of immacuately equipped walkers setting out from Edale, brimful of confidence, only to return several hours later, ashen-faced and peat-plastered,

shaking their heads sadly in disbelief and heading for home.

But if Dark Peak walking is for the macho bogtrotter, then walking in the White Peak is the feminine equivalent, a kind of genteel Mozartian minuet compared to a Wagnerian opera. For students of prehistory, however, the southern limestone plateau is as rich in relics as anywhere in Britain. Layer upon layer of human occupation has been deposited like a palimpsest across these gently swelling contours since the arrival of Neanderthal man, and every emerald green field holds its own story of the emergence of civilization. Even in the craggy dales, like overpopulous Dovedale, lovely Lathkill Dale and the magnificent Manifold valley, almost every cave and crevice has revealed evidence of early Man. The enigmatic stone circle of Arbor Low, remote and still unexplained, is a Neolithic power centre which retains its ancient mystery.

Every 'low', paradoxically sited on the highest points, marks the burial mound of some longdead chieftain, and the later bumps and hollows running across the meadows mark the labour of 't'owd men', the Peakland lead miners who delved deep into the limestone for the precious ore during the region's Lead Rush of the eighteenth century.

The conversion by the National Park authority of derelict railway lines, most of which had fallen under the Beeching axe, into easy walking or riding routes has opened up large areas of the limestone plateau for family walkers, and provides a perfect counterpoint to the sterner walking farther north.

Summer or winter, wet or shine, Dark Peak or White, when you're in this robust part of the world you can always reckon to come across walkers, either the solitary bog-trotter or the club outing from the surrounding cities. It is probably true to say that more people walk and climb in the Peak District than in all the rest of the hills of Britain put together. This is a region, by the accident of geography, where walking has taken on the nature of a religion, and is still usually practised on the Sabbath. 'I may be a wage slave on Monday,' sang Ewan McColl's Manchester Rambler, 'but I am a free man on Sunday.'

FOOTPRINTS IN THE PEAT

Some days before I left for an exotic trip across what used to be called the Belgian Congo, Harrison Matthews, then Scientific Director of the London Zoo and a much-travelled man, catechized me at some length on such points as the pursuit speed of large, rare and really aggressive snakes such as the mambas – relatively slow, about 5 miles an hour; the two mammals which, if disturbed, are most clearly out to do you (buffalo and leopard) and things to be avoided in the open bush without careful circumspection (tree-lined water holes). Since this was supposed to be a scientific expedition, before he offered a nightcap that old Africa hand, for so many years my mentor, leaned forward and asked: 'And when do you propose to write up your notes?' Every day, I said. He sighed and temporarily withdrew the bottle.

'No!' he said with a touch of asperity. 'Immediately! As soon as you can write them down. Details of what happens in the morning can easily be overlaid and forgotten by nightfall.' We touched glasses and I went home. That was over thirty years ago.

What, you may well wonder, has this got to do with Bodmin Moor, Dartmoor and peat bogs at both ends of the Pennine Way from Kinder Scout to the Cheviot Hills? I will tell you. Today, there are two or three dozen notebooks in a drawer of this desk. Apart from their dates, factual value to me as a walker and writer, they have more than justified the small effort of putting even unpleasant facts to paper. They have kept me going when, as Belloc put it, 'the small flame inside each one of us burns perilously low.' In 1965 the Pennine Way provided me with a convenient link between the West Midlands and the Scottish Border but there were long lengths of it, especially that damnable dissected peat, which I wouldn't wish on a Staffordshire terrier.

Mist shrouded the whole valley of Edale as I began the laborious but not difficult climb up the Grindsbrook, the classic start to the ascent of Kinder Scout. Not a soul in sight but at the top the peat had been heavily footprinted in many directions by the human traffic of the previous day, a public holiday. Up there I looked around, astonished, unutterably dispirited. A chocolate-brown labyrinth of groughs or peat hags. Unsure about which path to follow I took off my boots and waded bare foot through the crappy ooze. It began to rain.

What it is like today I cannot imagine but on that early Monday morning, over twenty years ago, the feeling was of straying into land at the end of its ecological tether. The faint slow cheep of a pipit could be likened to the last ticks of a Carbon-14 clock nearing its recording limits. More rain on

Saddleworth Moor and murder too. For half a crown a dreadful old woman offered to show me the first of the childs' graves to be discovered. In a nearby village, the home of the victim's parents, the atmosphere in the pub was that of a lynching party. They'd have them two flogged to death, they said, and that wouldn't be good enough.

Seen from high ground a succession of windswept reservoirs winked like watery eyes from the sockets of distant valleys. Thousands of footprints marked the detours around filthy-looking bogs euphemistically called mosses. Through the mist on the Haworth moors I saw a woman in a huge shawl who could have been Charlotte Bronte, for here it was that the sisters walked together, or alone, creating their private worlds. All that is down in my notebook, my sole companion. In five days I encountered only one Pennine trailer. It follows that observations on the calls of golden plover and the curious fact that all the grouse appeared to be feeding not on heather shoots, as we are led to believe, but on swarms of daddy-longlegs, are interlaced with oaths, notes on intemperance and pieties about the need for self-improvement which were quickly forgotten.

For me the Pennine Way opens up at Gargrave and becomes glorious up to and beyond Malham, Fountains Fell and Pen-y-Ghent, that hill of the winds, places I am vain enough to regard as my own country. With respect to Roly Smith, that champion of the bog-hoppers, I have little love for the southern gritstone moors where I have it from Adam Nicolson that the conservationists are now laying down bunches of heather pegged to the earth and overlying horizontal stakes just as the Neolithic people did on the marshes of Somerset, the Levels, over three thousand years ago.

The vast arboreal slums of the Forestry Commission to the north of the Wall are an ecological enormity for which the Minister of the Environment should be publicly boiled in oil and boiled slowly. Clearly I am a biased witness and a cheat, too, since the length of the whole Way is close on 250 miles. By cutting off not one but several corners it took me twelve days to trudge from Edale to Dere Street where I struck off for Jedburgh, arguing that a man is as good as his fancy takes him. On bad days I was sustained by the thought that better country lay ahead.

J.H.

THE PENNINE WAY

HUGH WESTACOTT

For the moors! For the moors! where the short grass
Like velvet beneath us should lie!
For the moors! For the moors! where the high pass
Rose sunny against the clear sky!

For the moors! where the linnet was trilling
Its song on the old granite stone,
Where the lark, the wild skylark, was filling
Every breast with delight like its own.

Emily Brontë

When one of the Rockefellers was asked what it would cost to take up deep-sea ocean racing he replied that anybody who needed to ask the question had insufficient means even to consider buying a yacht. If you have to ask how to set about walking the Pennine Way then you are not yet ready for high moorland walking and what should be an exhilarating and rewarding adventure will become a miserable, relentless slog. In the course of the last fifteen years I have walked the complete length of the Pennine Way no less than six times so I know whereof I speak.

Every year thousands set out to walk the Pennine Way. On any Friday night between Easter and September little groups of walkers can be seen huddled together in the bars of the Rambler's Inn and the Nag's Head Inn in Edale, midway between Manchester and Sheffield, examining guidebooks and maps, buying each other rounds of beer, shouting encouragement and exchanging good-natured banter with fellow walkers in an atmosphere reminiscent of the condemned man's last wish. In the morning tents will be struck, ruck-sacks packed at guesthouse and camp site, last-minute purchases of food and confectionery made at the village shop and a trickle of walkers will start up Grindsbrook on the first leg of their arduous journey to Kirk Yetholm, just over the Scottish border, 250 miles away.

A behavioural scientist would classify these would-be Pennine wayfarers into several distinct categories. He would observe high-spirited young people treating the adventure as a lark; groups of foolish, hairy, city-tough young men nursing hangovers and sporting an odd assortment of cheap rucksacks with cooking utensils and plastic bundles tied on with bits of string; and neatly dressed walkers, with well-packed rucksacks, striding purposefully with measured tread towards the Cheviot Hills. Many who set out will give up long before the end. Some will succumb to fatigue caused by the inhospitable terrain and mile after mile of slime-oozing bog into which a heavily laden backpacker can sink to his knees; others to such minor injuries as blisters and strained muscles; still more to inadequate clothing and equipment; another group to persistently foul weather and their inability to keep their clothes and sleeping bags dry; and yet more to a combination of these conditions which makes walking the Pennine Way such a formidable undertaking for the inexperienced.

The Pennine Way differs, too, from almost all other long-distance paths in that a number of very long days are unavoidable, with the first and last days being far and away the toughest of the whole

Kirk Yetholm, the northern end of the Pennine Way, in the Scottish borders.

158

journey. It is 16 miles from Edale to Crowden and there is no way of shortening this distance unless you can be met by a friend with a car on the Snake Pass. Moreover, at least 12 of these 16 miles are over appalling terrain. On the lunar-like landscape of Kinder Scout one has to scramble up and down the steep undulations of bare peat hags, leap over the oozing brackish water which collects in the bottom, and on Bleaklow cope with the miseries of water-sodden quaking bog. The final stretch over the Cheviot Hills is even more punishing. Unless backpacking and planning to use one of the two primitive mountain shelters, or walking off the route to Uswayford Farm for bed and breakfast, the 27 miles of boot-squelching peat between Byrness and Kirk Yetholm must be covered in a single day.

Another difficulty about walking this trail is its awkward length. Most walkers can spare only two weeks for their journey and will want to complete the whole of the route within that time. Unfortunately, this means an average 18 miles per day which, except for the strongest of walkers, is unrealistic. It is far better to take three weeks spread, if necessary, over two or three years.

Considerable stretches of the route lie above the 1,500-foot contour line and it is often more than 2,000 feet high. Rough weather is to be expected and if a deep depression comes in from the Atlantic the higher parts of the route are likely to be above cloud level and visibility will be poor.

ABOVE: *Cross Fell, the highest point of the way. Rough weather can be expected on many of the northern parts of the route.*
LEFT: *The Cheviot Hills, where the final stretch of the Pennine Way can be extremely punishing.*

But you may be lucky! In 1984 I walked the
Pennine Way during the first three weeks of
September and it rained on only two days. On one
of these days we set out from Dufton to reach
Garrigill, 16 miles away, on a fine but windy
morning. As we climbed the slopes of Knock Fell
the wind steadily increased and near the summit
of Great Dun Fell at 2,850 feet the wind reached
gale force and the first drops of rain were falling.
We dropped into a hollow beside the road to get
out of the wind and discuss our position. As
everyone in the group was a strong, fit walker, well
clad and shod, we decided to soldier on. At the
top of Great Dun Fell visibility was down to a few
yards and unable to find the path we marched on a
compass bearing until we were back on course at
Little Dun Fell. Here the wind was so strong that it
was difficult to stand and my fingers were so numb
with cold that I could not operate the zips on my
cagoule. We reached Cross Fell, at 2,930 feet the
highest point on the Pennine Way, rested thankfully in the lee of the wind shelter for a few minutes and then made our way down the steep
north-west flank to Greg's Hut.

Inside the hut a fire was lit and we brewed tea,
coffee and soup to warm ourselves and raise our
spirits. A group of walkers was anxiously discuss-
ing the fate of two friends. Their party had
become separated in the mist on Cross Fell, the
only map had been lost, their shouts and calls to
their missing friends had been blown away in the
strong wind and they had retreated to Greg's Hut.
There were not enough of us to make a sweep
search and so they left a note in the shelter and
hurried off to Garrigill to alert the police and the
mountain rescue team. The next day we heard
that the missing walkers had gone down to the
Old Corpse Road and walked south-west to
Kirkland where they had arrived safe and sound.

So many walkers use the Pennine Way every
year that some sections are subject to severe
erosion which can, at times, make progress difficult and slow. The problem is not entirely due to

*Haworth Moor, where Top Withens was the reputed
inspiration of Emily Brontë's* Wuthering Heights.

the constant pounding of innumerable feet because there is some evidence to show that overgrazing of an area by sheep can exacerbate erosion, but walkers are not entirely blameless. The Countryside Commission, the Peak District, the Yorkshire Dales and the Northumberland National Parks together with the local authorities responsible for the path have made heroic efforts to combat the problem. In places the path has been re-routed to allow the surface to recover; chestnut palings have been laid over bogs, steps cut in steep places, fellsides drained and duckboards laid. Walkers can help to prevent unnecessary wear and tear by keeping strictly to the line of the path and not treading on the extreme edge of it or cutting across switchbacks.

Why, then, with all these problems is this our most popular long-distance path? The unfortunate truth is that too many people walk it for the wrong reasons. Instead of appreciating it for its very real scenic merits and diversity many regard it as a challenge and attempt to walk it as fast as possible to prove just how tough they are. In the process they may gain nothing but a few blisters, some injury to their pride if they fail, and a lasting prejudice against walking and long-distance paths in particular.

But if you're tough enough it makes a very rewarding expedition. Roughly two thirds of it follows the Pennines, sometimes near the watershed of England. The bleak grandeur of the windswept moors contrasts with the delightful, sun-dappled valleys of the rivers Aire, Tees and South Tyne. It crosses the Newcastle to Carlisle gap, runs through a section of Kielder Forest and then climbs on to the Cheviot Hills and weaves in and out of Scotland, following the border fence before dropping down to the delightful village of Kirk Yetholm. There are surprisingly few really steep hills with perhaps three, Grindsbrook, which I've already mentioned, Pen-y-Ghent near Horton-in-Ribblesdale and Byrness Hill at the start of the Cheviots, classified as severe.

Every section has its own character. Edale to Lothersdale is desolate and melancholy uninhabited moorland on Kinder Scout, Bleaklow and Black Moss with man-made works – the M62, the chain of reservoirs, the dark satanic mills of the

ABOVE: *Malham in North Yorkshire. From Lothersdale to Malham the walking is easy and the scenery gentle.*

RIGHT: *Limestone pavements at Malham.*

Calder valley – and the evocatively remote Top Withens, the reputed inspiration of Emily Brontë's *Wuthering Heights*, on Haworth Moor. From Lothersdale to Malham we are in a different world; the walking is easy, the scenery gentle and the architecture pleasing as we cross over meadows by canal and streamside through enchanting villages and hamlets in the limestone country of Airedale. There is another change of mood after we climb Malham Cove, where a waterfall higher than Niagara once tumbled, to reach Malham Tarn where Charles Kingsley wrote *The Water Babies*, ascend Fountains Fell and Pen-y-Ghent and so to Horton-in-Ribblesdale. From here we follow the splendid elevated Cam High Road, now a green lane but once an important packhorse route, fast, easy walking to the lovely old market town of Hawes in Wensleydale. Good going, too, past the waterfall of Hardraw Force and over Great Shunner Fell to Thwaite in Swaledale but from then on the moors are bleak until reaching Middleton-in-Teesdale, which was beautifully laid out by the Quaker owners of the nearby lead mines.

We are now more than halfway along and follow the lovely valley of the Tees past spectacular waterfalls at High Force and Cauldron Snout over bleak, windswept uplands to High Cup Nick from where, on a fine day, the Lakeland fells can be seen 30 miles away across the Eden valley. Dufton, yet another beautiful village, provides a welcome break, then follows an arduous stretch over Knock Fell, Great Dun Fell, Little Dun Fell and Cross Fell, before we drop down to Garrigill and Alston in the valley of the South Tyne. The Maiden Way, which was an important Roman road, crosses some unattractive moorland pitted with old collieries to Hadrian's Wall which it follows for several memorable miles. We now cross moorland through characterless conifer forest to the charming Northumbrian town of Bellingham, and it becomes bleaker towards Byrness before the final, desperate push over the lonely, peat-sodden Cheviot Hills to journey's end at Kirk Yetholm.

And what are the highlights of the journey? Mine are the enchanting limestone scenery of Craven and Airedale dotted with the delightful villages and hamlets of Lothersdale, Thornton-in-Craven, Gargrave, Airton and Hanlith; Pen-y-Ghent, the only real mountain on the route; the Cam High Road, Gayle, Hawes, Thwaite, Great Shunner Fell, Middleton and the valley of the Tees; Cauldron Snout; High Cup Nick and the peaceful perfection of Dufton; Cross Fell, in fine weather, Alston and, finally, the wonderful section of Hadrian's Wall. To appreciate this properly, visit one of the Roman Army Museums and make the short diversion to see Housesteads Fort.

The Pennine Way seems to breed camaraderie among walkers. So many walk the route that groups are likely to pass and re-pass each other, meeting time and again at camp site and guesthouse before sharing a final convivial drink at the Border Hotel in Kirk Yetholm. This has encouraged some cafes, guesthouses and pubs to provide visitors' books in which they ask their customers to record their comments. The best known are kept in the Dalesman Cafe at Gargrave, the Pen-y-Ghent Cafe at Horton-in-Ribblesdale, Greg's Hut, the two mountain shelters in the Cheviots and the Border Hotel. Some of the entries make

entertaining reading. Most are dolorous, jejeune accounts of rain, fatigue, hunger, blisters and bog liberally sprinkled with exclamation marks, but occasionally a genuinely original contribution will appear like the mute, inglorious Milton who penned the following succinct summary of his misery in the visitors' book at the mountain shelter near Hen Hole: 'My balls are so cold.'

The Pennine Way is a route which attracts the odd and eccentric, where coincidences are everyday occurrences and the unusual is commonplace. I have seen two tall backpackers share a child's play tent which was so small that the lower half of their sleeping bags protruded through the doorflaps and were protected from the elements by a sheet of plastic. They camped in abject squalor and one night attempted to brew tea in an unwashed billycan still coated with rice they had burned whilst cooking their evening meal. The first time I walked the Pennine Way I encountered two young women in a pub in Hawes who were *drinking* their way along the route.

But my oddest encounter was on Cross Fell where I joined two young Dutchmen in the lee of the wind shelter on the summit. When I asked them how they came to be walking the Pennine Way one, with the manic eyes of a professional psychiatrist, told me that they had gone into a bookshop in Amsterdam and bought a copy of *The Walker's Handbook* and had been intrigued by

A stretch of Hadrian's Wall in Northumberland, one of the highlights of the Pennine Way. If you have time, make the short diversion to see Housesteads Fort.

the description of the route. They wouldn't believe that I was the author of that book and the mad psychiatrist, who, I discovered later, was a keen student of Krafft-Ebbing and must have heard plenty of tall stories in his time, was the more provoked. 'We buy a walking book in Amsterdam and meet the author on the highest part of the Pennine Way,' he said angrily, shouldering his rucksack and striding off. His companion rolled his eyes heavenward, spread his hands apologetically and followed him down the fellside.

Nearing Kirk Yetholm, after a wild crossing of the Cheviots, I was stopped by a man humping an old army rucksack, carrying a petrol company road map and wearing wooden clogs wanting to know if he was on the Pennine Way. He was the second of the three oddities I met that day. The first was a man wearing running shoes, elegant white trousers and carrying a sporty striped umbrella who overtook me without a word and seemed to dance his way over the bogs. The third eccentric approached myself and several other walkers in the Border Hotel asking us to sponsor him in his attempt to ride the Pennine Way on a horse. He wore a pale blue Charvet silk scarf and a white riding coat and was mortified when we laughed uncontrollably. Even after we explained that it would be impossible to get a horse over the innumerable stiles, even assuming that it got as far as Byrness without getting stuck fast and breaking a leg in the Cheviot bogs, he petulantly remarked that we were spoilsports. One wag suggested that the only animal capable of coping with the Pennine Way would be a cross between a hippopotamus and a kangaroo.

However, if you have not over-stretched yourself, if you have had your share of fine days, listened to the call of the curlew, the heartbreakingly beautiful song of the skylark and the drumming and whirring of the red grouse; and if you have happy memories to recollect, you will always remember with gratitude and just a hint of pride that you have walked the most famous Way of all.

IN TURNER'S FOOTSTEPS

Farnley Hall, originally a mullioned Elizabethan manor house, stands proud above Wharfedale some 7 miles to the north-west of that Victorian sprawl, the City of Leeds where I spent my boyhood. As a passionate fly fisherman this moody malcontent walked to the Wharfe and sometimes walked back for the cogent reason that often I couldn't afford the bus fare. It follows that, at the time, I knew that troutful length of the river more intimately than any other. I had seen the sun rise over the craggy crest of Otley Chevin and sink out of sight behind Almscliff Crag. Early morning mists wrapped their shawls around the shoulders of Harewood's place downstream and, when the barometer dropped suddenly, thunder echoed eerily in that harshly glaciated valley. An interesting landscape but not spectacular by contrast with, let us say, uppermost Airedale or those great gorges of the Swale above Keld.

Imagine then surprise bordering on astonishment when I learnt from David Hill whose book title prefaces this page* that Joseph Mallord William Turner had used the backdrop of the Wharfe I knew so well, a purling stream for most of the year, as the chaotic setting of Hannibal crossing the Alps during one hell of a storm. It is not my purpose to go deep into Turner's prodigious artistic powers beyond emphasizing that even when local topography had become of secondary importance compared with the combination of light and colour, he criss-crossed Yorkshire in an insatiable search for the raw material, only a few of the sketches of which became what he is best known for. He thought nothing of walking up to 25 miles a day, carrying a huge brolly which could be quickly converted into a fishing rod.

There are 541 oil paintings in all, many of which are unfinished. This is to be compared with 1,578 finished watercolours and over 19,000 pencil sketches, colour studies and unfinished watercolours. I shall now re-mount one of my favourite hobby-horses.

By looking at almost any of the sketches that show bare rock or craggy country lightly clothed in shrubs and trees, even an amateur geologist could tell whether the tubby little man had been staring intently at a variety of volcanic rocks, tabular limestone, Carboniferous limestone, Jurassic sandstone, grit, dolerite, irregularly bedded shales, chalk or clays. Transmute what he saw later on, as he so often did, initially, in the field – and he was almost always in the field or looking hard at the manifest strength of the sea – he was wholly absorbed by geographic essentials. Although I don't know whether he had any training in basic geology, visually he was at one with Coleridge who, intellectually, strove to see the history of the earth as a product of the power of life or, as he put it, 'the original fluidity of the planet'.

Although he travelled much further afield in later life, Turner might be considered as one of the first in Yorkshire's public relations business. The son of a Covent Garden barber and a more than slightly mad mother, his patrons were the Lascelles of Harewood and it was to Wharfedale he went in 1797, his first long journey, and he decided to use the opportunity to make a tour of the North Country as a whole. Ten years later he struck up a close relationship with another rich patron, Walter Fawkes of Farnley Hall, which became his northern retreat. He was probably happier there than anywhere else.

Napoleon's domination of the Continent meant that droves of romantic travellers were confined to Britain and where could they find more dramatic scenery than that sketched and painted by the man 'with a lobster red face, twinkling, staring grey eyes, white tie, blue coat and brass buttons, crab-shell turned up boots, large fluffy hat and an enormous umbrella'? He died miserably, a recluse in the company of pot-house whores, but very rich and famous. Roland Smith who knows the Dales intimately tells us about what inspired Turner.

J.H.

*In Turner's Footsteps (John Murray, 1984).

THE STRIDING DALES

ROLAND SMITH

It is curious how a particular piece of music can clearly evoke a certain place and time. Stevie Wonder's jazz-rock tribute to Duke Ellington, called 'Sir Duke', will always take me back to the Yorkshire Dales classic one-day excursion, the Three Peaks.

A ferociously hot June day. The sun reflected off the pearl-grey limestone walls and scars with the intensity of a photographic flash. We'd met friends from the Midlands at the camp site behind the New Inn by the bridge in Horton-in-Ribblesdale. Wonder's hit tune had been played constantly on the car radio on the way up to Yorkshire, and had firmly imprinted itself on our subconscious.

I had done the 24-mile route once before, and remembered the flicker of panic we'd felt after being caught in shifting mists and thickening light on Ingleborough's bald and featureless summit. Concerned about the possibility of being benighted, I'd encouraged my companion to *run* down from the col on Simon Fell Breast, risking twisted ankles, through the scars and pavements of Sulber Nick. Safe but breathless we eventually reached Horton in driving rain and almost pitch darkness.

Another unforgettable memory of that day came as we contoured across Souther Scales Fell on the climb up to Ingleborough from the Hill Inn at Chapel-le-Dale. We had walked into a sudden, drenching downpour of rain, and as we slowly gained height up the fellside, the sun came out with that crystal clarity which often follows a shower. Down the dale, the limestone pavements of Raven Scar shimmered and glistened like a newly polished suit of armour.

As the fellside started to steam in the sudden change of temperature we found ourselves surrounded by huge, black slugs which emerged from the tussocky grass to enjoy a natural Turkish bath. I don't know what the collective noun for slugs is, but a 'slither' seemed the most appropriate as we carefully picked our way through those slimy molluscs. I learned later that this could have been the annual slug mating session, and that all slugs are hermaphrodites. At least they are sensible enough usually to mate with another slug and not with themselves, for it can't be much fun being a slug at the best of times.

However, back to that June excursion, several years later. We didn't encounter many other walkers on the route then, but today the circuit has become the victim of its own popularity, and up to £750,000 is needed by the Yorkshire Dales National Park authority for footpath restoration.

Setting out from Horton through the hamlet of Brackenbottom, with the familiar 'crouching lion' profile of Pen-y-Ghent rising challengingly ahead, we joined Tom Stephenson's Pennine Way at Gavel Rigg and picked our way up through the delightful staircase of shale-grit steps of the Yoredale series to reach the flat summit and its superb panoramic view. One of the most attractive features of the Three Peaks is that you can usually see your next goal from each summit, and each has its own special character and identity. Pen-y-Ghent is many people's favourite, a lovely mountain form and a satisfying summit. Ahead of us, looking like a great stranded whale across the broad expanse of Ribblesdale, lay the next objective, Whernside.

There are some place names which precisely

Ingleton Glen near Ingleborough Hill in North Yorkshire.

match their physical characteristics, for instance Black Dub Moss, Long Mires and Dismal Hill, on the 7 miles of unrelenting bog-trotting between Pen-y-Ghent and Ribblehead. It is a relief to leave from under the still-threatened arches of the Batty Moss viaduct for the monotonous treadmill up Skelside to Whernside summit.

Whernside at 2,414 feet is the highest of the Three Peaks and the highest hill in Yorkshire – but it is also without doubt the most boring. It doesn't quite match the 4,050 feet credited to it by John Bigland in his *Geographical and Historical View of the World* in 1810, but then old Bigland (and perhaps the name was significant) believed: 'The mountains of Craven in Yorkshire, especially Whamside, Pennygant and Ingleborough are the highest in England.' It was an opinion he shared with many other early topographical writers.

Most modern walkers have elevated the next summit on the walk, Ingleborough, to the Everest of Yorkshire. It is apparently climbed by about 120,000 people a year, and has become something

of a pilgrimage to the young men and women of the county. It's said that a Yorkshireman cannot be called a true Yorkshireman until he has reached its spacious summit. Ingleborough imposes itself on the whole walk; possibly it has to do with a half-forgotten folk memory. Its millstone-grit cap is encompassed by a 15-acre Iron Age hill fort, thought to be the last stronghold of the Brigantian leader, Venutius, against the invading Romans.

One author has compared Ingleborough to Massada, the fortress hill by the Dead Sea where an army of fanatical Jews also held out against the Roman, before finally committing lemming-like mass suicide from its rocky summit rather than admit defeat. I have a sneaking feeling that if those ancient Brigantians possessed more than an ounce of good old Yorkshire common sense, they would have seen the futility of such a 'slammocky' gesture. If they were true Dalesmen, they would probably have ended up by inviting the Romans up and selling them some parkin for a few sesterce.

My final recollection of that sweltering day was the surrealist sight of the turquoise 'Blue Lagoon' under the glaring white cliffs of the eyesore of Horton Quarry, as we dropped back into Horton. How this kind of wanton desecration can be countenanced within a National Park is beyond belief.

It is the limestone dust dissolved in the water which gives the Blue Lagoon its unnatural colour, and it is this stone, known for good reason as the Great Scar limestone, which attracts both quarrymen and lovers of fine scenery, and gives the Dales their unique quality. Limestone is a fascinating rock, unique in that it creates landforms simultaneously both above and below the ground. Nowhere is this topsy-turvy, overground–underground world seen better than in the Craven area of the Yorkshire Dales National Park. Formed from the fossilized skeletons of tiny sea creatures which lived and died in a warm, tropical sea some 330 million years ago, the Great Scar limestones have a special, eye-blinking whiteness when the sun shines on them.

That authority on the geology and history of the Dales, Dr Arthur Raistrick, graphically illustrated the mind-boggling antiquity of these bones of the landscape in his description of Thornton Force, near Ingleton, in *The Pennine Dales*. At the end of a charming, family-length stroll up the waterfall-punctuated gorge of the Doe, which Wainwright described as the most delightful walk of its kind in the country, is a classic example of what geologists call an 'unconformity', which simply means that the rocks do not conform to their correct chronological strata.

Under the overhanging lip of the 46-foot waterfall – scramble behind it if you are feeling adventurous – there is a distinct shelf where the Carboniferous limestones rest 'unconformably' on top of the upturned slates of the incredibly ancient pre-Cambrian period. Here, says Dr Raistrick, 'a hand can span with thumb and little finger touching worlds more than 300 million years apart. No one with imagination can be insensitive to the experience.'

The Ingleton Glens walk, culminating in the lovely little cove formed by Thornton Force, can hardly be described as typical of the Dales. Water-

falls, in this land of disappearing streams and pot-holes, are uncommon and it was only prehistoric faulting which exposed the impervious slate and made their creation possible, as here at Ingleton and the spectacular Hardraw Force, near Hawes in Wensleydale.

As in the case of the sweeping amphitheatre of Malham Cove and in the numerous dry dales of the limestone, most of the waterfalls disappeared at the end of the last Ice Age. Wayfarers wending their foot-tired way up the new, man-made staircase by the side of Malham's towering cliffs should ponder that the former Malham Force, fed by the meltwater of the retreating glaciers, exceeded Niagara at its height. Some idea of the immense power of those post-glacial rivers can be gained from that great gash, Gordale Scar, a short walk to the east, which was also scoured out by those primeval floods. That manipulator of light, J. W. Turner, caught it exactly.

For the pleasure of exploring Halliwell Sutcliffe's 'Striding Dales', follow the stone-walled switchback known as Mastiles Lane, an ancient monastic track linking the sheep-ranching estates at Kilnsey and Malham. To walk along this grassy green highway is to follow the white-robed Cistercians who created enormous wealth by harbouring huge flocks on these curlew-haunted pastures. In doing so, they changed the face of the Dales. It is humbling to think, as you stride across Kilnsey Moor via High Long Ridge and the quarries of Coolscar, that you might be stubbing your toe on the same stones as did those sandal-clad Cistercians of seven centuries ago.

The great overhang of Kilnsey, frowning down on pastoral Wharfedale, marks the high point of the last Ice Age glaciers. It reminds me of the white cowls of those monks who lived beside the former glacial lake on the floor of the valley. Besides their thriving trade in wool the monks of Kilnsey also cut thatching reeds and quarried lime as modern quarrymen still do today.

The great overhang of Kilnsey Crag, frowning down on pastoral Wharfedale.

LEFT: *The remains of Fountains Abbey in Nidderdale.*

RIGHT: *The rocky confines of Gordale Scar near Malham, North Yorkshire, formed in exactly the same way as Trow Gill.*

Kilnsey and Malham Granges were both out-lying farmsteads of far-off Fountains Abbey in Nidderdale. The tremendous wealth won from the soft, long-stapled Dales-bred wool is reflected in the size and magnificence of what's left of the abbeys.

Perhaps the most impressive, and complete, walk in the Dales is the 9-mile ascent of Ingleborough, the region's legendary capital, from Clapham, via Trow Gill and Gaping Gill. None other shows the fascinating and subtle mix of limestone (above and below ground) and mill-stone grit than this very satisfying trail.

Leaving the pretty little village of Clapham, with a pottery which produces warm, flowerpot-red wares from locally dug clay, you pay a small fee and pass through the grounds of the Ingleborough Estate of the Farrer family. Reginald Farrer (1881–1920) was a great Edwardian botanist and collector of rare plants which he brought back and introduced round a delightful ornamental lake formed by damming the Clapham Beck. The walk through the Reginald Farrer Nature Trail is a charmingly sylvan prelude, along well-engineered paths, to the pleasant moorland above, though it's

surprising to find great stands of Himalayan bamboo in the heart of the Dales.

Breaking out of the higher beech plantations by an ugly grotto, you enter Clapdale proper. Generations of walkers have wondered at the rhythmic clanking emitted from the low blockhouse to the right of the path by the beck. It comes from an ingenious ram pump which transports the waters of the beck to Clapdale Farm, 100 feet above the path to the left. Passing the summertime picnickers tempted by the gurgling beck and the grassy sward of the valley, you soon reach the impressive low entrance to Ingleborough Cave at Beck Head. One of the great show caves of the Dales, this extends far beyond the public galleries into the cold, grey heart of the limestone towards Gaping Gill. For 146 years cavers sought for the connection between the Gaping Gill and Ingleborough Cave systems, but the famed missing link was not found until 1983.

As you leave Ingleborough Cave, the path rises steadily and then turns left by a wall into the rocky confines of Trow Gill, a Lilliputian gorge formed in exactly the same way as the more celebrated examples at Malham and Gordale. There's an

The dramatic Hardraw Scaur near Hawes in Wensleydale.

entertaining little scramble up the boulder choke at the top of the gorge and then suddenly, over a stile on Clapham Bottoms, you enter the other, moorland world of the Dales. A short step across the open fellside past the capped-off shafts of other minor potholes leads to the great, yawning gulf of the grandfather of them all, Gaping Gill.

Normally, pedestrians can only stand well back from the edge of this chasm and watch as Fell Beck drops 365 feet into an underground cavern said to be big enough to swallow York Minster. But for two weeks every summer, members of two local caving clubs erect a winch and bosun's chair so that the daring can, for a fee, explore the underground delights of Gaping Gill. (The cavers crack the rather ponderous joke that the trip down is free; the charge is only made for bringing you back up.)

Passing, by chance, at the right time a few years ago, my daughter and I made the exhilarating descent into the depths of the earth, and then were led on a mucky scramble to another chamber appropriately called Mud Hall. This was a taste of *real* caving – cold, wet, muddy and very dark – and a world away from brightly illuminated Ingleborough Cave down the hill. It was a memorable experience nonetheless.

Back on the surface, you head across the boggy open fell for the cairned ridge end of Little Ingleborough, contouring up the stony slopes to the main summit which is guarded by craggy outcrops.

In the frequent mists, it is easy to imagine yourself back in the days of Venutius and his Brigantes, waiting anxiously for the Romans on their commanding hilltop. When those mists clear, and the view extends across the Dales to Bowland, Morecambe Bay and the hills of Lakeland, you begin to understand why Venutius thought he could rule the world.

That's the magic of Ingleborough and the striding Dales.

SOME YOUTHFUL IDEAS

One of them, of course, was the feeling that I would never grow old, an illusion shared by all my generation, a fancy that will last as long as youth endures. All the evidence stood against me on two wind-bitten tomb-stones in the old churchyard at Pontefract in West Yorkshire which proclaimed in almost indecipherable lettering that two remarkable old men, my great-grandfather and my grandfather, both called John Hillaby, both top-grade walkers, had died in their mid-eighties.

But that was many years ago and I now know that fancy cannot cheat for long. The cormorant years gobble us up; the dear delusion dies. The asp accomplished what age had not done to Cleopatra and the Flying Dutchman comes at last to port.

Youth may not be all that the Shropshire Lad put to stirring quatrains but by the blessed Saint Willibrord, who once walked two leagues south of Rome during some pious introspection, there are few things better than pedestrian athletics to ensure contentment in riper years. By youth I haven't so much in mind an army of likeable teenagers who don't often get the press the majority of them deserve.

Rather, I am thinking of those from unsure-footed toddlers who can be carried on your back on their first walkabouts, to children up to the age of nine or ten for whom a few hours in the country, the more free the better, is just pure adventure with grassy slopes on which to roll, daisies to make into crowns and coronets and mud to be splashed through without any pious finger-wagging. A hollow tree, a gaunt rock face or a plank over a ditch is always a good setting for an old-fashioned folk-tale and it's not too difficult to make magic touched with a bit of basic biology about what lies behind the songs and calls of a dozen different kinds of common birds. No one more than children is more subconsciously aware of beauty and the sheer joy of being alive. Women know this. It is fitting therefore that our sole woman contributor should start by describing how she brought up two lively youngsters in a distinctly exotic environment.

J.H.

WALKING IN THE FAMILY WAY

KATHLEEN BURTON

I was pregnant at the time. Second child due to arrive pretty soon. In that exotic part of the world there were no ante-natal clinics so we consulted Dr Spock who advocated daily walking as a desirable routine. Fortunately my three-year-old daughter loved walking too. But being extremely hot at that time of the year she had more energy than I had. Swelling hands and feet told me when to turn back and change the regimen from exercise to relaxation.

I suggested we should return home. But she just wanted to go on and on. On narrow paths bounded by tea bushes she didn't run away, she simply lay down, flat on her back in front of me and refused to move. How did she know I couldn't bend down and lift her? Anyway she won.

In a district where the lie of the land is comparable to the Peak District or the Yorkshire Dales and criss-crossed with tracks, tea estates afford ideal walking conditions. The tracks were created for the labourers to reach distant fields for plucking, weeding, draining and pruning on widely scattered parts of the property, and the planters walked miles each day to superintend these activities. I put this in the past tense because even before I left, technology had started to creep in with mopeds and motor scooters.

The labourers had no choice but to walk. It was their only mobility. They did it not for the pleasure of the exercise, as we did; simply to reach the nearest village, or the main road to catch a bus to the town several miles away.

Each estate had its own lorry, sometimes more than one, to transport plucked leaf to the factory and fertilizer to the fields. The roads were often dreadfully rough but when a lorry driver saw us walking he would invariably stop to offer a lift. He couldn't understand that we walked for pleasure rather than necessity.

Most planters kept dogs in the dual role of companion and house guard. They were bitches rather than dogs, as the males of the species tended to stray to the native 'lines' when the mongrel 'pi' dogs were on heat – distinctly undesirable in a country where rabies had not been eradicated. It was truly a dog's life with a master to be accompanied on long adventures most of the day. Dogs everywhere cover far greater distances than humans on the same outing. Could it be that they have four legs and we have only two? Or that they are constantly doubling back on their tracks?

I can't now recall what wiles or gentle bribery I used to entice small girl back home, but I do know that within a few days our family had been increased by the arrival of a son and in due course he, being a normally healthy child, also learned to walk. I'm not the sort of Mum who frequently recalls her children's first faltering footsteps, but our son's were rather unconventional. Sally – short for Salote as she was, like the popular Tongan Queen, a large black lady – our gentle Labrador, was his constant companion at that time. She would stroll slowly round the lawn with a small boy's forearm resting along her spine whilst he tottered along beside her. But all that now seems long ago and far away, a short exotic instalment in the long-running serial story of my walking in Britain.

When we were kids – a word my mother would never allow me to use saying that it should only be applied to goats – everybody walked everywhere.

Or so it always seemed to us. By 'everywhere' I don't mean that we didn't use trains and buses, I mean that we could walk safely on grass verges even alongside major roads; children could roam happily without parental supervision or concern for their safety. We could cross farmland, using recognized paths, never dreaming that within our lifetimes the question of public footpaths and rights of way would become a national issue.

The local Infants' School had a kindergarten class which to my intense delight I was allowed to attend at the age of four. I don't think my mother accompanied me on the three-quarter of a mile's walk from home after about the first day. I walked down with the greengrocer's son of the same age who lived across the road, my first male escort. I was teased about my young boyfriend and according to Mum wept when shortly after the affair started an epidemic of some childish disease caused the closure of the kindergarten class and I had to await the important fifth birthday to resume my education.

Come to think of it, I've done my fair share of walking with boyfriends since that early start. But my early male walking companion was usually my father. Not just the two of us. Two sisters were included in the outings and perhaps Mum as well, though I suspect sometimes Daddy just took us off to let her go about her domestic duties without interference, or give her a break from childish chatter.

With hindsight it's impossible to gauge how much of our family walking had been dictated by the fact that my parents never owned a car. Neither did those of so many of my schoolfellows but I have no recollection of similar outings within their families. We didn't regard it as a hobby, nor as walking with a capital W as it seems to be regarded by some organizations nowadays. It was simply a part of our way of life.

The outbreak of war – World War II, I mean – more or less coincided with my reaching the status of teenager. By this time my elder sister and I had a circle of friends, a mixed gang of about a dozen, mostly slightly older than myself, who spent innumerable happy hours together. Sixpenny seats in the local cinema at the first house on Saturday evening. Early winter darkness drove us indoors

after the show; my parents kept open house and we played darts or bagatelle. But on light summer evenings we walked – all of us, on the cliff-top patch, or along the seashore until Coastal Defence Forces closed the beaches with barbed wire and we had to revert to the country roads, producing identity cards as we passed through military barriers on the outskirts of the town.

Air-raid warnings sounded frequently as Hitler's bombers droned in to pulverize yet again what was described as 'one of our north-east towns'. The revolving beam of the local lighthouse, the nightlight of our childhood, no longer accompanied our evening outings and was replaced by stabbing searchlights. The gang gradually dispersed as the boys exchanged their school cap badges for military ones and even before call-up age we had more important ways of filling our leisure hours.

Walking now started to play a different role in

'Taking the grandchildren for a walk in Yorkshire.'

179

my life although unlike so many of my contemporaries I didn't have it imposed on me in the form of route marches. Formal higher education seemed an unnecessary luxury when so many of my friends were in the forces, so after gaining a school certificate I took an office job in that north-east town. Unable to walk to work at twenty miles' distance we travelled by train. 'We' because my father was then working close by and we often met during lunch breaks. And what did we do? We walked.

My father, an unambitious man, a man of moderate appetites, was an avid reader with an unquenchable thirst for knowledge. From him I inherited a vast curiosity about almost everything. He taught me to explore. Not the Sahara Desert or the Amazon Valley but what could be found at the end of the next street and around the next corner. He knew the history and the topography of the Old Town and the names of most of the flowers and trees, and as we walked we talked. And as we talked I learned.

Outgrowing family holidays at a time when travelling was difficult and my budget rather small, an aunt suggested I might try guest house holidays of the kind which cater for organized daily walking parties. I delighted in the added dimension of what we then called rambling. We were divided into groups of A, B or C standard, depending on the toughness of the outings. I loved the chance to meet new people, make new friends and explore fresh countryside.

Two or three hours by train to Sheffield brought us to the little local railway which in those days chuffed along into the real walking centres of the Peak District, an area I grew to know and love. After the flat lands of my native Holderness even the Peak hills were something of a challenge and never before had I appreciated the feeling of luxury engendered by a hot shower and clean clothes at the end of a 20-mile day.

When travel became easier again we moved further afield and before long I exchanged annual holiday journeys for a much longer one to what used to be called one of the outposts of Empire. After rearing the children in the tropics eventually at the sad end of a marriage I brought them back to settle in my native Yorkshire.

After hot seasons alternating with monsoons the English spring and autumn colours attracted us to the countryside again, and the seasons came and went. Now I am back to walking with children again. My daughter's first-born, Rebecca, has been a joy and delight ever since her first appearance more than nine years ago. Not only does she love walking but also she is already a very receptive budding naturalist and we are required to identify all the trees, birds and flowers en route.

A couple of years ago after a school visit to the seaside she had a catch question: 'Nan, do you know what is a decapod?' I suggested she might be thinking of a crab. Response: 'Hooray! Nan knows. And it's called a decapod because it has ten legs. That's from the Latin.'

But grannies must keep their ends up so I countered by asking her why an octopus is so called. Only a very slight pause before 'The same reason, Latin again because it has eight legs.' It's much

'Rebecca, my daughter's eldest child, taking her grandmother for a walk.'

more interesting than computers, isn't it? And that's my comment, not hers.

Around that time we took her walking – a slog for her of about 9 miles. She got a little bored on some stretches. We stopped to investigate a bird on a fence which made a ticking noise like a rusty old grandfather clock. A resident stonechat or migrant whinchat? Both look and sound much the same. Then I asked her if we could get to the next bend in less than ten minutes, well knowing that we could do it in no more than six. Of course she was awarded winning points when we beat my suggested time. This great game continued until we reached a spot which we, but not she, knew was under an overhang with an excellent pub only two minutes' walk on the road above. Then it transpired that the day-sack we were carrying with rainwear 'just in case' also contained a picnic lunch so she and I stretched out on the grass whilst her beloved 'poppa John' disappeared to return – no doubt duly fortified with a pint of something or other – with cans of lemonade to sustain us on the way back. I'm a fairly law-abiding citizen, but I think bribery is justified on some occasions.

When I visited my daughter last year Rebecca decided it was her turn to take Nan for a walk. They live in a farm cottage in open agricultural country at the north end of the Vale of York. Mum had warned that there was only half an hour left until teatime. We followed a motorable road and I was instructed about the lark rising from the cornfield and had to ponder why we didn't see the usual pheasants, then was abruptly told to turn left on to an almost unidentifiable path – which she with her superior knowledge assured me was a right of way – alongside a field of growing corn, higher than my waist, with vicious nettles and thistles the same height in the hedge bottom on the other side of the path. She was wearing her play jeans. As I had called on my way home from town I was not so suitably dressed. Like her mother thirty years before, I felt she'd got the better of me.

Grand-daughter number two is not yet three years old. Kate-Mary was named after me and whether in being an early walker and a late talker she takes after me I don't know. Nowadays when I see them, not as often as I would like, and Rebecca

'A lovely walk on a blowy day in good company.'

comes for her expected cuddle, Kate pushes Big Sister aside and says 'No, she's my Nanna'. My heart is torn between the two of them and I dearly hope she will get as much out of this walking business as Rebecca and I have always done.

Although she is still at the age of trying to run before she can walk I do my best to encourage her. As my father taught me, and I have realized even more since, there's so much to be learnt by walking. I think to have an older sister or brother with whom to compete in any field is a valuable asset. With the young you must always be assured you are not putting them in any danger, nor any position from which they may have to be rescued. If you avoid difficult places and teach them how to tackle bad weather conditions, they will appreciate the comfort of knowing that walking is an exercise without any fears.

You may be a loner yourself, but if they are gregarious by instinct encourage them to join groups, always first making sure that they are welcome. It

is downright bad manners just to tag along with other people because they happen to be going in the same direction, like intruding in a private conversation. These are lessons I have yet to impart. But now I must jump backwards quite a number of years.

My daughter was one of the children who walk before they talk. Though never a great walker she's made up for it by talking ever since. Son, on the other hand, talked first and has been walking ever since. During one university vac. he walked alone across the north of Scotland, pioneering his own route by poring over maps which have been one of his passions since early childhood. He used to be a non-gregarious animal until he met his wife, now my dear daughter-in-law. She is not a great walker but he still devises long treks when she needs to be left peacefully about her own pursuits.

Before he eventually flew the parental nest just over ten years ago his cousin came to spend a few days with us. Neither of them had transport then and so I, working full time, said that if they would amuse themselves meantime I would drive them to wherever they chose for a day out on the Saturday. They selected Rosedale where Cousin had happy memories of camping when involved with the Scout movement. I had my own recollections of a happy Easter weekend I'd spent there in my courting days, though I didn't care to recall how long ago, so I readily agreed on the one condition that I wouldn't stand them a pub lunch unless the three of us *walked* first. We did. The pub lunch arrived. So did a man I'd never met before. Five years later I married him.

I soon got back to walking 20 miles a day. On my second honeymoon I backpacked and camped for the first time in my life. I still walk every day – no – I must say *we* still walk every day. Wherever we are. I am still asking questions about all I see. My husband has many of the answers and also an extensive reference library to be consulted. His name is John Hillaby.

Rosedale Head from Blakey Ridge in North Yorkshire.

SPIRITUAL TRAILS

They walked. From the north-east coast of ancient Northumbria, especially Lindisfarne known still as Holy Island, they walked the length of Europe. The irregular movement of a horse disturbed their long hours of prayer and meditation and it would be unseemly for a humble priest to be seen in a cart. So they made it in that most exhilarating of ways, on foot. In the eighth century that great scholar and theologian, Alcuin of York, walked at least twice a year to Herstal, now an outskirt of Liège, where Charlemagne, that King David of the Dark Ages, held high court and put his seal to all manner of important decrees. Alcuin, his spiritual adviser, brought him news of the brotherhood, of Peter the Grammarian, Paul the Deacon, Godescal the Illuminator, Clement the Irishman, Dungal, Durcuil and many more. All Gospel spreaders walked, those Athletes of God, a phrase I have borrowed from the life of St Willibrord of Holderness whose feast day is still celebrated at Echternacht on Whit Monday by thousands dancing through the streets, led by the princes of the Church. To a man those missionaries feared the Vikings, the sea-wolves whose longships with their terrible prows had already been sighted off the Humber, a sinister, exploratory fleet from Jorundsfjord and Borre.

J.H.

THE ATHLETES OF GOD

JOHN HILLABY

From the age of nine or thereabouts I heard a great deal about Holy Island but with scant enthusiasm since, in a vain effort to stem an irrepressible urge to go walkabout, entomologizing, collecting rocks and fishing in the nearby Dales, I had been unwillingly recruited to add my childish pipe to the choir of St Chad's, Headingley, a hilly, self-conscious suburb, half an hour's stride from the centre of soot-blackened Leeds. There, it must be faced, I wasn't among the most promising of choristers. I disliked cricket which, locally, came close to blasphemy; nor was I much inspired by weekly talks from the Vicar on the life and times on Lindisfarne when four brothers, Chad, Cedd, Celin and Cynebil, the first two eventually canonized, spread the word of God among the heathen Angles. Angles themselves, they were all pupils of saintly Aidan, successor to St Columba, who brought The Word from Ulster to Iona on the West Coast of Scotland and from thence to the beautiful island of Lindisfarne.

We must pause awhile for another war to end all wars and my need afterwards to earn the price of a roof and bread by reporting the derring-do of others. It happened, no matter how, that I spent over a month of exciting days in the Hebrides with the late Gavin Maxwell, gifted poet, painter and travel writer who had started a shark fishery based on Soay, an islet off Skye, a ruinous adventure that led him on to many more abroad and eventually a sad death.

After a buffeting both from a gale and a 20-foot basking shark that refused to die quietly, we lay literally holed up in Tobermory where shipwrights were imported from Clydeside to put the *Sea Leopard* to rights and I walked round the spectac-ular volcanic debris of Mull before settling down for two or three days on Iona, the Mother of Lindisfarne. Among the visiting pilgrims were several Benedictines led by their scholarly prior whom, since I forget his name, I shall refer to as Father Theodore. He was an authority on the ancient Celtic churchmen, especially those anchorites who lived in extreme austerity on bread, water, beans and a few wild herbs. He and his brotherhood were there to study aspects of the astonishing life of Columkille or, as he is better known, St Columba, the first Celtic missionary to Britain, and this is how he related it.

Born in 521 in north-west Ireland, 'The Dove of the Church' was the descendant of a notable king called Niall of the Nine Hostages, an aristocratic Christian with a powerful *fianna* or blood-bound clan of warriors. Those were days when it was unsafe to move about unarmed. Columba, to simplify his name, was ordained as a priest at the age of twenty-four and for the next fifteen years he travelled round Ireland founding, some say, over a hundred monasteries which may be likened to universities since the communities were threefold in structure. The novices were taught to read and write in Latin; afterwards they tilled the land, served meals and built additions to their retreat until their abbot considered them fit for a life of prayer, meditation and religious instruction or missionary work elsewhere. And then a most curious thing happened.

Finnian of Moville, a friend of his, possessed a new copy of the Gospels which Columba coveted. Rather than risk a refusal, he copied it secretly in his cell but he was seen. Somebody told Finnian who was incensed at his friend's behaviour and

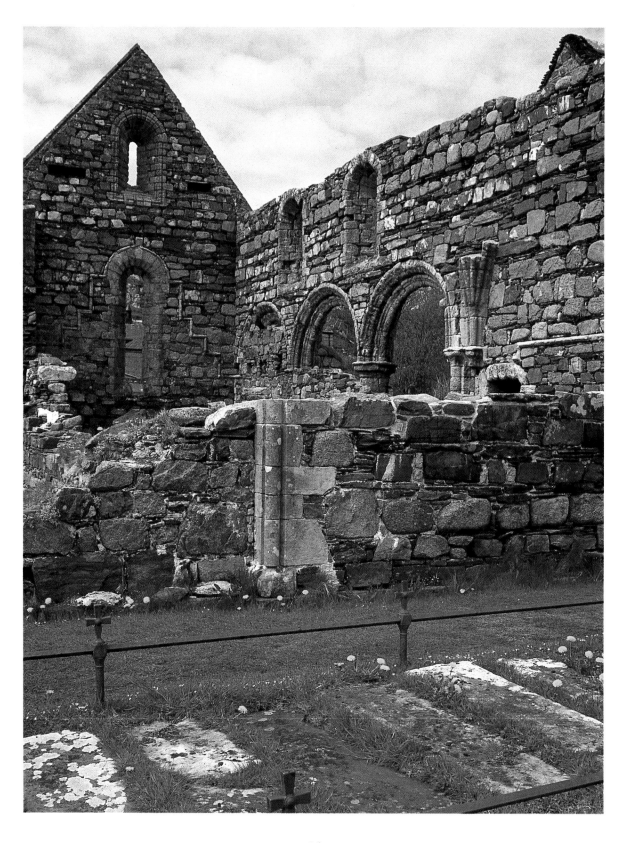

ABOVE: *Lindisfarne Castle on Holy Island.*

LEFT: *Remains of the Benedictine Nunnery at Iona.*

claimed that both the original and the copy were his own property. Arguments ensued and the matter had to be put to the King and his counsellors who, after much debate, adjudged in favour of Finnian on the grounds that 'the calf belonged to the cow', from which sprang the tradition and, many centuries later, the laws of copyright. Unbidden, Columba's family *fianna* rallied all those traditionally bound to their lord by the *sippe*, the blood-tie, and from a simple act, right or wrong as it may have been, skirmishing took place which, when the news got around, culminated in the great battle of Clonleve, the Battle of the Books in which thousands are reputed to have died, some killed after being captured. Columba, the story goes, was implicated in atrocities and whether banished or whether he fled intent on a great act of penitence nobody knows.

The fact is that in 563 that temperamental lord who became the priest known in Gaelic both as

'The Dove of the Church' and *Crimthan*, the Wolf, together with ten companions including his close friends, Brothers Finn Breenagh and Oran The Learned, set sail for south-west Scotland where half a century earlier his fellow countrymen had established the spreading colony of Dalriada. They landed at Iona where they knelt and prayed, planted a cross on the highest point they could find and dug a shallow grave. Then comes the strangest part of this tale.

Columba declared that, as he intended to take possession of the little island and build a monastery where he could no longer see his own country, it was necessary to make a human sacrifice. Oran promptly volunteered and, after embracing them all and in turn receiving Columba's blessing, he lay down in the grave with his arms outstretched and his legs crossed in the manner of his Redeemer, while the weeping brethren covered him gently with earth. He prayed audibly until they could no longer hear him. They kept silence for a week but collected stone and clay and wattles and cut and trimmed a dozen trees for the foundations of cells like beehives.

'But how could such a thing be?' I asked Father Theodore. 'They were Christians, all of them.'

'Christians yes,' he said, 'but you must remember you are dealing with an Iron Age society newly converted from the gods of barbarism about which we know very little. Cernonus, perhaps, the huge-horned stag. Or Epona who was both a queen and a riggish mare. This is what we've been trying to find out in Ulster.'

The sequel to the protracted death of Brother Oran is no less surprising than its inception. A fortnight passed. The brethren built a double stockade of pine stakes interwoven with willow strikes. A torrent was dammed and the water filtered through a mattress of ling. For the sanctuary they needed old oak beams, *Cranoch* from the ancient lakeside dwellings of Mull. Columba yearned for a last look at his friend. Oran was partially disinterred. He was still able to speak but, instead of pieties, he just managed to whisper: 'There is no wonder in death, nor is hell as it is reported.'

Columba was shocked. 'Throw dust on Oran's eyes,' he shouted, 'lest he blab further.' We hear no more of his friend who eventually became known as *Baw un Geeah*, the Lamb of God.

From Iona there emerged almost two centuries of ceaseless evangelical work. The brotherhood built more cells and recruited novices. Bibles were written on parchment made from the skins of calves and goats and carried to new-founded communities on neighbouring islands where they were copied out yet again. Could there be psychological reasons behind Columba's almost obsessional preoccupation with Bible production and distribution? Visitors arrived both secular and religious. The sick were healed. Miracles were attributed to the Dove of the Church. With interpreters in his retinue he journeyed up the Great Glen in an effort to convert the Picts, those shadowy war-like tribes we know almost nothing about except that they were understandably hostile towards those earlier immigrants from Ulster behind the shields of Finn McCumhal. We don't know with what success except that when the King of Dalriada died, Columba managed to secure the succession of Aidan, not the austere monk who was eventually canonized but a man outside the matriarchal line which must have been a very difficult thing to do. He was eventually consecrated on Iona.

In 593 when nearly 72 years old, Columba had a premonition which the Church called a vision that told him he would die within four years. After that he seems to have predicted accurately the moment of his death to within a few hours. His biographer tells us in detail of his last day:

'He went slowly round his island for the last time, blessing it and predicting a great future for it. His aged white horse came up to him, showing touching signs of distress and affection: Columba remarked how marvellous it was that a beast could know of his approaching death by instinct while the men nearest to him had not known of it until he told them. He spent some time copying the Scriptures, always a loved activity for him, and gave his last message to the community. When the bell rang for the midnight service he used his last strength in stumbling to the little church and there before the altar, in a blaze of unearthly light, he died.'

Meanwhile Oswald, a Christian convert, following years of exile in Scotland, defeated Cadwaller, King of North Wales, and reunited the kingdoms of Bernicia and Deira. From his capital at Bebbanburgh near the gaunt re-built coastal castle of Bamburgh, 20 miles south-west of Berwick-on-Tweed, he established Northumbrian supremacy from the Humber to the Forth. It was Oswald who sent to Iona for a missionary and after a somewhat unhappy experience with Brother Corman who didn't get on at all well with the Northumbrians, describing them as 'an uncivilized people of obstinate and barbarous temperament', in 635 the King besought Aidan, the man who was eventually canonized, to return to Northumbria from Iona and set up a community 'wheresoever he pleased.'

The gaunt re-built coastal castle of Bamburgh.

188

Aidan chose Lindisfarne because it was close to Bamburgh and he thought, wrongly, secure in its island position as the site for his church and monastery. Thus began years of blessed discipleship. He preached the Gospel throughout Northumbria, King Oswald sometimes acting as his interpreter. He walked thousands of miles and inspired others to do so since he and his successors believed that they might be overwhelmed by the Northmen and, if Christianity were to survive, its precious flames had to be lit and encouraged in as many places as possible. The missions flourished not least because lands were gifted for ecclesiastical purposes. Among the children who arrived at his school were the brothers, Chad, Cedd, Celin and Cynebil, and Hild, the first Northumbrian woman to take the veil. She was appointed Abbess of Hartlepool and later of Whitby. At Aidan's death a shower of stars were reported to have lit the night sky and were seen by a shepherd in the Lammermuir Hills who asked a priest what they signified and on being told that the Bishop and Abbot of the See of Lindisfarne had slipped away after days of almost incessant prayer in his lonely cell, he asked for instruction. The name of the shepherd was Cuthbert.

It has happened at first quite fortuitously that I have either crossed the trails or have been told about these athletic men of God: St Chad at Headingley, though not in circumstances to my credit; St Columba on several visits to Iona inspired by Father Theodore; St Cedd because in the early 1950s the conservationists with whom I was associated became alarmed that warm effluent from the new atomic power station at Bradwell in Essex was inhibiting the growth of the seagrass, *Zostera*, the food of vast flocks of wintering wildfowl. It was to Bradwell that St Cedd and three companions were sent from Lindisfarne to teach and baptize the Middle Saxons at the request of Peada, the young and newly converted King of Mercia. On a European walk I slipped through Holland and the Ardennes to Echternacht in Luxembourg often in the footsteps of St Willibrord and his eleven monks who set up mission stations in half a dozen kingdoms in days when it was unusual for an assertive foreigner to die quietly in his bed.

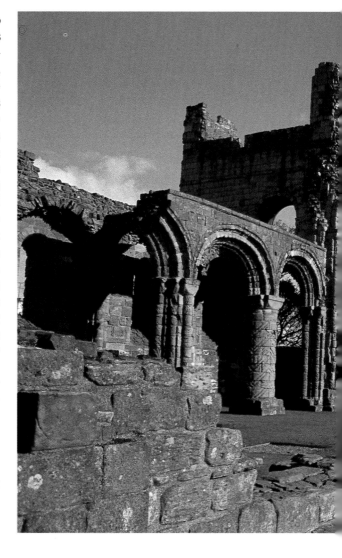

On the way to our moorland cottage in North Yorkshire – where this chapter is being written – we pass our parent church of Lastingham, a groin-vaulted treasure house described by Nikolaus Pevsner as 'unforgettable'. The Venerable Bede was much of the same opinion but for quite different reasons when he wrote that 'The craggy and distant mountains looked more like lurking places for robbers and retreats for wild beasts than habitations for men.' St Cedd walked there in 654 to seek out a site on which to build a monastery and it was there that he and thirty East Saxon monks died from a devastating outbreak of the plague. He bequeathed the abbacy of the monastery to his younger brother Chad.

ABOVE: *Statue of the blessed St Aidan at Lindisfarne.*
LEFT: *Lindisfarne Priory on Holy Island.*
BELOW: *The inscription on St Cuthbert's tomb in Durham Cathedral.*

From time to time we cross over to Lindisfarne, which is over-populous in summer but a superb retreat in the cold months. Together with the North Yorkshire Moors, the Cheviots and the fringe of the Border, this to us is where we feel most at home, especially on the coast for what Ronald Blythe describes as 'the need for the noise which the shore makes. Sea sounds became the concomitant of Celtic prayer. It sounded thin without sea cadence.' On our way there we rarely pass through Durham without standing for a few minutes, looking down on that huge slab of death-grey dolerite in the cathedral into which has been deeply chiselled that one word: CUTHBERTUS, the saintly shepherd from the Lammermuir Hills.

POETRY AND PLACES

'It is ironic', wrote Ronald Blythe,* 'that the landscape which provided the features for this country's finest spiritual allegory should be that of one of its least regarded counties where scenery is concerned.' He goes on to say that 'for years denied his wanderings across country to village meetings or to repair household utensils, prevented from preaching, cooped up, Bunyan's reaction to Bedford Gaol became that of an unstoppable river which, dammed its natural course, floods its banks.'

Although Bedfordshire may be one of our least regarded counties there is in its very soil and distant prospects some of the elements of Christian's enormous journey of the soul, as anyone may discover who has sought out the granite block in the field within the hamlet of Harrowden near Elstow that marks the site of Bunyan's cottage. Except in dry weather the going is heavy and the foot-clogging mud a chastening reminder of the Slough of Despond. But look south across Ampthill and Toddington and the eye is caught and the spirit lifted by the prospect of the Delectable Mountains, the gleaming white whale-back of the Chilterns.

On the lines of William James's *A Variety of Religious Experience* there is an evocative book to be written about the Saul-like conversion of writers with recurrent themes which must have glowed at some vital moment and then, suddenly, burst into flame on their particular roads to Damascus. It would of course abound in contraries. What possible connection could exist between E. M. Forster's *The Eternal Moment*, *The Longest Journey* and *The Celestial Omnibus* and Stevenage, his birthplace and childhood home? We may imagine what happened to Paul Verlaine and Rimbaud together in the stews of Soho in 1872 and how the Malvern Hills he loved influenced much of Masefield. There are still glimpses of John Clare's innocence around Helpston in Cambridgeshire and his fearful trials, too, if you try to walk on the A17 or press on a public right of way through a waist-high field of wet corn newly sprayed with an adhesive and irritant fungicide.

Surely it was more than fortunate coincidence that John Aubrey, the great seventeenth-century antiquarian, was born within a short walk of the skyline barrows of the Wiltshire Downs and it is not difficult to guess why D. H. Lawrence, his wife Frieda, Katherine Mansfield and John Middleton Murray sought solitude in the almost lost village of Zennor in North Cornwall. But W. H. Auden is an enigma.

A farm on the North Staffordshire moors.

   In his Preface to the *Selected Poems*†, Edward Mendelson says: 'Auden was the first poet writing in English who felt at home in the twentieth century. He welcomed in his poetry all the disordered conditions of his time, all its variety of language and event. In this, as in almost everything else, he differed from his modernist predecessors such as Yeats, Lawrence, Eliot or Pound, who had turned nostalgically away from a flawed present to some lost illusory Eden where life was unified, hierarchy secure, and the grand style a natural extension of the vernacular. All of this Auden rejected. His continuing subject was the task of the present moment, erotic and political tasks in his early poems, ethical and religious ones later. When Auden looked back into history, it was to seek the causes of his present condition, that he might act better and more effectively in the future.'

   Auden was born at York and spent his boyhood in Birmingham where his father was a distinguished physician. The scenery of his early poetry was almost invariably mountainous. He loved industrial ruins and Adam Nicolson tells us how the lead-poisoned soils of the Pennines were smelted in his superb imagination.

J.H.

Divine Landscapes, Viking, Penguin Books, 1986.
†Faber and Faber, 1979; Random House Inc.

AUDEN'S LANDSCAPE

ADAM NICOLSON

A uden avoided the obvious. 'Hate Switzer-
land,' he wrote in an account of a tour
abroad. 'Cooking rotten and architecture
hideous. Personally, give me a good hotel and a
petrol pump or city streets in a fog.' He always
maintained that scenery did not interest him. The
wild lava fields of Iceland looked, he said, 'like a
party after which no one had tidied up.'

But this, in part, was a line, because Auden was
more attuned to landscape and the layered
meanings it can carry than any English poet since
Wordsworth. And his development as a poet,
from the time he went up to Oxford as an under-
graduate in 1925 until his death in Austria in
1973, can be seen in terms of one landscape that
meant a great deal to him: the lead-mining dales
of the northern Pennines around Alston and
Nenthead, centred on the point, high on Killhope
Moor, where the borders of Northumberland,
County Durham and Cumberland all meet.

It is a deeply dissected country, where the
world of the valley and of the high, austere and
barren ridges are quite unconnected. Simply put,
Auden's poetry begins on those loveless ridges in
winter, looking down with an unresolved mixture
of envy and contempt into the warmth of the
accepting valley, and ends in the comfort of that
valley, in the summer, looking back up without
regret. Nowhere does his poetry relax into the
simple description of place. Auden was in fact
chronically short-sighted and was never – and
never wanted to be – one of the great English
observers of the natural world.

'To me Art's subject is the human clay,' he
wrote, 'And landscape but a background to a
torso.' The exact transcription of place into poetry

never interested him. 'Coming out of me living is
always thinking,' he once wrote and his poetry is
always dense with thought, with the implications
of place, with the metaphorical weight of the landscape that was neither exactly his subject nor the
background to his subject, but his subject itself, a
moral and dramatic one, seen in the precise and
concrete language that the physical world provides.

> See frozen buzzard flipped down the weir
> And carried out to sea,

is not a description of a real thing but of an
extraordinary *idea*, bound into the tangible fragments of an almost-real world, one that could be
nobody's but Auden's. The place is never removed from the mind that is considering it. The
substance and connections are never elaborated.
The hint is always enough, the fragmentary knowledge all that is available. And to walk in these
northern valleys now, as Auden often did as a
young man, with the astonishing rhetoric of his
poetry in your mind, is to experience a part of
England soaked in this harsh and altering light. It
is to walk with your mind full, to spend long, hard
days in which walking is always thinking.

These valleys and their surrounding fells –
Weardale, East and West Allen Dale, South
Tynedale and Upper Teesdale – are still a curiously unknown part of the country. They are
somehow hidden between the great routes running north on either side and overshadowed in
the obvious mind by the glamour of the Lake
District to the west and the charm of the more
famous Pennine dales southwards. Both these
dales now, and the peculiarly haunted landscapes

View of between Stanhope and Edmondbyers in Weardale, Durham. The valleys and surrounding fells in this part of the country are still curiously unknown.

of Auden's early poetry which stems from them, are parts of a hidden country, thick with its own private meanings and private history.

The time to walk there is the winter. It needn't be a hard winter because every winter is hard here. It always snows and frosts will often last all day in the wind. The passes will be blocked with snow, and the rough tufts of the moor grasses will emerge from the snow that is blown away from them in the constant wind. The hard lines of the stone walls remain sharp on the valley side 'disciplining the fell' as one Auden poem puts it and the whole landscape is stiffened into black and white. You will crouch with relief in the crook of a stone wall against the wind, where sheep have sheltered before you and the stones are bound together by old ice and snow. You will learn to recognize the look of each valley simply by the cut of its walls, where the intake makes angular slices up on to the high moor. The houses are set apart, joined together in the day-time by the field walls, but at night becoming separate points of light like yellow stars, fragmenting into private lives and mirroring, as if through a marginally warmer filter, the sparse constellations above them. The map is covered with the angular consonants of Norse names – this is Viking country: Staneshaw Rigg, Bleagate, Low Skydes, Northgrain, Annat Walls, Howgillsike, Hartleycleugh, Holmsfoot, Intack, Foreshield-grains, Blagillhead, Black Band, Killhope Law and Seldom Seen. There is a harshness already here which is foreign to England. Or at least it is a foreignness, which like so much in Tolkien, whom Auden greatly admired, has been half translated into English and remains only half-articulate. It is a country depicted in its own rigid fragments.

And underlying it all are the mines. There is – or was: they have been picked clean now – an extraordinary concentration under these fells of mineral veins, some of copper and iron but most of lead, with a tiny but valuable fraction of silver mixed in. The first miners, who were here at least as long ago as the twelfth century and may themselves have found the remains of Roman workings, did little more than pick away at those places where the veins broke surface. Those places were soon exhausted and the miners took to 'hushing'. A stream would be dammed above a small valley. When a large enough head of water had built up, the dam would be breached, and the water would surge down the valley, stripping the top layers away and revealing with luck the minerals beneath them. But even that in time was not enough. In the eighteenth and nineteenth centuries, when lead mining reached its peak in these valleys, every vein was chased and removed from these hills. There was some magic in it. The veins had characters. Some were reliable and long-lasting; others whittled away to nothing in a few feet.

A nineteenth-century guide to the mines, a copy of which Auden owned as a boy, describes how the miners here assumed 'a sort of volition in the mineral world. Thus they speak of a vein being *frightened* to climb the hill, and she therefore *swings away* to the sun side (a feminine appellation being generally used). The throw of the strata is attributed, as it were, to an *act* of the vein, – "*she throws* the north cheek up."'

Shafts hundreds of feet deep were sunk to reach them. Levels many miles long were driven through the 'dead ground' to meet them. Many adits, to drain the mines above, were hacked by hand, one of them almost the whole way from Alston to Nenthead through the rock underground. It was possible in places to walk through the levels from one valley to the next. There was a story that one winter, when the passes were blocked, a man who had died in West Allen Dale was carried in his coffin through the underground passages to home and burial in Nenthead. There were giant chambers underground where lunches for the Freemasons were occasionally held. On the surface, where the shafts and the haulage levels emerge in little toothless mouths, the tramlines

disappear into the darkness, and the 'dead' was piled in mounds of useless rubbish, evidence of the rifled hillside. Here were the dressing floors and the crushing mills, with their giant water wheels, where the ore was broken and sorted by water, and the poisonous smelt mills, where the galena, the lead sulphide, was burnt so that the metal could run out into moulds, and the corrosive and fatal smoke from the fires was carried in long flues to chimneys on the tops of the fells.

By the late 1920s and 1930s most of this was in ruins. The huge machinery rotting or dismantled, the corrugated iron on the roofs of the mine buildings shuffling in the wind, the miners' houses, many of them on their own smallholdings where the women farmed, abandoned and the roofs fallen in. This air of retraction and the disintegrated moor-edge houses are still there today. The map is pockmarked with the words Mine (dis), ruin, Shafts (dis), ruin, ruin. And these

elements – the austerity and northernness of the place, the knowledge of the riddled mass of rock underfoot, the abandonment and decay, the sense of something active in the past and now forgotten, the harshness in the names of the farms and fells, the strict look of this 'lean country' as Auden called it – all this provided exactly the metaphorical landscape (you might even say the psychosomatic landscape) for the intense, dark dramas of his first real poetry.

It is a poetry of departures, enemies, incomprehension, lies, bafflement, darkness, 'the eyelash barrier', vengeance, bitter bonding and disintegration. The full story is never clear, the language residual.

'The strict look of this "lean country" ' – Milburn Forest and Trout Beck in Cumbria.

On northern ridges
Where flags fly, seen and lost, denying
  rumour
We baffle proof, speakers of a strange tongue.

It is the language of the ridge, bitten-off and
unconnected:

Travellers may meet at inns but not attach,
They sleep one night together, not asked to
  touch;
Receive no normal welcome, not the
  pressed lip,
Children to lift, not the assuaging lap.
Crossing the pass descend the growing
  stream
Too tired to hear except the pulse's strum,
Reach villages to ask for a bed in
Rock shutting out the sky, the old life done.

A boy is born fanged like a weasel, a brother shot
like a dog. 'On Cautley where a peregrine has
nested, iced heather hurt the knuckles.' Fragments of the real past appear in a strange light:

. . . one died
During a storm, the fells impassable,
Not at his village, but in wooden shape
Through long abandoned levels nosed his way
And in his final valley went to ground.

But 'This land, cut off, will not communicate,' and

Beams from your car may cross a bedroom wall,
They wake no sleeper; you may hear the wind
Arriving driven from the ignorant sea
To hurt itself on pane, on bark of elm . . .

An exact description of the lead dales becomes,
without elaboration or invention but in the
rhythms of Anglo-Saxon poetry, a description of a
state of mind:

Head-gears gaunt on grass-grown pit-banks,
  seams abandoned years ago;
Drop a stone and listen for its splash in
  flooded dark below.

Squeeze into the works through broken
  windows or through damp-sprung doors;
See the rotted shafting, see holes gaping in
  the upper floors;

The intense romanticism of this poetry, which at
times has the air of something like *Kidnapped* in
modern dress, Auden came to see as a sort of
bogus temptation into which he had been led by
the apocalyptic glamour of its rhetoric. It is a feeling to which we have all at times succumbed,
dreaming up something heroic from our isolation
on the ridge, reading the landscape in the way of a
schoolboy-guerrilla (when he was at school,
Auden always made a point of going for walks out
of bounds), seeing the valley clogged with dull
legitimacy and darkened by what Auden called
'the immense bat-shadow of home', and hearing
'The sound behind our back/Of glaciers calving.'
It is an attitude that comes easily and excitingly to
the lonely walker, removed and superior, distant
and even supercilious, burying his isolation in a
cloak of grandeur. It is what Auden often called
'the hawk's vision', distant and precise, able in one
sweeping overview to survey the breadths of
continents and history with an enormous and
prophesying exactness.

This view lies behind a great deal of his best
poetry of the 1930s, cold ridge-poetry which pre-
dicts disaster for the muddled beings it surveys.
But buried within it is an acute awareness of its
fascist tendencies, its natural drift towards an adu-
lation of the totalitarian vision. Even as early as
January 1929, when he was 21, he wrote a poem
that begins 'From scars where kestrels hover'
where all the lean elements of the ridge world
reappear – the curlews and sleet, acrid streams and
the drumming of snipe, along with the familiar
apparatus of the leader and his doomed companions, 'Fighters for no one's sake' dying beyond the
border. The rhetoric is undimmed. The tall,
unwounded leader takes a short look into the
happy valley and then turns away to move across
the fell. But the poem moves on and another character and setting appear, the *host* who waits, with
lights and wine ready, for supper by the lake. He,
patient and generous, emerges as the real hero:

And bravery is now
Not in the dying breath
But resisting the temptations
To skyline operations.

This is the first sign of Auden's movement into

LEFT: *Stanhope-in-Weardale, Durham.*

RIGHT: *The main street of Alston in Cumbria.*

the comforting valley and his abandonment of the winter ridge. But a mind does not move forward in single file; it is more like a crowd or a flock shuffling forward in patches across a hillside. The two elements and Auden's sympathy for both coexisted for many years. A reluctance towards comfort, the real strength of those temptations towards skyline operations – you must know them as you come down towards the valley after a day in the wind, the idea that coming back inside is simply a form of giving up – are forces which cannot easily be dismissed.

The northern austerity begins to slip out of Auden's poems as he matures and its place is taken by the valley and the city within it. Brief moments arise in which the contentments of the valley are accepted and recognized,

> Where the sexy airs of summer,
> The bathing hours and the bare arms,
> The leisured drives through a land of farms,
> Are good to the newcomer.

And where, for a moment, on one incomparable evening in June 1933,

> The lion griefs loped from the shade
> And on our knees their muzzles laid,
> And Death put down his book.

But those moments of valley certainty are hedged around by doubt and longing. 'Wandering lost upon the mountains of our choice,' he wrote almost at the end of the 1930s,

200

We envy streams and houses that are sure:
But we are articled to error; we
Were never nude and calm like a great door,

And never will be perfect like the fountains;
We live in freedom by necessity,
A mountain people dwelling among mountains.

But the language has changed. Warmth and connections have entered it, a stream-like ease and fluency. 'From scars where kestrels hover' admired the valley host in the language of the ridge; this poem remembers the romantic unease of the upland in the comforting and comfortable language of the valley. It is a crucial change.

All this has come a long way from the lead-mining dales of the northern Pennines. But I would maintain that everything that develops in Auden's poetry through the 1930s, and particularly this tension and opposition between the claims of valley and ridge, which walkers above all others can appreciate, is implicit in that first landscape. One might even say that the warm summer valley where his poetry comes to rest is no more than the image of the valley that runs along the edge of the Pennines one pass west of Alston, the Vale of Eden, blonde in summer with squares of wheat and watered with streams that come down off the fellsides.

This is not the last word. When on holiday in 1948 he wrote to a friend in America: 'I hadn't realized till I came how like Italy is to my "Mutterland", the Pennines. Am in fact starting on a poem, "In Praise of Limestone". . .' In this poem, he looks back with the wonderful relaxed strength of his maturity at the same landscape which had been the ferocious matrix for his early fragments. But now he chooses to see everything that was ignored before. The hard mineral veins that lie embedded in the limestone of the Pennines are not mentioned, neither the abandoned levels nor the broken machinery. Here he concentrates on the acceptance and humanity of the rock itself:

> If it form the one landscape that we the
>   inconstant ones
> Are consistently homesick for, this is chiefly
> Because it dissolves in water.

Instead of the indifferent mineral veins, the rock is riddled with running water. Each spring fills a private pool for its fish. Even the cliffs which the streams make *entertain* the butterfly and the lizard. It is a stone that responds, making a region of definite places and short distances, where life and the world are

> Adjusted to the local needs of valleys
> Where everything can be touched or
>   reached by walking . . .

In the long development of Auden's moral landscape, founded in all the early resonance of the lead-mining dales of the northern Pennines, this represents some sort of culmination and solution: the absorption of the ridge, the limestone ridge, into the embracing humanity of the stream and the valley.

FOOD FOR FOOT-MEN

On my first long walk, the British one, I carried more weight than a sensible man should in an old-fashioned Bergen-type rucksack without a waist strap, a serious omission since, even when braced up tight, it bulged and wobbled about, impairing my stride. I fancy I resembled a badly dressed camel. It follows that I had precious little space for food and all the gadgetry that goes with romantic suppers alone under millions of stars.

Except in the north-western wilds of Scotland, many of my evening meals were prepared. The important thing is carefully to avoid the middle of the catering spectrum. I rarely failed to get substantial meals in cottages, transport cafés, small pubs and big hotels, the bigger the better. In time I learned to avoid places with a set menu, especially those half-timbered genteel guesthouses on the fringes of country towns where the guests speak in whispers, nervous about the retired soldiers on half pay who usually run them.

Let us take what used to be The Radnor in the old shire of that name, a three-star place, littered with the dubious accreditations of foreign inspectors of British *haute cuisine*, an elegant restaurant not 5 miles from Offa's Dyke. No dubiety there. I cleaned up in a ditch before walking in as hungry as a hyena. Too late for dinner? In nicely Welshified English the owner said, 'We are open until our last guest chooses to leave.'

What they laid out I have long since forgotten but it went down as well as that bottle of Pope's best Newcastle on the Rhône. And out of home-made brown bread the chef made game sandwiches, water-cressed and garnished for my next morning's breakfast on a hill in Housman country. That's the pattern I have so often enjoyed: a late meal in a good restaurant and then out and on again.

Since what follows these note-booked reflections is by a wine and food expert, Christopher Driver of *The Guardian* and former editor of *The Good Food Guide*, I trespass, I feel, on his opinions but cannot resist recalling a night on the outer walls of Italy when, not too tired for a supper light years beyond all this dehydrated stuff, I tickled a few immature trout, lit a fire of larchwood and steamed them, wrapped up in the tin foil around the main dish: rolls that bulged with creamed eggs and veal, prepared in a mountain restaurant at midday. Although one or two fish exploded in fits of posthumous pique, raising a shower of ashes, the two-course meal went down extremely well, fortified as it was with half a bottle of local stuff the colour of venous blood.

Those intent on *déjeuner sous les belles étoiles* in the light of a wood fire ought to know that most coniferous wood, dead or alive, especially Scots pine, burns well but living hard wood has something of the combustibility of wet asbestos. Make use of what can easily be got hold of. In *Food for Free*,* Richard Mabey has told us how to snip and boil a variety of common wayside plants but I have never got beyond fruit and berries. In the early part of the nineteenth century one man, the famous Dean William Buckland, anatomist and prehistorian, asserted that he could eat anything organic and treated the most tolerant of his guests to experimental meals of grilled mice on toast, curried hedgehog and crocodile steaks from a salted specimen in his laboratory. Several guests left the table hurriedly when they knew what they were in for.

In Scotland I have felt that I could live for ever on brose, that is dry oatmeal well moistened with burn water to which raisins or chopped-up slices of fresh onion were added, but the thought of it still brings tears to my eyes. As for Christopher Driver he is, he says modestly, 'A useful cook on an expedition.' Aged 55, he has twice recovered from a rapid ride from a mountain to a hospital. Next time? That last question is his.

What had he in mind for next year? I asked him.

'Mont Blanc,' he wrote. 'Skin chestnuts. Cook them soft in milk and vanilla with sugar to taste, and drain. Rub them through a wire sieve into a ring mould like vermicelli, and turn out on a dish. Fill the centre with cream Chantilly. Knowledgeable alpinists can achieve other peaks with the cream. The chief hazard is your doctor.'

J.H.

* Collins, 1972

EATING HIGH

CHRISTOPHER DRIVER

On mountains, bring me muscles. Not the kind of muscles that pull you up mantelshelfs and chimneys and keep you upright for the twenty-fourth mile. You will allow an old hunter-gatherer the old spelling of muscles: those splayed-oval, mauve-indigo marine shells, belayed to rocks in clusters at low tide, each encasing a morsel of orange flesh no larger than two fingernails, inviting hungry beach-combers to a Stone Age feast.

Mussels/muscles can stand for a division of mountain mentalities between different people, perhaps within the same person at different times: the absurd and the physical. Sometimes they need each other. Next time you pass a fishmonger, pick up a bag of mussels and feel the weight. Now consider what kind of young maniacs, 30 years ago, would have carried rucksackfuls up a long valley to their tents under Garbh-bheinn of Ardgour after a day at the seaside.

The physical mentality – the Cape Canaveral calculation of the energy needed to counteract gravitational pull – would have dumped the lot and settled for dried beef and potato powder. Tomorrow is another Munro. But the absurd mentality – the Brillat-Savarin stretch for the stars with the discovery of a new dish – prevailed on this occasion. If you doubt my word, mussel shards must lie to this day in the bed of Amhainn Coir an lubhair where the water ran shallow across sun-warmed rock, even if the taste of the garlic butter and the smell of the charring rowan branches have fled. No doubt in my lackadaisical fifties I would settle for *sous-vide moules marinières* from Marks and Spencer in the camp-fire pot – though I rather doubt whether M & S has crossed

Corran Ferry yet. But in that year I was in love with mountains, food and a girl and I would have been hard put to it to tick the order of priorities.

It was the same when a friend and I aspired to that *summum bonum* of British hill days: the Cuillin ridge of Skye from Gars Bheinn to Sgurr nan Gillean. I cannot remember what we carried as refreshment apart from grapefruit, and the eleven hours we took on the ridge has become a time for one-legged men or ladies with hats on.

But I do recall the celebratory dinner we cooked next night at the Glen Brittle Youth Hostel after a gentle day gathering mussels – some of the juiciest and tastiest I remember, done with a Mornay sauce, preceded by a soup seasoned with the drips from the socks of fifty people drying above the iron range, and followed by a rice pudding so compact that no one could finish more than a teaspoonful: somebody's mother had failed to teach him the physics of rice absorption.

From satiety to famine, and with the same companions, up to the far reaches of Glen Nevis and along the tussocky waste to Loch Ossian, another long day. No warden nor food greeted us at that youth hostel, but Robin fancied himself with a rod and he would supply the trout from the loch upon our arrival: no need to carry tins, just a bag of oatmeal. But the trout in the loch were cannier than that. The self-appointed caterer fished for a solid 48 hours and at least that gave him something to do while the rest of us meditated upon our pangs: never have I been nearer to the Oxfam look. I seem to remember that the catch amounted to two little fishes between five persons. The fisherman went into the ministry after that, and his sermon on the Five Thousand always brought tears

204

The Cuillin Hills in the Isle of Skye, near Sligachan.

to all the congregations whom he favoured with it.

Do all these vividly recalled feasts and fasts also express the taste for contrast that takes us up into the mountains anyway? Our overcrowded, thermostatic, flattish land is designed for temperate experiences. Only our mountainous fringes hold out to the human body the possibilities of extremity: daunting climbs and scree runs straight into the lake, Arctic cold and an Easter heatwave in the same week, a 50-mile view or damp cloud

pressing against your nose. That is why mountains are meant not for walkaholics with tomato sandwiches but for hedonists who take their pleasure twice: once in luxury, again in relief from just-tolerable pain.

I hesitate to quote my children in case I should be taken for some Hunter Davies clone, but of our three daughters, the one who can do without mountains and fine food showed her disposition early at five. She glumly trailed uphill behind her parents on some rain-sodden Welsh hill near Tregaron, muttering: 'I am talking to God. I am asking Him to make all the days sunny and all the hills flat.' No sense of contrast, you see.

One of the solaces of British mountain country is the thoughtfulness of hoteliers and restaurateurs who have taken up residence at a boot's distance from mountains which they would never dream of climbing. Indeed, the only excuse for several rather opulent Lakeland hotels is their location. I always hoped to hear an account from some Good Food Guide correspondent who had visited one of these establishments and had leaked out mud and rain from every chink of his or her cagoule or decapitated a vase with an ice-axe on their way to the *fricassée de sole aux suisses* and 'the chocolate and grapefruit *gouache bombe* on which an inspector met a bluebell'.

The English Lake District is particularly rich in places of this kind. But one or two have been real mountaineers' hotels too. At the Old Dungeon Ghyll Hotel in Sidney Cross's time we once sat down and demanded tea and scones in the lounge without realizing that the dinner gong was about to be sounded – and we got it.

But we should celebrate other ranges, other hotels, other characters. Think, for instance, of Robert Irvine – now better known as father of Castaway, Lucy Irvine. (This happens to fathers.) His hotel at Achiltibuie became an unmissable stage on the long road to Quinag and Stac Polly because he kept good claret, grew the only vegetables north of Stirling, and smoked everything that ran or swam (including his customers, I wouldn't be surprised, when they annoyed him).

No other country in the world worships its mountains with its tummy in this practical way. I do not underestimate the cheeses and the snails of the Pyrenees ('*Chasse gardée – même escargots*' I once read on the slopes of Mt Canigou), the chestnut-fed *jambon Corse* and *omelette de brocciu* served in desultory hotels on the spine of Corsica,

ABOVE: *'Up to the far reaches of Glen Nevis . . .'*

LEFT: *Aerial view of Skye and the Cuillins from the Inner Sound.*

RIGHT: *Ullswater in Cumbria.*

and the 'wild' trout – as we now have to call it to distinguish it from the all-too-tame kind – in the Vercors. But the great French restaurants are not to be found within a boot's tramp from serious peaks partly for the simple reason that wealthy French holiday-makers and retired but active couples do not walk: ours do. The British salariat – or a noticeable section of it – likes to earn its fleshpots at night under the daytime anonymity of its anorak.

But whatever a restaurant's altitude, there comes a point beyond which no meals can be served nor for that matter can waiters be persuaded, and the pleasures of the table have to be carried in the mind. This stratagem is worth trying: I have persuaded a reluctant child or two most of the way up the nose of Bowfell by playing alphabetical feasts: A for aubergines, B for brains, C for chump chop and so on. And sooner or later you have to pack your tastes and nutrition knowing that you have to back your own choices – literally back – for the day or week or month, summer or winter. No second chances.

Winter, though it makes heavy porterage, is in some ways easier to cater for: every man carries his own refrigerator on his shoulders. Water and bilberries apart, there is no summer food and drink that tastes better on a hill than it does in your garden, and most of it tastes markedly worse. (After one summer night out under the stars below Dow Crag we woke up to Noilly Prat and lemon in a thermos and it was *horrible*.) Winter treats, by contrast, come into their own as the altitude rises and the temperature falls. Christmas cake, for instance, never tastes right at a table, certainly not at a Christmas table. But it tastes exactly right when the sweetness is reviving tired muscles for the long trek home to soup, and the tooth print in the icing is echoing the crunch of boot in the snow round the summit cairn. Snow, too, supplies jam ices – a pot of strawberry jam upended into a likely drift and turned over by the ice pick. It would never occur to me to try it after a Kent blizzard. But since Chernobyl, shall we have to christen this carefree Helvellyn dish *glace Kiev*?

CROWDS AND
<u>CLOUDY LONELINESS</u>

It has always surprised me more than a little that, from a pictorial point of view, Turner didn't make much of the Lake District beyond two or three pictures of the Cumberland mountains seen across Morecambe Bay from Heysham near the muddy mouth of the Lune. Thereafter we have him tramping up the most serpentine lengths of that river in the vicinity of Hornby Castle. Could it be, as David Hill has suggested, he felt uneasy about what he saw in his mind's eye? He couldn't arrange the vistas to his satisfaction. Strange this in a man who was born to bring order to geological chaos in the way that Samuel Johnson grappled with whole libraries.

When I come to think about it, a more likely reason for Turner's prompt return to the Yorkshire Dales is that among those fells which caused Southey to pull his coach blinds down to block out the view of some of those *horrid* mountains was that up there rich patrons were pretty thin on the ground. Other artists thought differently. We have Christopher Steele, Daniel Gardner, Peter de Wint and, eventually, John Harden, first of the diarrhoea school where today in that much trampled on but (almost) indestructibly beautiful country, painting is now mostly art for postcard manufacturers. Among my own favourite views is the one from a high-flying plane.

The complex asymmetrical structure of Snowdonia is far from evident; the outer walls of the Weald, that is to say the North and South Downs, are deceptively simple. The broken jaws of the Pennines, riven as they are by lateral gaps, require only a little geological knowledge and imagination. But take a map, take a plane or look more carefully at the satellite pictures during the TV news of the weather, and you have a mega-landscape of superb simplicity.

Let us assume you have an atlas open at the page where north-west England is depicted. Place the point of a pencil held vertically on the Borrowdale Crags and you are at the axle of a wheel the spokes of which, read out clockwise starting from the north, are Derwent Water, Thirlmere, Ullswater, Hawes Water, Windermere, Coniston, Wastwater, Ennerdale Water and Crummock Water cum Buttermere.

Except where vast landslides and the blocking, dam-forming action of glaciers has warped their original pre-glacial axes, they all point to that wreckage of volcanoes centred on what the Northmen called *Borgarardahl*, Borrowdale, 'the valley with a fort.' I shan't go on about how that mighty collision occurred beyond mentioning that where climbers now risk their necks, some four hundred million years ago that region was covered by a 2-mile deep layer of

An approaching storm in the hills.

volcanic debris. Today, the beauty of the landscape is such that a friend of W. G. Collingwood who wrote of it with love and learning said: 'Your poor children! It is hard on them to bring them up at the Lakes; they will never be happy anywhere else.'

My grandfather, Old John, a hugely entertaining ne'er do well to whom I attribute most of my imperfections, boasted among much else to cutting a fair figure as a fell walker and Cumbrian-style wrestler. For this and many other reasons, my wife Katie and I set off from Ravenglass on the west coast, not far from that infamous atomic power station, for our honeymoon walk and reached Shap Fell in four days as a warming-up exercise for an east-to-west traverse and south ambulation that brought us back here to Hampstead within a month.

This is not at all to the fancy of my friend and neighbour Hunter Davies who's paused, ready and waiting, champing at the bit to give us his views on crowds and cloudy loneliness. So, I beg you, be indulgent. He's a thoroughly good fellow at heart, learned in much except perhaps natural history.

J.H.

LAKELAND WALKING

HUNTER DAVIES

Walking is easy, one foot in front of the other, so why make all this performance about it? These professional walkers who pontificate and lay down rules, just as I am about to do, make it all so much more difficult and unattractive and offputting by overstressing two elements: clothing and distance.

I'll take clothing first, in which I include associated walking gear. The experts and the organization men and officials would have us dressed for a simple walk on the fells as if we were going up Everest. I'm talking about walking, not climbing. If you are dopey enough to go up sheer rock faces or tackle solid ice walls, then that's a different activity. Yet I have read so many pamphlets put out by so many worthy bodies which say that *all* fell walkers should have ice picks, emergency supplies, flares and crampons, whatever they are. If you like carrying all that clutter to make yourself look the part then go ahead, knacker yourself.

Lakeland purists go spare when I say such things, accusing me of causing accidents, of encouraging people to be silly and unprepared. You *do* have to prepare yourself. Even walking over Catbells is not the same as walking down to Tesco's. But there's no need for oxygen masks. Every year there's a published list of Lakeland accidents and it makes appalling reading. The worst in recent years was 1984 when twenty-four people died. Every year I analyse these figures very carefully. There's always a percentage who have died from natural causes, such as heart attacks. Of the so-called 'accidents', you will find that over ninety per cent have happened to people who *were* adequately equipped, wearing recommended clothes. One can only assume that they

were too daring, too foolhardy, especially in snow or ice. But I've seen no proof of deaths from bad clothing.

What I wear for walking, repeat walking, is trainers in the summer and wellies in the winter. Trainers are brilliant these days, if rather expensive. Did you notice that Ian Botham, on his John o' Groats to Land's End charity walk, wore trainers all the way, dozens of them? Present-day trainers are so soft and easy on the tootsies, yet strong and reliable. I even feel they are safer than boots. You have much more flexibility with trainers, compared with those hefty clod-hopping leather things. Boots do admittedly protect your ankles, but they make you very clumsy and slow. That's the reason why professional footballers gave up those ankle-length boots. They can manoeuvre much better in modern slipper-type boots.

Wellies are best for keeping your feet dry. No argument about that. Boots eventually let in water, or the rain gets over your socks, and they become heavier and heavier. If the sun comes out, then you do sweat in wellies, and coming down a steep bit of grass you can slip if it's wet, but that can happen in boots as well. People have it against wellies and they can make you look a right amateur or a child. I do have a pair of light-weight leather boots for show and occasional rough work, but I'm always glad to get them off.

There's only one real rule when it comes to clothes, and the Blessed Wainwright agrees with this – comfort is all. The second rule, at least in Lakeland, is that it won't last. You might set off in bright sunshine, but it's best to take some sort of rain wear and an extra pullover. I also take plastic leggings if it looks at all dodgy, but then I'm a softy. I hate it when the rain runs down your anorak and goes straight for the knees. And if you are walking alone, it is sensible to tell someone where you are going, and take a whistle, just in case the old heart needs help.

Next, friends, we come to distance. I simply do not understand people like John Hillaby who go on these marathon walks. How can they see or experience or enjoy everything? It becomes a route march, clocking up their 20 miles a day, keeping to their self-imposed targets. He has written elsewhere (or even here) that the real enemy of the serious walker is not physical but mental pain. Yes, but Hillers old boy, the mental pain is because you've taken on too much. You've turned it all into a long-distance trudge, a mental

Ullswater in the Lake District. 'Lakeland is by far and away the best area in all England for real walks.'

marathon, setting your mind these ridiculous tests. For the same reason I hate joggers, and I suspect they mostly hate what they're doing, turning pleasure into pain, concentrating on the time and distance, hoping to drain virtue out of the agony suffered. In my opinion those long-distance walking slogs are just as potty, marching against the clock. It also means you have to carry your gear with you, or you cheat and use hotels, or a helper drives behind who of course never gets a mention in the book. Imagine having to hump all that stuff on your back every day. Daft, I call it.

Right, let's now have the elements I personally look for in a good walk. I don't always find them, but one can try, one can hope, one can dream.

I do two walks every day of my life when I'm in London. Half an hour in the morning, then a one-and-a-half-hour walk in the afternoon. The first is roughly round the block, to make myself feel good that I'm not travelling to any office, to smirk and feel smug when I see the cars, bumper to bumper, and those poor sods queuing up to give their life away. The second is always a big walk, usually round Hampstead Heath, taking in a selection of my favourite spots. Once a week, I do Regent's Park and surrounds, just to vary the pleasures.

For three months of the year, we are in the Lake District; what bliss, what perfection, because Lakeland is by far and away the best area in all England for *real* walks. (Notice I said England, thereby excluding Wales and more particularly Scotland.) But wherever I am, I have in mind these five requirements. Not in any particular order.

1. Refreshments Yes, the wizened walkers, the long-distance wonders will scoff at this, but I do like to be able to take in a pub or a caff on my walk. At the beginning, the middle or the end, I'm not fussy. I plan my Heath walk round the place I have chosen for my afternoon capuccino. In the Lakes, I like to know there's a nice hotel or tea place I can work in. And in the Lakes, doing a day-long, I always need a picnic, otherwise I'm not going. I like looking forward all the way up to the thought

Near Ulpha in Cumbria. One rule of walking in Lakeland is that the weather won't last.

of the coffee and sandwiches on the top, then perhaps a choccy bikky to help me come down. I am human. Not a machine.

2. Roundness I hate a walk that is there and back, straight up and down, repeating what you've just done. That's for fell runners, long-distance sloggers and other cranks. I want my walks to be round, so that I end up where I began. Hard to do in the Lake District, because of the terrain, and you often have to repeat bits, but it's always my ambition to walk a complete circle.

3. Openness Is there such a word? I mean open country, without roads, without fields or farm land or private pastures. We did have a cottage once near the Cotswolds and how lovely it looked in the photographs, but the restrictions drove me mad in the end. Life and leisure were totally circumscribed. You have to know the farmers to use their land, or it's a hanging offence. You have to make enormous diversions to get a proper walk. You end up on roads, looking across *at* the good stuff, not being part of it.

Only in Lakeland can you be certain of a 20, 30 or even 50-mile walk where there are no restrictions, where you are walking on God's own earth which, at this moment, happens to belong to or be controlled by you and me, even if we are masquerading as the National Park or the National Trust.

4. Variety With age, and with the residue of two cartilage operations which never properly cleared up, I am not so keen on the steep stuff, the long continuous slog, only to come down the other side. I still want *some* climbing, some height on my walk, rough bits as well as smooth bits, wild tops and frightening crags if only to look at, plus lush pastures and low valleys to linger in. Ideally, I want variety in every aspect of the walk, in the vegetation, the houses, the weather, the terrain, the people, the paths, and I certainly don't want all my sandwiches to be tuna fish, didn't you bring any cheese, oh Gawd.

5. Views I want a top that is a top, where I can look back and think terrific, Hunt, what a great walk, haven't you done well! And I also want to look ahead, preferably towards a lake, to savour the sight, bask in the beauty, imprint it on my mind's eye so that come the rotten days in boring old London I can turn the mental clock back and

recollect the wonders.

Those then are my five requirements, which in a perfect world I would always try to achieve. As a family, we also have minor modifications, little extra rules we impose upon ourselves, such as a maximum of forty minutes' drive to start the walk, no screes as my wife hates them, and each walk must be new if we're with any of the children, because newness is all to the young. We oldies can quite enjoy the old walks, retracing steps where we have been, knowing the pleasures to come, the views round the next bend. I spend hours with the O.S. maps and Old Wainwright, working out a new route, trying to find a way back to the beginning without any repeats, ensuring it will excite the children by the very fact that we haven't done

it before, yet at the same time trying to manage at least three out of my five major requirements. I have been known to set off without any refreshment place in sight, but in that case we take an especially good picnic. The incredible thing is that every year we do discover, or should I say create, at least one new Lakeland walk which provides most of the qualities we so desire.

We now have a store of about twenty Lakeland walks, which last no longer than a day, though some of course score better on one or two elements than on others. If I were forced to choose just *one* walk, told that's it, you're not allowed into Lakeland ever again, the one I'd go for is not in fact very good for refreshments. But on the other scores, it is absolutely sensational.

This all-time favourite walk is around the shores of Ullswater, on the southern side, not on the other bank where the road is. We always drive there, to Martindale, to start the actual walk, but one of the many attractions is that you can take a lake steamer, sailing from either Glenridding or Pooley Bridge, to Howtown.

Basically, the walk takes you round Place Fell, without having to climb up it, yet you still get marvellous high views and then, down below, you hug the shores of Ullswater itself. Only 10 miles, all perfect. We usually park at the little church of Martindale, above Howtown. There's no point in exhausting yourself before you begin by climbing up that switchback road below. Just admire it.

The first stretch is very easy, down and along

LEFT: *Lake steamer on Ullswater.*

BELOW: *Looking north down Deepdale towards Dent in Cumbria.*

the little twisting road and into Boardale. It's rather Beatrix Potter, roly-poly countryside, smooth and rounded with twee cottages, neat fields.

In the Boardale Valley itself, the fields and the farmhouses gradually run out as you slowly find yourself climbing higher, but it's still pretty easy. At the head of the valley there is a hause, or pass, which looks quite dramatic from a distance but turns out to be quite simple, if a little rougher underfoot, though still walkable in trainers. On the top, it can be a bit boggy if there's been a lot of rain, so it could be a day for wellies. Then keep heading right towards Patterdale. We usually have our picnic here, once the lake and Patterdale are definitely in sight.

You come down and hit the shores of Ullswater, following a path which twists and turns with the shape of the lake, up and down, high and low, flat and then rocky, but all of it clearly marked, giving endless vistas which change with every bend in the lake.

At Sandwick you can carry on, taking in the path round Halin Fell, or turn right up the little road and back to where you left the car. By going on round Halin Fell you end up at Howtown, which means you have the switchback road to climb, but it does give you a chance to visit Howtown Hotel where, if you've timed it properly, the bar will be open. If not, you can always order afternoon tea with home-made scones.

On the walk itself, there are no pubs or caffs. We can't always have everything in life. What it does have is all the wonders of Lakeland, every sort of sight and sensation, from lake views to crags and wild fells, pretty farmlands, empty marshland, all of it in a short distance.

It was Wordsworth who first noted that the unique thing about the Lake District is that in a 'narrow compass' you get every variety of light and landscape. I like to think that my Ullswater walk encompasses all the best of Lakeland, and almost all the best things that any walker anywhere could ever desire.

Boys fishing on the shores of Ullswater. The lakeside path provides endless vistas which change with every bend in the lake.

THE INS AND OUTS OF GAELDOM

From the Mull of Kintyre to the topmost tip of Cape Wrath the west coast of Scotland has an uncommonly dissipated appearance on the map. The headlands are slashed by sea lochs and studded with islands that look as if they've been shoved into place like ill-fitting parts of a jigsaw puzzle. Their purpose, you might think, was to protect Drum Albyn, the great ridge of the Highlands from the ravages of the Atlantic. But the forces that beset the landscape thereabouts were plutonic, not marine, and if I've succeeded in imbuing the ins and outs of that ridge with a degree of bewilderment bordering on awe it reflects accurately what I felt after poring over twelve sheets of the old-style one inch to the mile O.S. maps of the Western Highlands that year (1966), when *The Times* put news instead of ads on her front page.

How best could I bridge the gap between the northern end of the Pennine Way in the Cheviots and the Highlands by way of the Border shires and, having got there, how could I get out again and tramp off north-east towards Caithness? As far as I can make out there is still some dispute about the axis of the Highland Line, that subtle division between Saxon and Celt, the breeches and the kilt, especially between the inhabitants of Dumbarton who see themselves in florid tartanry, but at the risk of re-opening old conflicts I'd place it north of Stirling, a region which may be likened to a huge brooch that clasps together the Highlands and the Lowlands. With help from that fine man, the late Donald Moir of the Royal Scottish Geographical Society who advocated the use of drove roads, the old cattle tracks, I struck through Jedburgh, Selkirk, Peebles and the Pentland Hills to Callander and Strathyre and thence north-west to Rannoch Moor and Glen Coe by way of the bonnie Braes of Balquhidder and Glen Dochart.

Nowadays, instead of striking Crianlarich from the south east I should go almost due north from Loch Lomond which is but a vigorous day's stage from the centre of Glasgow. This is now the West Highland Way, a half-signposted route which left Scottish walkers unimpressed when it was prematurely launched in 1979 on the grounds that they didn't want it and the Sassenach who'd written a book about it (Tom Hunter) didn't seem to realize that access problems which beset English trail blazers simply didn't exist north of the Border. I happened to be present at that shindy and thanked God that the bottles laid out for our refreshment were not chucked about. But now it's a still somewhat unacceptable fact to the Scots and this is how our delightfully mad mile-slayer Stephen Pern recalls it, starting with that slide show with dubbed music which he put on for his Aunt Mabel in South Ealing.

J.H.

WEST HIGHLAND WAY

STEPHEN PERN

'No, Aunt Mabel. Not Long *Island*. Loch *Lomond*.'

'Sugar please.'

'Oliver! Will you put Cissy *down*!'

'Not there Oliver. I can't see.'

'Sophy, don't whine.'

'More tea, dear. Another mince pie? Can we have the lights for a moment?'

'Phone.'

I shut my eyes, bit my lips, gnawed the projector cable and tried to recall the commandment that thou shalt not swear at thy nearest and dearest. Nor shalt thou storm out of the room in a huff. Neither shalt thou remember that Aunt Mabel still thinks thou art three, nor mind that thy brother, thine only beloved twin brother, seems to have important business to conduct on the telephone in a very loud voice at the other end of the room. Thou shalt not resent the man-hours wasted marshalling slides into painstaking sequence; nor, while we're at it, the fact that no one's yet noticed the soundtrack, the waggish selection of 'Chariots of Fire' to cheer our backpacking hero north out of Glasgow.

Not that the music now mattered. With the show hard-frozen because of the phone the tape was way ahead of the pictures, the crowded pavements of Sauchiehall Street mocked by a vigorous passage from Beethoven's Sixth and I still on my blocks at the bus station. Where Aunt Mabel was only Auntie knew.

'How Nairobi's changed,' she sighed.

'No dear, Nairobi was last year.' At least my mother had the dates right. 'This is Scotland. His walk up the West Highland Way.'

'Ah,' said Mabel, reading aloud from the map I'd flicked up on the screen. 'M-I-L-N-G-A-V-I-E.'

'The suburb where the waymarked trail begins,' I explained, abandoning my tightly conceived script. Why cast hard-won pearls of the presenter's art before these . . . these . . .?

They were all at it now, five not-unintelligent adults mouthing place names like confused boy scouts, though Sophy and Oliver, both under ten, remained commendably silent. Their father had at last put the phone down. 'Milngavie to Fort William, eh? Not one of your epics, then?'

I said nothing. Ninety-five miles isn't that far. And hundreds walk the Way every year. Thousands for all I knew, flooding along Scotland's first long-distance footpath, though in the eight June days I spent on the trail I saw very few of them – neat lines of rucksacks outside the first rural pubs, but through the Highlands almost no one. Red deer, ptarmigan, the occasional stoat, the bliss of remote solitude. Except for – and I smiled – that afternoon with Dr Snodgrass. While Oliver spills tea and is sent for a cloth let's slip 20 miles up the trail and meet him.

The route had been easy till then, a gentle warm-up, the suburbs behind me and on through verdant Strathblane, but somewhere around mile fifteen I crossed the river Endrick and the Highland Line. No more sun-splashed dragonflies. Scarcely any sheep. Just incomparable silence as I climbed Conic hill, six or eight hours' walk from Scotland's largest city, to stare down on her largest loch.

A puzzle of fronds between me and the sky, I lay drowning in the young bracken, heather and myrtle slung forward across the rising moorland; a cuckoo calling the evening down from a stand of

ABOVE: *Sunset on Loch Lomond.*

RIGHT: *Loch Lomond, looking towards Ben Lomond.*

white-flowering rowan. Not an epic, no, though this was just the first day.

The orange moon rose; Loch Lomond turned black; restless curlews whiffled in the night. By dawn the clear skies had vanished, the white silence around me broken only by dispossessed bleats. Compass in hand, I set off in the hope that the mist would not become rain.

But here's Oliver back with a cloth to mop up the spilt tea and we still haven't met Dr Snodgrass. Never mind; we will. Meanwhile, back to Miln-gavie and verdant Strathblane, glorious summer leaping straight off the screen. Out, then, through the newly opened shopping precinct and straight into Mugdock Wood – sappy bluebells but des-pite the deep shade in 4 miles I was a puddle of sweat. I jumped into the Blane, gasped, jumped out, and recovered on my back in the grass.

On Queen Street station, a soiled busker had been singing about this 'Cellophane flower of yel-low and green, dee diddle dee diddle dee dum . . .' I'd never seen open pasture shrug off littered streets so abruptly: only 12 miles from a big city centre and waters choked with delirious trout.

RIGHT: *Glen Falloch, in central Scotland.*

BELOW: *Winter view of Ben Nevis hunched over Fort William, seen from Corpach.*

Next stop – I could already see the croft-like walls – was Glengoyne Distillery, a white splash against the rising fellside. I hate whisky but love the smell of its manufacture, the barley, the bran, the pine vats frothing mush, the ethnic gleam of the copper condensers. I couldn't refuse a drink at Glengoyne, though, not touring the still with a group of visiting publicans, and when I got to the next river I fell in. Which is about all I have to say about the hamlet of Gartness, except that the inventor of logarithms once occupied a castle downstream of the bridge.

Aren't interesting facts a pain? I'll scatter a few for form's sake en route but – be honest – have you yet missed Rob Roy? He lived in the area too. Marauding and such. Walter Scott got some of the details wrong so I'll nae bore ye furrther.

The last thing about Gartness was the fête, audible but obscured by a hedge. I marched past to the strains of 'Waltzing Matilda', coaxed, I think, from a squeeze box, and almost before realizing I'd forgotten the words had pitched camp on Conic Hill. So, there we are. Day one just about over, and tomorrow our fogbound meeting with the doctor.

Fortunately for me, Ben Lomond's 3,194-foot peak is a popular spot. Despite the murk of that second afternoon the summit trail was difficult to lose, though the question why I was on it and not youth hosteled below is unanswerable. Hauling my way uphill I was damp, chilly and bored, the meteorological equivalent of a thick plastic bag pulled firmly down over my eyes. Why *was* I doing this?

A fleshly scourging – if that's what I'd required – was at hand along the roadless lakeside: floundering on, I might have reached the loch head by nightfall, called for hot gruel at the Inverarnan Hotel, a massage, a bed . . . and I'd postponed all that by ascending the invisible mountain, my motives as obscure as the fog.

But the patron saint of travel writers stood by me. The view from the summit, marked by a cairn, might just have overlapped a dartboard, but by a stroke of monumental good luck I'd scored a double top. Caviar in some hands, champagne in others, a group of friends were celebrating the ascent by Dr Anthony Snodgrass, Professor of

Archaeology at Cambridge University of his last 'Munro' – those 276 summits listed by the Victorian traveller Sir Hugh Munro in his *Tables of heights over 3000 feet*. Whether Dr Snodgrass was a typical Munro bagger I couldn't say. Self-effacing, bespectacled, he passed me a beaker of Moët et Chandon.

'Left Ben Lomond till last because of the view,' he told me as we began the descent. 'My voyage to Ithaca, what?'

I dined, that night, in the Duke of Montrose's hunting lodge – chips, beans, condensed milk and canned peaches to follow. It is now Rowardennan Youth Hostel. The visitors' book recorded three hundred hikers already that year, and, speed-reading the comments, perhaps a thousand attempts to spell 'knackering'. Not that this applied to the third day. I'd met an economist – hostels these days aren't all wet boots and flea powder – and we pattered north very gently, the steep valley sides, tumbling wedges of green, restricting us to the lake shore, irritated cattle, like herds of squat gonks, wading clear of us into the water.

Though mild anaesthetic fantasy has its place on the trail I should have dumped mine at the door of the Inverarnan hotel to which I stumbled through the dark. The bonny barmaid of my dreams turned out to be about six feet two and his name was Duncan Macgregor. I had supper but skipped the massage.

The West Highland Way, plus the A82(T), the national gridline, me, the railway to Mallaig and the river Falloch itself now entered Glen Falloch. There was a certain amount of jostling but, 6 miles later, we emerged untangled into Strathfillan. The gridline turned right; I and the remaining lines of communication turned left.

I've nothing against Highland glens as such, but a walk through western Scotland by valley alone is like touring London by underground train. You don't see an awful lot, my guidebook at this point admitting as much by veering suddenly way off the trail to bog down in the lives of the saints. Strathfillan, it seemed, had been a sort of Celtic St Peters, littered, apparently, with old armbones in silver and bits of Robert the Bruce. Perhaps I'd got that wrong – by now almost halfway to Fort William the guide book had lost several pages, so I

White Corries at the mouth of Glen Etive.

of jam from my moustache at the summit. The best thing about long-distance walking is that you don't need a plate.

The next best thing is to be free on a high top like Ben Challum. The view was colossal, from the insects and spiders in the bog at my feet to the tumultuous cloudscape overhead, Ben Nevis 30 miles away hunched over my destination at Fort William. It seemed hardly to get dark that night,

called at the Spar grocery at Crianlarich for another, a long shot which didn't come off. But they did have Battenburg cake. I bought three and, climbing Ben Challum, ripped blushing pink chunks from the first, sucking delicious globules

green was an overnight cattle stance, the hotel itself originally a drovers' inn. In September, 1803, Dorothy Wordsworth stayed there with her brother.

'Seven or eight travellers, probably drovers, were sitting round a large peat fire, each with a mess of porridge in a wooden vessel on his knee, a pot suspended from one of the black beams boiling on the fire. Children were playing on the floor . . .'

She doesn't say if the drovers spoke Gaelic. Decimated by Hanoverian grapeshot, drained south by new military roads, the clan system was already stone dead by Miss Wordsworth's day, the Victorians yet to dig up the coffin, though to what extent they actually reinvented the Highlands is difficult to say. As a Victorian shooting box, gabled Forest Lodge, set in a pine plantation across the lake from my camp site, was hard to beat. The Breadalbane estate of which it was part succumbed to death duties and damp in the twenties, though things had evidently been going downhill, for some time before that.

'In 1904,' the last Marchioness writes, 'I was not for the hill. A long sojourn at Bad Nanheim in the summer tells its own tale, and the tale told me I should never go to the high tops again.'

I understood her feelings precisely. As I climbed Stob Ghabhar – the Hill of Wild Goats – I grinned up at what I fancied was her cloud and invited her to come along with me, I in my vibram soles and stretch breeches, she in her hobnails and tweeds; I spotting deer through my lightweight Pentax, she with her brassbound spyglass. The gear has all changed, her world upside down, but the stark loveliness of the hills she so missed remains.

I'd abandoned the West Highland Way for a day, the official path skirting the dreary moorland below, high passing cloud singing passions in grey to lakes flat and aimless as soup. Rannoch Moor slept through the last Ice Age under roughly a mile of ice, a scarcely churned gathering ground whose spreading columns gouged out the radiating glens. Looking down from the Black Mountain Ridge, the impression was of a hastily abandoned HQ, boulders big as tanks left studding the treeless peat. Bad-ankle country, I reckoned; and up here,

and next day the good weather continued, breezy sunshine speeding me down Glen Orchy to the muted prospects of Rannoch Moor. I decided to avoid them – 120 inches of rain a year was more than I could handle – and swung left around the shores of Loch Tulla, pitching camp on the nearest thing to a lawn I'd seen since leaving the outskirts of Glasgow. Margaret Gravell, who runs the nearby hotel, told me that this small patch of though the going was easy, no place at all for loose dentures: the rash of Gaelic all over the map was a killer – comfortably anglicized round Loch Tulla behind me (Forest Lodge, Black Mount, Victoria Bridge), but here on the 3,000-foot contour line it was Beinn Mhic Chasgaig and Stob a' Bruaich Leith and streams like Allt Creagan nam Meann. Eleven miles later I'd hardly needed to look up from the map to know I was about to descend – 'White Corries', I read, and 'Blackrock Cottage' and – yippee! – the Kingshouse Hotel.

What a day, what a day, the wild wind in my hair, wild ptarmigan clucking round my feet. I'd seen mountains for miles, been Monarch of the Glen and was glowing as I hit the bar. I could, of course, have been coming down on a stretcher. It could have been foggy, I could have broken my leg. As well as being a warmly run hotel the Kingshouse is a Mountain Rescue Post, and, as it so happened, there'd been an incident that very afternoon – nothing much, so the manager said, just a careless couple helicoptered off a cliff.

To say that I met them the following day isn't, strictly speaking, the truth: I had notes and letters to write; they'd just been rescued, so I set off intent to catch up, but the old military road which I had rejoined was dropping to the head of Glen Coe.

Glen Coe! Scotland's Transylvania. Even the deserted A82(T) looked scared as it tiptoed between Stob Dearg and Stob Beinn a' Chrulaiste. As massacres go it was a routine but sordid affair – two companies of the Earl of Argyll's Regiment billeted on the unsuspecting clan with specific orders for its extirpation. Not a man below seventy to be spared; houses and barns to be torched; women and children left to the mid-winter night, the penalty, in 1692, for failing to appear on time to take an oath of allegiance to the Crown.

And it actually happened. The bleak crags, the peat hags, the scudding clouds tell you that: four hundred people, some shot, some frozen to death. It was cold here even in June.

Following the rescuees up the Devil's Causeway and out of the glen it had started to rain, the windswept expanse of the Blackwater reservoir frowning under an uncertain sky. From the west-

ern barrage piped water plunges 1,000 feet to the loch-head turbines of the Kinlochleven smelter, fuelling the annual production of 10,000 tons of aluminium. Was nothing sacred? I wondered. Shop stewards, newsagents, a company town in the Highlands? But I ran into a fellow called Archie Mitchell and ended up staying the night. The only Pakistani in town was from Kenya but no one could pronounce his name so they called him Pratiki Macdonald. Gave him a kilt eventually, and a dirk to stick down his socks. Archie had organized the whole thing. Kinlochleven was all right.

Head still in a vice, I crawled out of town some time after midday, walked up one hill, down another, turned left and ended up in the youth hostel at the bottom of Ben Nevis, an unfocused sort of afternoon, flavoured only by this conversation with a frog.

'Hallo matey. Got any aspirins?'
'Arrrrk.'
'Wanna fag?'
'Arrrrk.'
'See you.'

The guy in the bunk below me didn't think it funny either, and I climbed Ben Nevis alone.

The snow at the top was delicious, the small silver plaque set among the rocks salutary. At 4,408 feet, Britain's highest peak can be a killer, but today there were girls in bikini tops and families with dogs on the summit. Ben Nevis inspires lunacy. In 1911 one Henry Alexander drove his model T Ford to the top in three days. More recently Jean-Franck Charlet, no doubt with a sportif 'Vive la France' on his lips, skied down it in just fifteen minutes, though the 13-mile descent to journey's end at Fort William took me rather longer.

'I said, "The thirteen-mile descent to journey's end at Fort William took me rather longer".'

'Yeah?' said my brother. The others had gone to bed.

Glen Coe, Scotland's Transylvania!

THE VIEW FROM THE TOP

By far the easiest climb up on to the gable of the Western Highlands is by way of the Devil's Staircase above the Pass of Glen Coe, renowned for its mountaineering, its mists and memories of the massacre. By climb I mean trudge for, although this old military road looks perilous, it swings from side to side, ascending gradually to a height of about 2,000 feet. There is no arguing with that onward-going track. It knows what it's about.

If you are fortunate enough to get up on to that bare sandstone shoulder of Lismore and Appin on a clear day – which, I'm inclined to think, is a rarity – the views of snow-capped Ben Nevis due ahead, the Grampians almost all around with Rannoch Moor to the south, are tremendous. Look up with proper respect at those intrepid climbers strung like conkers on strings from the ledges of the Buachaille, the Shepherd. As for myself, I'm all for *terra firma* and, as some half-wit remarked, the more firmer the less terror. Look down before you strike off for Kinlochleven and Fort William some 20 miles to the north-west for I have it from Adam Nicolson that it was down that Staircase that four hundred reinforcements scrambled on the morning of the massacre. But several hours too late to be of any assistance. Perhaps purposively. It would leave more blood on the hands and the consciences of the followers of Sir John Campbell of Glenorchy, a man described as having neither honour nor religion except where they were mixed with self-interest.

Since that fine writer my friend Ivan Rowan will tell you how he reached the Fort from the most northerly point, Cape Wrath in Sutherland, my purpose here is merely to give some remembered impressions of life on the high tops as I have seen it there, particularly through the flaps of a small tent at first light.

Moorland, mountain-top and upland grazing occupy over a third of the total living space of the British Isles and of all kinds of land have suffered least interference by Man. It follows that they provide the widest scope for studying natural wildlife on land. I quote from William Pearsall's *Mountains and Moorlands*, one of the early volumes of the Collins *New Naturalist* series. I first met Professor Pearsall when as a youth I went a-rambling to the north of Leeds. In later life on committees which had to do with conservation issues I met him often, sometimes in the company of the late Frank Fraser Darling, another pioneer in the then new science of ecology. Without the influence and tutelage of those two men I would no more have adventured high alone than joined in a mass walk anywhere.

Herdwick sheep grazing in the snow.

Gatherers of fundamental biological data are obliged to walk far and watch for days, weeks, usually for seasons. But sometimes they will set off on a marathon both for enjoyment and comparative data. It is just ten years since Wynne-Edwards, a learned Fellow of the Royal Society, walked round the six main Cairngorm summits in under ten hours, an exercise in which the previous year (1967) he was beaten by Eric Beard who, Hunter Davies please note, galloped round in half that time. And what have these ambulatory naturalists discovered? The inexorable law that governs life up there is simple but all-exacting. Despite its rugged exterior, its extremes of weather, frozen in winter, baked in summer and wind-thrashed for many months of the year, the region of the High Tops, viewed as an ecological entity, displays a sensitive mechanism. Plants can survive only by cultivating thick skins, cushion-like growth forms or furtive, strictly economical habits. If they are fertilized by insects and not by wind-borne pollen, they must stand out star-bright and offer reward to the moths and flies that gently stroke their anthers.

As with plants, so too with animals. For shelter and insulation hares, foxes and ptarmigan are competent to dig holes in the snow. The deer move down into the glens during bad weather. In the days when the Picts and the Scots buried their dead on islands to keep them from wolves, the deer were creatures of the Great Forest of Caledon. This struck me as curious. How can a startled stag with a mighty spread of antlers move rapidly through trees? Though red deer have never threatened me, moose on several occasions have lowered their horns and showed signs of charging as I trudged through narrow trails in the forests of Maine and Vermont. To my intense relief they never pressed home the attack. They plunged into the trees. They did this by raising their heads so that the bulk of their antlers lay almost flat on their neck and shoulders and the projecting tines enabled them to crash their way through thick undergrowth with a noise that can be imagined.

The red deer is the largest wild land mammal in Britain. Their social life is founded on a matriarchy. For ten and a half months of the year the sexes remain in separate herds; the hinds in large, close-knit family groups with outlying sentinels that bark like dogs at any sign of danger; the stags aloof in loose companies that might be likened to mens' clubs. During the rutting season, they run about and roar and wallow in peat dubs from which they emerge black and awesome, ready to round up their harems. But when all the commotion of multiple mating is over and done with, the winter over and the calves are born and hidden away in the heather and bracken in June, you may witness heart-touching scenes.

On the high plateaus between Loch Arkaig and Quoich, above the glens of Dessary and Carnach where the short grass is bright with saxifrages, moss heaths and small pink azaleas, the fawns fall about and gambol like young lambs, warded and licked by the ever-attentive hinds. Frank Darling puts it in words* I cannot equal:

'The deep and precipitous corries and the spiry summits may cause awe, but the high grasslands on a summer day have an idyllic quality. They are remote and quiet. They are green and kind to the eye. They are ease to the feet. The flowers have great variety and a new beauty, and the very pebbles among which they grow have a sparkle and show of colour. To climb one of these alps and grass and descend again in a few hours is not enough. Take a little tent and remain in the quietness for a few days. It is magnificent to rise in the morning in such a place. The only sounds breaking the silence, if you get the best of early July weather, will be the grackle of ptarmigan, the flute-like pipe of the ring ouzel, and perhaps the plaint of golden plover or a dotterel. See how the deer, now bright red-coated, lie at ease in the alpine grassland. Listen, if you have stalked near enough, to the sweet talkings of the calves who are like happy children. Of your charity disturb them not in their Arcadia.'

J.H.

* Collins *New Naturalist* series.

CAPE WRATH TO FORT WILLIAM

Ivan Rowan

Grey clouds rolled overhead like an inverted ocean, and the moorland itself took up the theme. Great breakers of heather, grass and rock swept to their crests and plunged down to ravines and stream-beds, rose again up hillsides with a spume of wildflowers and grass cotton blowing off the wind, then fell away to deep troughs of peat and bog, an endlessly heaving green, brown and purple swell that by late afternoon had me near to drowning and still hours from my landfall. And still only 5 miles south of Cape Wrath, with another 245 miles to walk.

Nothing prepares you for the daunting scale of distances in the Scottish wilds. I know Wales from the Brecons to the Carnedds, but Welsh hills have good access roads, the lack of which in northern Scotland prompts me to declare that a Welsh mile is worth barely one Scots kilometre. North Highlands approaches are long and arduous, the weather is so notoriously unpredictable you can meet a blizzard on a summer's day, and you can journey all that summer's day and not meet a soul.

These factors combined mean that any Highlands foray is fundamentally serious. Not for me John Hillaby's pragmatical, fast-moving ways – lightweight shoes, 20 miles today, and the same tomorrow, feed off oatmeal cakes, keep going, God will provide. I am not and never will be as fit as Hillaby, and I planned Cape Wrath to Fort William as Montgomery planned Alamein, all the artillery in place, compass bearings worked out, lightweight foods despatched to await collection at infrequent Highland village post offices, rucksack load pared down from what at one stage threatened to put a pound on my back for every one of my 55 years.

What I wanted, and with my newspaper's indulgence obtained, was a walk that perhaps no one else had done, a Pennine Way or Offa's Dyke Path of my very own that I could mould out of the modelling clay of ordnance survey maps, and it rapidly became clear that for this purpose only the far northern latitudes would do. The paths there are usually good, but thankfully there are few Ways. It may seem eccentric that I decided to start at the north-western extremity of Scotland and move down, but I reasoned that I had better defer my confrontation with the true Highlands until my body had marched off some of the worst excesses of a hack's life.

And thus, Sedentary Man 36 hours out from London, wearied by the rough and trackless walk from the lighthouse, I looked around for shelter on this, the first evening of my expedition, and above Keisgaig Bay found myself staring at what was perhaps the remains of the founding walls of a cottage, but roofed with grass like a burial mound. Inside, bending double, I found an alcove topped with planks and a sheet of black polythene, and an earth floor strewn with dried, blackened heather twigs. I emerged, wondering whether to stay or go on, and up on the moor the bog cotton swayed in the wind like sheaves of white feathers deriding my indecision. Five minutes later I had my sleeping bag down and packaged farmhouse stew heating up on my stove, while enjoying an incomparable view of the cool Atlantic merging with the dusk. I turned in, knowing that this night on my heather bed I would have the sleep of kings.

Next day I pushed on to the Strathan bothy, one of those refuges Scottish climbers and walkers establish against the magnitude of their landscape

and fickle weather. Strathan! A three-roomed cottage, bare save for a table and two stools, over-looking a dancing river. There was a visitors' book – E. J. Thribb of *Private Eye*: 'Ate off the floor, blessed place.' Back through the pages: 'No booze left, sober again. Thank God.' I smiled virtuously.

From the lovely village of Kinlochbervie I glimpsed between the fishing-smacks' masts the long white quartzite ghost of distant Foinaven, before entering on the stuff I suppose that dreams following a late supper of curry, over-ripe crab and Stilton are made of. At the head of Loch Stack I found a small hut with its door ajar, holes in the roof, rolls of old fleece and excrement fouling the floor, rotting wall plaster, a permeating smell of damp and decay. To insulate myself against the dirt and rot, *I put up my tent inside the walls*. On leaving, like other people before me, I tried to put my name in ballpoint on the plaster – it was like writing in quicksand.

I left feeling like a dosshouse down-and-out and contoured round the slower slopes of Ben Stack, once resting by a lochside surrounded by burnt heather like a charcoal sea. Six miles to go to Kylestrome, said my map, and once again the map was a cheat and a scoundrel. More or less hobbling there with a sore left heel, I asked the guesthouse landlady if it was all right to take ten minutes over a pint before accepting her offer of soup and sandwiches.

'Ten minutes? I should take longer than that,' she recommended. And so I did; much longer.

The joy of northern Scotland is that it is almost the last piece of Britain to evade the full impact of the tourist. You do not find there the car parks, lavatories, tearooms, litter bins and litter un-binned that disfigure so much of the central and southern Highlands. But by the same token the north's desolate virginity is an unforgettable reminder of the Highlands' history of depopula-tion; you cannot go there without asking whether anything can be done to reclaim a region seem-ingly given over in perpetuity to the deer estates, the Forestry Commission and the White Settlers (weekenders and craft shop owners from England and the Lowlands), a wet desert unredeemed by plough or beast, the sufferings of the clearances superseded by a prevailing indifference to any possibility of repairing their consequences.

I looked north across the loch. Two hundred years ago George Leveson-Gower, later Duke of Sutherland, came into ownership of every acre of land extending to Cape Wrath. To make it profit-able he evicted 15,000 people, burnt their homes, furniture and crops and destroyed their livestock. Impossible not to stand here and experience a moment's sadness, a spark of anger, at such great wrongs done and never righted.

At Skiag Bridge, my tent up near an empty farm, my personal stream only 150 feet away, I visited the ruins of Ardvreck Castle, where Neil MacLeod sold Montrose to the hangman for

LEFT: *Cape Wrath at the north-western extremity of the Scottish Highlands.*

RIGHT: *Fishing smacks at the lovely village of Kinlochbervie, on Loch Inchard.*

The sinister ruins of Ardvreck Castle.

£20,000 and a consignment of rotten meat: a sinister place, you would not want your children to play there. Loch Assynt looked as big and blue as the eight o'clock sky. I watched two oyster-catchers calling to each other from their orange beaks and later spent half an hour reuniting a lamb and ewe my to-ing and fro-ing had inadvertently separated. The farm manager came along and we talked of the Highlands' future or, in his view, lack of one.

'All this land is fit for is trees,' he cried. 'And there's too many of them already.'

The road now afforded the only plumbline south. It would have been perverse to take any other route, and from it I climbed Spidean Coinich in a screaming young gale, and at Knockan was lucky enough to be housed for the night by Tom Strang and his wife – he is the author of the classic guidebook to the area, *The Northern Highlands*. The Strangs gave me a fine dram and talked of the poor, acid soil, the ferocity of the weather which renders it impossible to make hay for winter feed, defeats attempts to grow potatoes or greens, and visits hillsmen with a melancholy Dr Johnson understood immediately when he came to the Highlands: 'The phantoms which haunt a desert are want, and misery, and danger; the evils of dereliction rush upon the thoughts; man is made unwillingly acquainted with his own weakness, and meditation shows him only how little he can sustain and how little he can perform.'

They told me about the crofter who drank too much after a devastatingly lethal lambing time and decided he had sustained enough, could perform no more. He was the third recent suicide in their community.

Every journey has its crux, and after a hotel stopover at Ullapool and a journalistic diversion which has no place in this account, I now faced mine – the Maree-Broom mountains, what W. H. Murray in *The Scottish Highlands* calls the most remote wilderness in the land. I got to the excellent Shenavall bothy in an icy downpour and found myself stuck there while the bailiff rain boarded up the mountains and empty glens on one of those days which saturate boots and breeches in minutes and turn hill walking into a dismal, sightless trudge voided of all joys and rewards save those of safe arrival or return.

I lit a fire, went to the woodstore and chopped a lump of bog-pine until it looked like a grotesquely mutilated turkey, then joined the merry company of five young Glaswegians who had arrived back after me. One of them, a medical student, talked about the 'incomprehensible' party of the previous night.

'Foreigners?' I hazarded, and the lad knew a lead with the chin when he heard one.

'Yes. I did notice some of them had English accents.'

They all rolled about. Kids? They were like kittens. A golden eagle was announced, and they grabbed binoculars and ran barefoot for a glimpse. A trick of the light turned Beinn Dearg Mor to molten copper and they looked on transfixed, as though someone had given them ringside seats at Genesis 1:1.

My transistor gave a better weather forecast. 'Gentlemen,' I said grandly, 'we have a fighting chance,' and I was lying upstairs, still hearing their sleepy voices from below, when my mind went out like a candle in the wind.

In the morning the boys set out for the great ridge of An Teallach while I forded the Sealga river and ascended the Gleann na Muice Beag to its 1,800-foot crest, where by a secret loch in bursts of high speed morse a sandpiper signalled my achievement to an audience of none.

You know the fluted majesty of organ pipes in cathedrals, and that is how the amphitheatre of Carnmore greets you as you begin your descent: a peal of music from the gods, crags and buttresses soaring tier on tier above the glen and falling to a silence of great lakes and green shores where

stunned vision can recover from the ringing in its ears. There was a hunting lodge there, from which people could go out, and for their pleasure kill a beast and return to a good meal and clean sheets; a hundred yards away was the bothy, a filthy little slum with two iron bedsteads drawn up like a Victorian workhouse reception for the undeserving poor. I pitched my tent under the stars. Nothing could ever dim my first impressions of Carnmore. Naples? Well, perhaps another life!

The iron smelters felled much of the Letterewe Forest in the eighteenth century and I presently wished they had finished the job, losing my way among dead trees, slimy, moss-wrapped boulders and ruined crofts as unkempt and overgrown as long-neglected graves. To complete my discomfiture, the evening turned wet and humid and out of the July monsoon the voracious Highland midges swarmed into my face like handfuls of pepper before I could zip up my tent's mosquito net. The following morning I rubbed my bitten ankles together like a demented cricket.

Having secured a room at the decent hotel in Kinlochewe, with washing machine and spin dryer expurgating wriggling horrors from my shirts and underclothes, I had a drink with the warden of the 11,000-acre Beinn Eighe Nature Reserve. A wild thought struck me – suppose 10,000 desert-transforming Israeli pioneers were flown in with a remit to re-transform the Highlands into a national home for Highlanders – could they pull it off?

He smiled politely; after all he was a conservationist not a revolutionary, his real task was to safeguard 350 acres of indigenous Caledonian pine and its associated wildlife of wildcat, pine marten, otter, eagle and merlin. He gave it as his personal opinion that something could be done by reintroducing the slow-growing native Highland cattle to enrich the soil and divest it of some of the coarse moorland vegetation sheep won't touch, but that the problem could not be solved by throwing money and bulldozers at it.

Next day I met an English forestry manager who thought differently. Could 10,000 Israelis . . .? 'Yes. They could. And would.' Then why couldn't the Highlanders? 'Part of the trouble is that people here don't want to do anything about it.'

I knew by the map how the descent from the

Coulin Pass was going to end, but still felt I had stumbled into a Hans Andersen setting updated by Walt Disney: a railway station set in a forest clearing, a little house I trembled to go near lest my boots scuffed up the marzipan. The hotel at Strathcarron turned me down. Someone suggested that the local station house did rooms, so I knocked and a tall man with a long, thin Calvinist face and expression met me: 'No, we do not. And you are interrupting our Sunday service.'

A few minutes later one of the hard-drinking, sinful men servicing the Kishourn oil rig stopped his car and gave me a lift to an hotel on the other side of the loch.

My intention was to go through the mountains to Alltbeithe, possibly Britain's most remote and isolated youth hostel, but peering with pure hatred at the rain and mist I suddenly lost my nerve. So I travelled more than 20 miles by road to Shiel Bridge. Each man has his own answer to the monotony of route-marching – Hillaby, perhaps, would occupy himself with the mating customs of the Slavonian grebe. However, sadly I have no such resources.

Dumping my tent and some gear at a camp site I advanced on Alltbeithe, a far-off red dot glimpsed like a mirage among enfolding dunes of bog and grass. It consisted of two huts with about fifteen two-tiered bunks and a kitchen with butane stoves and paraffin lamps; help or supplies involved either a two-hour drop to the inn at Cluanie or a 20-mile round trip down Glen Affric. There was company, including a Czech student whose imperfect English nearly cost him any chance of supper. He sat on his bunk while the rest of us ate. I asked if he had any food with him. He pointed impatiently at his foot: 'Yes. I have food. That is my food.' We fed him, and when he loped down the glen to Cannich I think I heard him say he was going to buy more feet.

I climbed the long and splendid switchback ridge of Sgurr nan Ceathreamhnan to 3,770 feet; it yielded heady mountain views and I sat in the warm sun and poured them slowly, like a decanter in paradise. Back at the hostel the estate owner's notice said: *These hills are out of bounds, north and south, after August 10.* If I came back in a month's time, I would be a trespasser in paradise.

Well south of Shiel Bridge, on another perfect day, the sweat stinging my eyes like liquid nettles, I missed a crucial river fork and found myself on a 2,000-foot pass overlooking a loch both my compass and my common sense told me could not possibly be on my route. Yet on that same day I surged up steep slopes with a verve and ease I had not known since I was nineteen; that is what hills do for you, they are reverse Shangri-Las, you go into them an ageing man and come out with intimations of your youth.

That said, I came down over the heights where Prince Charles Edward broke through the redcoat

RIGHT: *Shiel Bridge, near Glen Shiel and Loch Duich in the North-western Highlands.*

BELOW: *The shaggy, slow-growing native Highland cattle, which enrich the soil and divest it of coarse moorland vegetation.*

lines after 1745, 5 to 10 miles off course and grateful for the cool brown river I camped by at Kinloch Hourn.

From Greenfield I followed the faint tracks of some giant caterpillar which treated moorland like an outsize cabbage leaf, then put up my tent for my last Highlands evening, eating the end of my packet foods, cheese and onion snack and banana and custard mix, over a cup of black coffee, reliving so many skylines and secret places, good companionship, hilarious comedy.

Next morning I descended to the Dark Mile and thence to Fort William and home. The mountains withdrew behind a curtain of rain as I squelched through the forest. Only a month, 1/660th of my life, yet it was like walking away from a time machine.

BY COURTESY OF BUTLIN'S

In very wintry conditions in February, 1960, that remarkable creator of holiday camps, Billy Butlin, organized a race from John o' Groats to Land's End, the whole length of the mainland of Britain, a distance by road of about 900 miles. The race caught the imagination of the public in a quite extraordinary way. Nearly a thousand entries were received and seven hundred actually started off from John o' Groats. This extract from *The Big Walk* is an account of an early stage of that marathon, the one down the west side of Loch Ness. It was written anonymously by one of those taking part. Nobody has been able to discover his or her identity and I am grateful to the Butlin Organization and to Roger Smith, editor first of *The Great Outdoors* and currently *Environment Today* for bringing it to my attention and allowing me to reprint it. At the very least it shows that some walkers seem curiously determined on self-punishment.

J.H.

THE BIG WALK

ANON.

Shortly after Drumnadrochit, the glen road divides on either hand of a small bay inlet of Loch Ness, the left-hand fork going to Inverness and the right one down the Great Glen to Fort Augustus. It was not too dark to see the outline of the hills, and in this light one had an impression of gigantic size on reaching the lochside proper.

Towards Inverness, the water seemed to stretch away into endless distance, giving an illusion of looking out to sea. In this direction, it was as if one was looking slightly uphill along the line of the water, which grew lighter in hue as it neared the imagined sea until it ended in a haze of dawny light.

The other way, between the great mountains on either hand, the loch flowed gently downhill into dark depths of unknown mystery. No doubt this contrast of impressions was due to the hills becoming gradually lower towards Inverness, and higher in the other direction, towards the very heart of the Highlands. The loch weaved an atmosphere of obscure secrecy and fascination about its hidden depths, as it does at all times, but perhaps more so to a person walking its shores alone on a winter night.

There was none of the ice and snow on the road here that we had heard about, and I made good speed for the first two hours, almost catching up with the Yorkshireman. He was wearing steel-studded boots, and at one point I could hear their echo in the stillness of the night a short way ahead. But that was the closest I ever came to him, for after putting on a spurt my blisters were burning the soles of my feet so badly that I was forced to stop for a break.

Starting again five minutes later was like going through hell. It was as if hundreds of little devils, each with a tiny red hot pitchfork, were prodding my feet continually. I could almost see the wide grins on their ugly little faces as they danced about me. They were quite naked, with flaming red skin, big ears and polished white horns – like those of a prima donna dairy cow ready for a show. On their feet they wore white boots, laced tightly to the tops and glowing phosphorescently in the dark. Standing only half an inch high, they leaped and danced soundlessly round my feet, and I imagined that somewhere behind, a group of reserves were heating their pitchforks in a mobile brazier, ready for their turn to join in the bloodthirsty sport of pricking my feet. The pilgrims of old who put stones in their shoes when they walked cannot have suffered more than I did that night alongside Loch Ness, and I felt that if I had been doing this walk as a penance, I would have been absolved from and forgiven many sins. All the same, I wished that the monster would appear and gather the little wretches with her tendrils into the icy depths. What a sizzling there would have been as their red hot bodies touched the surface! Perhaps the monster knew this, and that the waters of the loch would have boiled and made things uncomfortable for her. At any rate, she stayed where she was and I never had a glimpse of her.

There was little traffic on the road; only two cars passed me the whole night. About halfway to Fort Augustus I met a tramp walking the other way, and passed the time of day (or rather night) with him. He should have been on the walk, I suggested. Yes, he had thought about it. He was used to walking long distances on the roads, but had

An aerial view of Loch Ness near Dores. 'The Loch weaved an atmosphere of obscure secrecy and fascination about its hidden depths.'

heard of a job he might get near Inverness. He was on his way there from Glasgow, and his last long stop had been in Fort William. He had seen quite a few walkers in Fort William and had passed occasional ones or groups every few miles since then. He had seen the Yorkshireman just one mile down the road, having a rest.

Some way on I came to a house on the lochside, and rested awhile in the porch of an outhouse. I was becoming sleepy and thought I could snatch a few winks sitting on the concrete floor. I dozed for a minute or two but was soon chilled and aching all over, so got up to continue. As I was emerging round the side of the house, a voice from the darkness called out: "Ullo, 'ow are you?"

Thinking that this was the house owner, I started to explain that I had just used his porch to rest a few moments. Then he told me he was the wee fellow with the bad leg – the one I had overtaken near 'Drum'. I tried to persuade him to come on with me for company, but he said he was all in and would stay the night. As he appeared to be crouching on an upturned bucket, I have no doubt he did not enjoy his rest very much, but he was obviously in great pain and I let him be.

I met him again later the same day, as I was leaving Fort Augustus; at that time he had given up the race and was going home. He was very miserable at his failure – not so much because he had not lived up to his own expectations of himself, but rather because he felt he had let down his family and friends.

This attitude was not uncommon; indeed, I think we all suffered from the same mental outlook at one time or other, if not all the time. There was no conceit in the perception that those we had left at home depended on us to do well, or at least to complete the journey. The encouragement we received from our home areas, individually, was a very real thing, and may well have been the reason for some of us keeping going long after we knew we had lost all hope of winning any prize.

As dawn broke, a tall young Englishman

BELOW: *Near Drumnadrochit, on the western side of Loch Ness.*

RIGHT: *A serene summer view of Loch Ness near Dores.*

wearing a duffle coat caught up with me. I had left him asleep in the hotel at Drumnadrochit; he had left at 2 a.m. and had not stopped since, but was now very sleepy. So was I.

We arrived at the hamlet of Invermoriston at 7 a.m. and, deciding we must have a nap before completing the remaining 7 miles to Fort Augustus, rested on seats on the verandah of a hotel. We were woken ten minutes later by three lusty youths who arrived for breakfast, and banged on the door for service. When they got no answer, two of them joined us on the seats. The third said he was going on, which he did.

The other two were steel workers from Bradford, good chaps both, and I saw quite a bit of them over the next week. We had all been sitting there for five minutes or so, eating chocolate and biscuits, when someone suddenly realized that the road the other man had taken was signposted to Skye. We tried shouting, but he had obviously gone too far to hear us and no one had the energy to get up and follow him. We all thought this was a

hilarious joke and laughed our heads off at the thought of a Butlin walker solemnly plodding his way through Glen Shiel and then finding himself on the west coast.

However, the wandering stranger returned after a while, realizing his mistake, and we all set off together. This was much easier than walking alone or even than being with just one other. For if one of us eased up a little, the others all bullied the offender into keeping up. We were no longer tired, but felt very hungry, and the thought of

breakfast kept us going at a steady four miles an hour.

I can remember few more pleasing and more beautiful sights than Fort Augustus as it came into our view that morning. Nestling serenely amongst trees at the end of the loch, it seemed that here was heaven after the hell of the night. The little town appeared to be coming to meet us in its image on the surface of Loch Ness, and when we were still a mile away we could almost smell the bacon and eggs.

EAGLES, WILD CATS AND WALKERS

We were at Boat of Garten between Aviemore and Grantown-on-Spey at the time, that is about a fortnight after Dunkirk when, after spiking our twenty-five pounders in Normandy our regiment of Yorkshire gunners, the 71st, was reduced to mock battles in the Cairngorms and polishing the eye-holes in our boots. Deep boredom except on the part of this gunner, a walker-naturalist who, with the welcome task of catching trout for the colonel's breakfast, roamed around a dozen Lochans between Rata Mhurchuis, the Fort of Murchus and Oban Neithic, the Confluence of the Pure Streams. Gaelic place names sound pretty impressive until you learn that Loch Mhic Ghille Chaoil merely means the Lake of the Thin Man's Son.

As for myself I saw several herds of deer on the flanks of the Lairig Ghru, the Gloomy Pass, and barking ravens were mobbing a hole under a rock where, I never could have guessed until a local shepherd pointed it out, a snarling wild cat crouched, indignant at being awakened after her nocturnal prowl in search of grouse chicks and field voles. They are rarely seen by people except in the headlights of a car. I saw several golden eagles to whom, soaring high above the peaks on thermals, the Cairngorms must have been mere bumps. Some conservationists have put it about that the most exciting birds in the world are primarily scavengers, feeding on such stuff as placental remains but we have it from Desmond Nethersole-Thompson that some Speyside pairs preyed largely on blue hares, red grouse, ptarmigan and, formerly, rabbits, in that order. He had never heard of an eagle killing a live sheep or lamb in the Spey valley but the head keeper at Glen Tanar told him how he had seen an eagle dive-bomb a young roe six times.

'Each time it made a slanting dive and then flattened out. The first time it hit the fawn on the shoulder, but the mother roe rose on her hind legs and lashed out. She did this five more times, always forcing the eagle to zoom upwards.' He had watched an eagle chase a gaggle of greylag geese too, like a Spitfire on the tail of bombers.

My friend, the local shepherd, had seen an eagle soar to a height of about 500 feet above the Coire Sputan Dearg, The Corrie with Red Spots, with a writhing wild cat in its talons and drop it on some rocks, but to judge from the bird's swoop and quartering the ground before it flew off, the cat had not lost one of its lives on that unwelcome free ride. Maybe it bounced as squirrels appear to do when they miss a prodigious jump from the top of one tree to the lower branches of another. How did he feel about wild cats? I asked my informative friend who pointed out the first dotterel, greenshanks and snow buntings I had ever seen. He shrugged his shoulders. 'What harm did they do?'

This charitable attitude is not shared by gamekeepers who, since the prodigious rise in grouse moor rentings, nowadays boast of how many they have killed. Nethersole-Thompson reported that one man in Glen Cova claimed to have killed up to a hundred in one year. I have yet to see one, alive or dead, but the chances are that these ancestral mousers have benefited more by the decline in numbers of keepers rather than by the vigilance of the World Wildlife Fund.

I have gone back to the Cairngorms several times but can describe that spectacular hill-walking country and all that lies to the south and the east with no authority, certainly not with the familiarity of Cameron McNeish who, as an editor, author and mountaineer can write about that exciting world with knowledge and love.

The most dangerous animal thereabouts is Man, not just the maker of ski-lifts and mountain roads. Worse by far are the heavily subsidized foresters who cling to the notion of efficient monoculture in the hideous shape of vast corduroys of exotic spruce. They are into a monocultural whirlpool which involves epidemic outbreaks of pests, followed by aerial spraying of lethal chemicals which do much more than kill the pests. Waters are polluted, fish food is destroyed, fish are killed and raptorial birds become sterile. The Great Caledonian Forest first reported by Pliny has been reduced to relics. What little is left of stands of Scots pine range in age up to three hundred years so there are not many generations between their earliest predecessors of about 9,000 years ago and those growing today. To stand among them is to feel the past.

But Eastern Scotland still provides the most extensive and spectacular hill-walking country in Britain. A few landowners tried to forbid access as late as the Glen Tanar Right of Way litigation in 1931 but some notable court cases have maintained the traditional rights of way of the Scottish people.

J.H.

THE HIGHLANDS
OF THE EAST

CAMERON MCNEISH

In the days of long ago when all men strove to make their peace with their gods, both the good ones and the bad, the Gaels that clung to what we now call the Cairngorms held to the belief that *An Fearlas Mor*, the Great Grey Man, had his home on the heights of Beinn Macdhui, the second highest mountain in Britain. They had good reason for such a belief as you may discover for yourselves.

Up there are no mighty *sgurr* or *stac*, the Gaelic words for sharp conical peaks, but rolling *meall* and *monadh*, high moor-clad plateaux which are all too often *glas* and *fliuch*: dour, grey and wet. In short, the summit of Beinn Macdhui resembles North Britain not long after the great glaciers melted. In winter it is a white waste, thrashed by tremendous winds known to the Northmen as the *Bora* from which even the camouflaged and warmly feathered ptarmigan flee. But when the air softens and the deer trudge up the corries to graze among the exquisite rose-pink flowers of the moss campion, the roof of Macdhui slowly achieves the glory of the arctic tundra in late spring.

But all hazard is not over and done with. Macdhui is a mountain of many humours and when the wraith-like mists float around mysteriously, there are those who claim to have seen the Great Grey One as he strode towards them like a terrible Titan. They saw no more. They turned round and fled.

But go there, go across the high plateau from Cairngorm, or up the long Riach ridge from Luibeg near Braemar on a crystal-clear heaven-sent day and you'll lord the whole of the east of Scotland. A granite and marble direction indicator close to the cairn on the summit draws the

picture incisively: to the north the outline of Morven in Caithness and to the south the Lammermuir hills beyond Edinburgh. Those are the heady boundaries reserved for the favoured few.

Far away to the west the Highlands of Drum Albin could be in another world for you are standing atop the Grampians, rounded hills whose summits were left untouched by the grinding glaciers. The glory of these hills is not to be found in gazing upwards at serrated skylines, but in gazing downwards, down into great chasms and trenches, scoured corries and mighty hill passes. Essentially, the Torridonian and quartzite peaks of the north-west have an impoverished flora by comparison with that of the undulating heartland of the east which is composed of granite and metamorphic schists, rich in nutrients.

The Lairig Ghru, running below Macdhui, is one of the truly classic passes. It splits the granitic massif of the Cairngorms into two halves at a height of 2,750 feet. There is, thank goodness, no heavily trampled long-distance path southwards but one of great antiquity as the best ones always are. Up in those roads in the clouds, cattle drovers bullied and beguiled their shaggy beasts so well adapted to the austerity of the Highlands over the boulder-strewn screes of the pass to the great trysts of Falkirk and Crieff. The going was too arduous for the young beasts so they were taken on a diversion, through the other great pass of the Cairngorms, the Lairig an Laoigh or Pass of the Calves where the going was longer but less difficult.

The classic route of the Lairig Ghru breaks you in gently through a relic, a mere fraction of what

The ruins of Rothiemurchus Forest . . . but what's left today?

used to be the great Forest of Caledon, an immensity of Scots pine which once stretched from coast to coast. The relic is at Rothiemurchus, a treasured nature reserve, a living museum of yesterday. Look at those trees with respect. They are rock-hard and anchored deep in the ground. They have a trunk like the foremast of a sailing ship, golden-red at the cross trees, a colour perfectly offset by the bottle-green colour of the foliage. In the streets of the mountains they have about them the quality of a bugle blast and they are tenanted by pine martens, crossbills, crested tit and capercaillie, that huge grouse of the woods.

What happened to that truly enormous forest was meticulously investigated – among much else – by the late great Frank Fraser Darling, scholar, humanist and one of the Founding Fathers of the science of ecology, the study of the homes of plants, animals and Man. For him the Highlands were a living laboratory.

Looking back over a period of three or four thousand years he envisaged the first Highlanders who were not merely wandering predators and scavengers. They were the Picts or proto-Picts, a polyandrous, matriarchal series of societies constantly preoccupied with looking for or creating clearings among the fearful forests that harboured wild beasts such as wolves and bears. The young sons were obliged to move further and further away from their parents' holdings, to shielings that were progressively enlarged by the use of the axe and fire. The Roman influence on the Highlands can be ignored but not that of the ruthless Northmen who burned their way into the interior.

The process has been repeated over the centuries and reached a climax with the terrible evictions in the early part of the nineteenth century when, to make grazing grounds for sheep, countless thousands of Scots pine were incinerated by the fire-sticks of the flockmasters. A small but noble example of what they left behind can be seen at Rothiemurchus.

Who then was this Murchus who, presumably, had a fort there? An ancient chief? A contemporary, perhaps, of Finn McCumhal who invaded those hills with his *fianna*, his warriors, the fair-haired giants of Ireland? We shall never know but Finn's wife is said to have been carried away by the angry waters of the River Avon in the heart of the Cairngorms and you'll pass the spot in the Lairig an Laoigh, that is if you believe the plaque of the Ordnance Survey marked Ath na Fionn.

LEFT: *The hills near Braemar in Grampian.*

RIGHT: *'The angry waters of the River Avon in the heart of the Cairngorms.'*

BELOW: *Balmoral Castle, with proud pines and ever-present views of distant mountains.*

The Lairig Ghru pass carries you high over the boulder screes of its summit and on down by the infant River Dee towards Braemar. The Dee is high born amid the tundra of the Braeriach plateau but it soon matures, crashing over into the deep bowels of An Garbh Choire, the Big Rough Corrie. Losing its youthful vitality it becomes sedate and even regal when beyond Braemar it assumes the title of Royal Dee. Proud pines crowd its banks as one walks through the beautiful Balmoral estate enjoying ever-present views of distant mountains.

One such mountain is Lochnagar, a ruggedly handsome hill beloved by Queen Victoria and immortalized in Byron's verse. Its ascent is not difficult but should be left to the more experienced walker while the same heady atmosphere can be enjoyed less strenuously on a walk around Loch Muick.

Easily reached by car from Ballater, Muick is a long sheet of water surrounded by the high Grampians with the backside of Lochnagar to the north and the Mounth hills to the south. A rough track at the head of it leads to the smaller Dubh Loch which reflects a long beetling cliff, the Creag an Dubh Loch, Crag of the Black Loch,

well-known to climbers. This is a worth-while diversion taking you high above Loch Muick into its high and remote corrie where I have often enjoyed the company of red deer. I distinctly recall camping there recently and thoughout that October night the place rang with the great primeval lust-roars of rutting stags which boomed back from the dark crags.

South of Braemar the road climbs high over the rough hill country of the top Cairnwell and down into Glen Shee, Gleann Sith the Fairy Glen. Sadly on either side the hills have been gouged and scarred by bulldozers developing one of Scotland's major ski areas, but it is still worth walking over the hill of the Cairnwell down to Loch Vrotachan, the Hill of Fattening traditionally so named for its fat trout.

Here on a still summer day the trout rise for the fly hatches and the shrill twitterings of the skylark enliven the air even at such a height. Nearby a battle was fought in 1644. A body of rievers from Argyll ravaged the rich lands of Glen Isla and Glen Shee but were met by a hastily roused band of men on the slopes of the Cairnwell. One local worthy known as Cam Ruadh performed feats of valour and skill, turning apparent defeat into certain victory. Unfortunately in the course of the action he was hit in the backside by an arrow.

The story goes that as he returned to Braemar the old women cried out to him: 'Chaim Ruadh, Chaim Ruadh, tha saighead na do thoine!' ('Cam Ruadh, Cam Ruadh, there is an arrow in thy backside!')

'Tha fios agam fhein air sin!' ('I myself know that!') came back the reply, and when the Cam came home his wife extracted the arrow by standing on his back, one foot on either side, and pulling with all her strength. It makes me wince to think about it.

West from the Cairnwell one gazes on the high hills of Atholl, a land set deep in the romance and legend of the Highlands. Here one finds Blair Atholl, the home of the Duke of Atholl. His castle at Blair, the policies of the estate and the long track which runs up Glen Tilt from the village are all worth exploring.

From the castle an ancient route wends its way through the hills to Badenoch. This thirteenth-century Comyns Road was reputedly built to carry barrels of ale to the Comyn castle at Ruthven near Kingussie. It seems that Comyn, passing through Atholl, stopped at Blair and so liked the local ale he immediately decided to import it, at great expense, to Badenoch. One can still walk by the headwaters of the Bruar and over into Gaick, reputedly the most supernatural place in Scotland. We are told that the *Leannan Sith*, the Faery Sweetheart, once appeared here before hunters who became so entranced by her great beauty that their earthly wives grew to fear their supernatural rival.

Stalking in the Gaick hills in 1958, Colonel Jimmy Dennis spotted a small moving figure dressed like a child in a green siren suit and pixie hood in the far distance, but approaching the spot near a stream and finding no trace of it, wondered if he had imagined it until he told the story to an old retired keeper from a neighbouring forest who identified it as the 'Sprite o' Gaick'.

The tiny hamlet of Bruar, remarkable for the Bruar Falls, is a few miles north of Blair Atholl on the A9. Park your car next to the hotel and walk along the signposted path by the river whose waters burst over falls and deep chasms between deeply tree-clad banks. Tree-clad, I say, but it wasn't always like that. When Robert Burns visited the area in September, 1787, he was obviously impressed by the rock features, the rushing waters but not by the bare moorland that embraced the stream. After his visit the poor ploughman poet wrote a short poem for his Grace.

> Wad then my noble master, please
> To grant my highest wishes,
> He'd shade the bank wi' towering trees,
> And bonnie spreading bushes.

The verses had the desired effect and Atholl began to plant what eventually became a vast wood. Could finer tribute be paid to a poet recognized by the whole literate world who realized, two hundred years ago, that Scotland needed her magnificent native trees?

Blair Castle in Tayside, the home of the Duke of Atholl.

EPILOGUE

Our tales are told. The narrators, like those fourteenth-century wanderers intent on shrines such as Walsingham, Norwich, Glastonbury or, maybe, Holy Island are off somewhere else. Before we wave to them in spirit with, perhaps, a touch of envy, we might take up what Adam Nicolson, re-appraising a vital aspect of Auden, said about 'hard days in which walking is always thinking.' Hard meaning not only hard going among arid landscapes but hard weather from spiteful rain that comes at you sideways to that most nebulous of opponents, an enveloping mist which gives the impression that the whole planet has plunged into cosmic cloud, leaving only a small circle of uncomfortable reality in which you are the sole survivor.

On serene mornings, especially at dawn in high places you may adopt the saintly tread of an elephant, both in ceremonial trappings and at large in the wild, which is delicate and almost soundless. Thoughts are there to be summoned up at will or lightly dismissed. But in periods of stress my experience is that despite stern reasoning about the need for self-discipline and that strange Platonic equation between courage and endurance, there are intractable areas of the brain that tend to race like a car engine with a slipping clutch.

I recall what I took to be an arête on An Teallach in Wester Ross which I took to with less enthusiasm since nothing could be seen on the invisible side of a vertical face. At intervals clouds drifted over and they were highly charged clouds for sheet lightning lightly flickered among them like a faulty fluorescent tube. A situation here for thought and mine were mostly that I was a damn fool to have got there in the first place because to retreat meant throwing away the better part of 2,000 feet of sheer slog. I scrambled, clumsily, and did what no mountaineer would ever have done, that is relied on a foothold which collapsed leaving no alternative but to scramble down, an exercise in which I was more fortunate than skilful.

On firm ground I rested and note-booked some notions which were an expurgated version of the brain race that actually took place when things seemed to be going progressively wrong. But these are mere specks on the mirror of great walks remembered.

Let us go back to one of those Arcadian situations about which Frank Darling writes with such affection. It is the Beinn Eighe reserve to the south-east of Loch Maree in Wester Ross. The dominant tree is that most noble of conifers, the Scots pine with its muscular limbs and trunk golden red below the crown. The juniper, birches, rowans and alders become thicker without competition on the flanks of the burns. In the spring you may hear the wonderfully weird wail of the loon from the dappled water below and maybe catch a glimpse of a pine marten, head upturned, furtive yet inquisitive. The woods are alive with those little foragers the crested tits, interspersed with the ripple of redstarts and the downward falling cadence of willow warblers. Cascades with different voices pour down from the gleaming white Cambrian quartzite where pairs of golden eagles soar and circle as if in praise of the One.

Climb on to the shelf between Sgurr Ban and Coire Domhan and look due west, far across the Minch where the Outer Hebrides stand out like the dorsal fins of basking shark cruising line astern. Between the Aird, the topmost tip of Skye

and Kebock Head on Lewis stands a strange group of islets, the Shiants with truly staggering cliffs, a minute sea kingdom owned, as I understand it, by Adam Nicolson's family. What a place for a retreat especially since, among his almost boundless enthusiasms, he numbers 'fulmars, thrift, basalt, sheep, seals, caves decked with pink algae, puffins and that amazing orange lichen.'

Not long before we went to press I heard that Miles Jebb was heading for the forests of Morvan in the very heart of Burgundy and I hope he's in time for the *vendage* in the Côte d'Or. Typically, David Bellamy will be walking the shores of Cornwall at a time when no doubt the weather would deter all but the crew of a lifeboat. Brian Le Messurier has been studying the bleak maps of Alaska for a trip that will take in Le Mesurier Point and Le Mesurier Island, two places which give him reason to believe that, although spelt differently, they were named after an ancestor, Captain Vancouver's navigation officer. Hunter Davies, that self-confessed workaholic is off, he says he

hopes, for somewhere between Venezuela and Loweswater in the Lakes, the first for his slowly on-coming biography of Christopher Columbus, the second a dream house to the south of Cockermouth, the birthplace of the Wordsworths. It came as much of a surprise to learn that Ronald Blythe, that passionate dreamer, had set off for Australia, a country not notable for introspective inhabitants, as it did to hear that Richard Mabey was flying to crowded Majorca, but not for the beaches. He has gone there for a quiet view of one of the rarest and most majestic of our avian predators, Eleonora's falcons which patrol the sea-cliffs of the Balearics, ready to pounce on luckless migrants. Stephen Pern was last heard of within a four days' march of Tierra del Fuego.

As for the rest of us we are mostly about more ordinary business at home, some keeping National Parks in order or guiding newcomers or exploring a promising new trail, fortified in our common belief that the land of our better selves is surely reached by walking.

J.H.

INDEX

Page numbers in **bold type** refer to illustrations

Abberley Hills 114
Abbots' Way, The 58
Abereiddi 93
Adam's Grave 15
aerial perspective 47
Aidan, Saint 188, **191**
Airedale 164
Alfred, King 28
Alltbeithe 236
Alston **200**
An Teallach 235
Anning, Mary 60
Aran Fawddwy 110
Ardvreck Castle 233–4, **234**
Arenig Fawr 109
Arger Fen 135
Arnold, Matthew 22
Arthur's Quoit 93
Ashdown House 13
Assynt, Loch 234
Aubrey, John 28
Auden, W. H. 193–5, 198–201
Austen, Jane 71
Avebury Stone Circle 24, **27**, 28, 31
Avon, River (Cairngorms) **249**

Balmoral Castle **249**
Bamburgh Castle **189**
Barbury Castle 28, 31
Bath 122
'Battle of Kinder Scout' 152
Beach of Morning, The 94
Beachy Head 12, **12**
Beaker people 28
Beinn Dearg Mor 235
Beinn Eighe Nature Reserve 235–6, 252
Beinn Macdhui 244
Ben Nevis **222**
Berwyns, The **110**
Birmingham 112–13
Bitches, The 92
Black Mountains **101**
Blair Castle 250, **251**
Blake, William 94
Blakey Ridge **182**
Boardale Valley 217
Borrow, George 33, 74, 107
Braemar **248**
Brantham **133**
Brecon Beacons **47**, **76**, 78

Bredon Hill 114, 118
British Camp 114
Broadway 126
Bronte, Emily 158, 164
Brown, Lancelot ('Capability') 123
Bruar 250
Bude **65**, 67, 68
Bunyan, John 37, 192
Butlins-organized walk 238–43
Butt, Dame Clara 31

Cader Idris 110, **111**
Caerbwdi Bay 90
Caerphilly Castle **80**, 81
Cairngorms 244–50
Cam High Road 164
Cam Ruadh 250
Cannock Chase 116
Capel Curig **107**
Cardiff 75, 77
Carnedd range 106–7
Carn Llidi 92, **93**
Carnmore 235
Castell Coch 77, **78**
Castell Mor Craig 81
Cedd, Saint 129, 190
Cefn-mawr 103
Chagford 55
chalk 10–17
Challum, Ben 224
charcoal for sketching 43
Chepstow 96, **97**, **98**
Chesil Beach 73
Chess, River 36–7, **39**
Cheviot Hills **161**
children and walking 177, 181–2, 205
Chiltern Hills 24, 34–5
Chipping Campden **124**, 126
Chirk Castle **103**
Churn, River 124
Cilgerran **79**
Clapdale 175
Clare, John 37, 192
Clent Hills 113
clothing 210–11
Clovelly **66**, 67
Clun Forest 102
cocoliths 11–14
Coleridge, S. T. 67, 169
Columba, Saint 185–8

Coniston **229**
coracles 79
Cornish Coast Path 68–9
Cotswold Way 119–27
Coulin Pass 236
Countisbury Church 67
Countryside Commission 29, 141
Cowper, William 37–8
Cranmere Pool 56–7
Crickley 124
Crossing, William 58
Cuckoo Tye 132
Cuillin Hills 204, **205**
Cut Hill 55–6
Cuthbert, Saint 190–1, **191**

Dark Peak 147–54
Darling, Frank Fraser 228, 230, 248
Dart, River 59
Dartmeet **59**
Dartmoor 52–9, **56**, **59**
Dartmouth 71
David, Saint 90
Dee, River (Scotland) 249
Deepdale **215**
deer 230
Defoe, Daniel 10, 30
deforestation of southern England 26
Dent **215**
Devil's Staircase 228
Devon Coast Path 66–7
Divine Landscapes (Blythe) 128–9, 192
Dorset Coast Path 72–3
Dovedale 154, **155**
Drumnadrochit **242**
Duck's Pool 58
Duich, Loch **237**
Dyrham 122

Edburton **11**
Edge Hill 116
Edington (Ethandune) 28
Eisteddfod 103
Eliot, T. S. 52
Emondbyers **195**
Exmoor National Park 67

Falmouth 68, **68**
family outings 179
Feldon, The 116
flint 12–13

Index

food 202–7, 213–14
Food for Free (Mabey) 203
footpaths, destruction of 141–2
footwear 210–11
forestry 109, 157
Fort Augustus 243
Fort William 237
Fountains Abbey **174**, 175
Four Stones 113–14
Frithsden Beeches 34
Fur Tor 56–8

gamekeepers 149, 151–2
Gaping Gill 175, 176
Gartness 233
George, Saint 31
Girald de Barri 85
Glen Coe 226, **227**, 228
Glen Etive **224**
Glen Falloch **222**
Glen Shiel **237**
Glengoyne Distillery 223
Glyndebourne **14**
Glyder ridge 106
Goodwood House 12–13, **13**
Gordale Scar **175**
Gower Peninsula **81**, 83
Grand Union Canal 30
Great Badminton 123
Great Maplestead **134**
Great Scar limestone 172
Greater Pennines 146
Green Roads 24
Grimes Ditch **35**
Grim's Ditch 31

Hadrian's Wall 165, **166**
Hailes Abbey 125
Hard Tarn **49**
Hardraw Force 172
Hardraw Scaur **176**
Hartland Point **64**, 67
Hartshill Hayes 116
Hawkes, Jacquetta 11
Hawkesbury Church 123
Haworth Moor **163**, 164
Hay Tor 54–5, **56**, 59
Hay-on-Wye 99
Hazlitt, William 33, 130
Heardman Fred ('Bloody Bill the Bog
    Trotter') 147
Hepworth, Barbara 69
Herepath 31
High Force 165, **197**
High Street (Hawes Water) 24
History of Mr Polly, The 31
Holy Island **187**, 191
Hopkins, Gerard Manley 111
Horseshoe Pass 107
hotels 202

Icknield Way 30
Ilkley Moor 24
Inchard, Loch 233
Ingleborough **44**, 170, 171, 175
Ingleton Glen **171**
Iona 185, **186**
Ivinghoe Beacon 26, 30

Ivinghoe Hills **26**

Jefferies, Richard 15, 31, 37
Joad, Cyril 149, 152
Johnson, Samuel 33, 234
Jones, Elwyn 104–5
Journey Home 137
Journey through Britain 6, 60
Jurassic Way 123, 125

Kelmscott **23**
Kemerton Camp 114
Kilnsey Crag 172, **173**
Kimball, Sir Marcus (Lord Kimball) 143
Kimmeridge 72
Kinder Scout 152–4, 159
Kingswear **70**
Kinlochbervie 233, **233**
Kinver Edge 114
Kipling, Rudyard 25, 67
Kirk Yetholm **159**

Ladybower Reservoir 149, **151**
Lairig Ghru 244–9
landowners' powers 141
Landslip, the 71
Langridge **121**
Lansdown Hill **122**
Leach, Bernard 69
Lechlade 19, **21**
Letcombe Castle 28, 31
letter-boxing 56–8
Lich Way 58
Lickey Hills 112, 113
Liddington Castle 28, 31
lifeboat stations 62
Limestone Link Path 123
Lincolnshire Wolds 138–9
Lindisfarne Castle **187**
Lindisfarne Priory **190**
Lindsey Loop 139
Little Down 122
Little Horkesley 133
Little Hucklow **150**
Little Sodbury 123
Llanberis Pass 109
Llangollen 103
Llanthony Priory 98
Lleyn Peninsula 109
Llyn Mymbyr 107
local exploration 180
Lochnagar 249
Lockley, Ronald 84
Lomond, Ben 223
Lomond, Loch 220, **220**, **221**
Lustleigh Cleave 54
Lyme Regis 60, 71

McColl, Ewan 154
Maiden Castle 72, **73**
Maiden Way 24, 165
Malham 40, 164, **164**, **165**, 172, **175**
Malvern Hills 114, **115**
Mariners' Way 58
Marloes Beach 88
Marshfield 123
Mastiles Lane 172
Mellte, River 78

Meltonian Marathon walk 116
Middleton-in-Teesdale 196
Midger Wood Nature Reserve 123
Milburn Forest **198**
mining 196
Moel Hebog range 109
Moel Siabod 106
Moelwyn 109
Monmouthshire and Brecon Canal 78
Montgomery 102, **102**
Morris, William, Lord Nuffield 31
Mud Hall 176
Mugdock Wood 220
Muick, Loch 249
Mumbles Head **81**
Munro, Sir Hugh 223

Nantlle Ridge 109
National Trust Book of Long Walks
    (Nicolson) 95
navigation aids 64
Neath, River 78
Ness, Loch 239, **240**, 243, **243**
Nethermost Cove **49**
Nevis, Ben 226
Newlyn 69
Norse place names 195, 208
North Kyme Fen 141
North Staffordshire Moors **193**
North Worcestershire Path 113
North Yorkshire Moors 7, 45
Northern Highlands (Strang) 234
Noss Mayo 71

Offa's Dyke Path 95–103, **99**, **100**
oil drilling 72
Old Sodbury 123
Overton Hill 25

Padley Bridge, near **149**
Painswick 124
Palmer, Samuel 16
paper for watercolour 44–6, 48
Parsons' Folly 114–16
Peak District 146–54
Peak District National Park 152–3
Pearsall, William 104
peat 147, 159
Pembrokeshire Coast Path 84–93
Pennine Way **154**, 156–67, **159**, **161**, **166**
    difficulties of walk 160
    eccentric characters on 165–7
    erosion 162–4
Pen-y-Ghent **95**, 170
Pen-yr-Ole-Wen **105**
Pilgrim's Way 125
Pipe Track 54
Piper, David 18
Plymouth 70
Polperro 64
Ponsticill Mountain Railway 78
Porth Llong 90
Porthclais 91
Porthkerry 82
Porthselau **93**
Powys, John Cowper 37
pre-historic remains 26–8
    Beaker people 28

burial chamber 93
Bronze Age 54
Celtic 28, **29**
hill forts **29**, 30, 31, 65, 72, 103, 154
stone circles 28, 65, 72
Windmill Hill people 26–8
Preseli Mountains 79
Purton Green **131**

rambling 180
Ramsey Island 92
Rannoch Moor 225
Ranny Point 81
Reginald Farrer Nature Trail 175
Rhinog Range 110, **129**
Rhossili **83**
Ridgeway Path 17, 24–31, **27**, **30**
rights-of-way 142
Roberts, Bartholomew ('Black Bart') 90
Roman remains 122, 138
Rosedale Head **183**
Rothiemurchus Forest **247**, **248**
Rowardennan Youth Hostel 223
Rowley Hills 113
Rumbolds Way 24

Saddleworth Moor 157
Sail Laith **50**
Saint Bride's Bay 84, 89, 90
Saint David's Peninsula 86
Saint Govan's 86, **87**
Saint Ives 69, **69**
Saint Mary's Well Bay 81–2
Saint Non's Bay 90, **91**
Salcombe 71
Salisbury Plain 24
Sapperton **124**
Saxon invasion 28, 31
Scutchamer Knob 31
Seven Summits Walk 109–10
Sgurr Fiona **42**
Sgurr nan Ceathreamhnan 236
Shaugh Bridge 54
Shaw, George Bernard 31
Sheffield Clarion Rambling Club 149
Shenavall 235
Shiel Bridge 236–7, **237**
Shropshire Hills 116

Shropshire Way 118
Sidmouth **73**
signpost removal 143
Silbury Hill 16, **16**, 28
sketching 41–51
Skiag Bridge 233–4
Skomer Island 84–5, 90, 92
Skye, Isle of **205**
Slaughter Lane 122
smuggling 64–5
Snowdon 107
Snowdon Ranger Path 107
Snowdonia 104–9, **105**, **108**, **109**
Solva **85**, 89
Somersby 138, **143**
South Devon Coast Path 70–1
South West Peninsula Path 62–73
Stack, Loch and Ben 233
Staffordshire Way 116
Stanhope-in-Weardale **195**, **200**
Stanton **127**
Stiperstones, the **9**, 116, **118**
Stoke by Nayland **132**
Stonehenge 24
Stour, River 135
Strathfillan 223–4
Strathan bothy 231–3
Streatley **30**, 31
Stukeley, William 16
Sully Island 77, 82
Swift, Jonathan 128

Talybont bridge 78
Tanat Valley **110**
Task, The (Cowper) 38
Tees, River **197**
Teesdale 165
Ten Tors Expedition 53
Thames Path 19–23
Thames, River **21**, **22**, 25, **30**
This Land is Our Land (Shoard) 141
Thomas, Edward 10
Tintern Abbey 98, **99**
Top Withens ('Wuthering Heights') 164
Trengrouse, Henry 64
Trout Beck **198**
Trow Gill 175
Trwncynddeiriog 90–1

Tulla, Loch 225
Turner, J. M. W. 92, 168–9, 208
Turnpike Acts 28

Uffington **29**
Ullswater **207**, 215–17, **215**, **216**
Ulpha 212

Viking Way 139

Walseby **141**
Ward, G. H. B. (Bert) 149
Waseley Hills 113
watercolour 44–6, 48
water-soluble pencils 45–6
Wayland's Smithy 28, 31
Weardale **195**
Webb, Mary 116
Wells-next-the-Sea 25
Welsh language 75, 79
Wendover 30
Wensleydale 164
West Highland Way 218–26
West Kennett 28
West Mendip Way 123
West Midland Way 118
Westerdale 45
Westminster Abbey 13
Westward Ho! 67
Whernside **44**, 171
White Horse Hill, Uffington 28, **29**, 31
White Peak 154
Whitesand Bay 92–3, **93**
Wick, The 84, 85
Widecombe-in-the-Moor **57**
wildcats 244–5
Win Hill 149
Windmill Hill 113
Windmill Hill people 26, 28
Wolfscote Dale **153**
Wordsworth, Dorothy 225
Wordsworth, William 67, 98, 217
Worm's Head **83**
Wotton-under-Edge 123
Wrath, Cape 231, **232**
wrecks and wrecking 64, 90
Wychavon Way 118, 125
Wye Valley 97, 98

Acknowledgements
Extracts from *The English Auden: Poems, Essays and Dramatic Writings* by W. H. Auden, edited by Edward Mendelson, reprinted by kind permission of Professor Edward Mendelson, Faber and Faber Ltd and Random House, Inc.

The Publishers have made every attempt to contact all copyright holders for permission to reproduce works included in this book. We apologise for any omissions and would be grateful to hear from any copyright holders of unacknowledged material included herein.

The Publishers would like to thank the Britain on View (BTA/ETB) picture library and British Tourist Authority for all their help with this book.